NIGHT AFTER NIGHT

NIGHT AFTER NIGHT

LUELLA LANGEVAD

Copyright © 2022 Luella Langevad

The moral right of the author has been asserted.

Apart from any fair dealing for the purposes of research or private study, or criticism or review, as permitted under the Copyright, Designs and Patents Act 1988, this publication may only be reproduced, stored or transmitted, in any form or by any means, with the prior permission in writing of the publishers, or in the case of reprographic reproduction in accordance with the terms of licences issued by the Copyright Licensing Agency. Enquiries concerning reproduction outside those terms should be sent to the publishers.

Matador
Unit E2 Airfield Business Park,
Harrison Road, Market Harborough,
Leicestershire. LE16 7UL
Tel: 0116 2792299
Email: books@troubador.co.uk
Web: www.troubador.co.uk/matador
Twitter: @matadorbooks

ISBN 978 1800465 091

British Library Cataloguing in Publication Data.
A catalogue record for this book is available from the British Library.

Printed and bound by CPI Group (UK) Ltd, Croydon, CR0 4YY
Typeset in 11pt Minion Pro by Troubador Publishing Ltd, Leicester, UK

Matador is an imprint of Troubador Publishing Ltd

This book is dedicated to the memory of William Meyer and all the men of RAF Bomber Command, to whom we owe so much.

CONTENTS

Acknowledgements	ix
Introduction: Early Memories	xiii
Chapter One: Standing Alone	1
Chapter Two: Joining Up	8
Chapter Three: A Journey to the USA	14
Chapter Four: Polaris Flight Academy	25
Chapter Five: Advanced Training	39
Chapter Six: An Introduction to the Lancaster	54
Chapter Seven: IX Squadron	63
Chapter Eight: First Ops	70
Chapter Nine: Uncle	87
Chapter Ten: The Battle of the Ruhr	99
Chapter Eleven: Rest and Recreation	111
Chapter Twelve: The Squadron Moves	116
Chapter Thirteen: Experience	129
Chapter Fourteen: Training Others	146
Chapter Fifteen: The Pathfinders	156
Chapter Sixteen: 97 Squadron	162
Chapter Seventeen: Life and Death	172
Chapter Eighteen: The Bleak Midwinter	188
Chapter Nineteen: The Rising Cost	205
Chapter Twenty: March 1944	216
Chapter Twenty-One: The Aftermath	223
Chapter Twenty-Two: Final Acts	229

The Afterword: Tracing the Past	233
Notes and References	257
Bibliography	265
Index	267

ACKNOWLEDGEMENTS

So many people contributed their help, expertise and time as I researched and wrote this book. I owe a huge debt of gratitude to all who helped me piece together William Meyer's story. I hope I have acknowledged everyone but my apologies if there is anyone I have missed.

Illustrations
Michael Turner kindly gave permission to reproduce the paintings of *The Isle de Chausey Combat* and *A Steeplechase Across Denmark*, and the IBBC Digital Archive gave permission to reproduce the photos of Lancaster 'B' Beer and her crew. The other photos are my own or come from families who kindly gave their permission.

I am very grateful for the help of the following who sadly have since died:
Roger Audis, the late IX Squadron historian, who first showed us the airfield at Bardney and was unstinting in sharing both his research and knowledge.

Ken Gilderdale, who generously shared his diaries, photographs and mementos covering the period of William Meyer's journey to, and training in, the USA.

Alan Hart, whose phenomenal memory and many wonderful anecdotes together with his photos helped bring to life both the nights on operations and day to day life on IX (B) squadron.

It was a privilege to talk to such veterans as Harry Irons DFC, Jack Linaker, and Jim Brookbank. A special mention must be made of Bob Lasham DFC & Bar, who, during a long correspondence, patiently answered my many questions.

Kurt Schneider, who had watched as Lancaster JB 361-B crashed. His vivid memories of the events of that night and its aftermath were invaluable as was his help in organising the unveiling ceremony of the memorial.

Dr Schimpf-Reinhardt of the Stadtarchiv Balingen, Germany, for his help with documents held there.

My heartfelt thanks also go to:
Brigitte Lorch, for her indispensable assistance in organising the memorial, its unveiling and the dinner that followed. Also for the many times she acted as interpreter and the long hours she spent translating documents and speeches.

Herr Helmut Reitemann, Oberbürgermeister of Balingen, Germany, who gave permission for the memorial and the use of the ground on which it stands.

Richard Lovelace, who had been a director of William Meyer & Co., whose memories filled in the post-war period until the company was dissolved and the Primus agency was sold back to Primus.

Archivists at the National Archives at Kew and the RAF Museum at Hendon for their assistance and the staff of RAF Personnel Management Centre whose disclosure of Bill's service record was such a help. Also to Dr Dan Ellin at the International Bomber Command Centre for his help with photographs.

Air Commodore Nick Hay, then Commander of IX (B) Squadron, who arranged for the Squadron presence at the unveiling of the memorial and visited it himself the following year.

Squadron Leader Dicky James, the IX (B) Squadron Association Historian, who welcomed us to the Association and showed us their squadron archives.

IX (B) Squadron for their presence at the memorial and the IX (B) Squadron Association, who made us welcome.

The Pike family, both the older generation, comprised of Tich, Nancy and Edna, and the younger generation, comprised of Jackie and Norrie Ferguson, Sue and Keith Fitzpatrick and Duncan Pike. They have generously shared memories, photographs and memorabilia.

Ken and Linda McCorkindale. Ken, Neil McCorkindale's son, not only provided a vital link to crews' families but also details and photographs and the moving letter from William Meyer.

Gordon and Catherine Taylor, relatives of James McLeish. They kindly provided both helpful details and photographs of James McLeish.

Dorle Steingraeber, who organised the reception at the memorial and helps maintain it together with Roland Kose and Herbert and Marianne Lorch.

Sue Rea and Susan Stewart for patiently reading the drafts and for their perceptive comments.

My dear daughter, Claire, for her love and support.

Finally, I am especially grateful to my dear husband, Brett, my indefatigable co-researcher and perceptive editor, without whose help, advice and support, this book would not have been written. His assistance with research, photographs and technical details has been invaluable. Any inaccuracies remain mine alone.

INTRODUCTION
EARLY MEMORIES

Few childhood memories stay with us. The ones that do are usually of special events, but for the rest the loop of memory runs on and with time is overwritten. Occasionally, however, a moment in an ordinary day fixes itself forever in the mind. One such memory would come back to me years later and ultimately result in the writing of this book.

At home there was a formal black and white studio portrait in a simple frame standing in a prominent position on a table. It showed the head and shoulders of an immaculately dressed man wearing a pinstripe suit. His tie is smartly knotted and his hair close-cropped; in one hand he holds a pipe near his mouth. There is something unusual in his watchful eyes and his grave and thoughtful face. I asked my mother who this man was and she replied, "That's Bill, darling. He was a pilot and was killed in the war. Bill was a wonderful man, your father's greatest friend." I have never forgotten her words. I was six years old at the time.

Many years later, after my parents had both died, I started sorting through their possessions and came across the photo of Bill. The memories of that day long ago came flooding back. The photo was dated 1941. Putting it to one side, I continued looking through boxes of memorabilia, letters, photos, postcards and mementos, all so carefully put away. Coming across a small cardboard box, I opened it to find, carefully wrapped in tissue paper, a leather wallet. Unwrapping the yellowed tissue revealed a small bronze plaque. Gently I pulled it out and read what was embossed upon it. On the top was a logo and under it the words 'Polaris Flight Academy'. Below that was engraved the name 'William A. Meyer'. It certified that William Meyer had passed his flying training at the Polaris Flight Academy, War Eagle Field, Lancaster, California in 1942. This had belonged to the man I knew as Bill, the man in the photograph.

Another box contained photo albums. Among them were pictures of holidays that my father and Bill had taken together in the 1920s and 1930s. There were photos taken on a cruise in the Mediterranean. Other photos show Bill in his car, a Wolseley, with the roof down, while yet more had been taken at a rather splendid picnic with a gramophone in the background.

Another sequence of photos shows my father with Bill on a pre-war Meyer family holiday. The photos were taken at a port, later identified as Boulogne-sur-Mer, and provide a glimpse of a pre-war lifestyle that was about to vanish. In the background waits a huge, elegant Rolls-Royce complete with chauffeur, while ahead of it, only half in the picture, is an SS Jaguar which we later discovered belonged to Bill. Sitting and standing around on the quay in front of it are a stylish group, including Bill, Bill's parents and my father.

My husband Brett and I were intrigued and wanted to know more about Bill. My mother's words, a photograph and a bronze plaque: it did not seem a lot to go on but one discovery led to another and we had some amazing strokes of luck. Our research led us in some totally unexpected directions, and the story was more complex than we could ever have imagined.

We were puzzled when we could find no record of Bill's birth and had almost given up when some papers concerning the family company led to an astonishing discovery that finally enabled us to find the certificate. We had been searching for William Alexander Meyer, but Bill's birth certificate was in the name of Wilhelm-Alex Meyer-Braselmann. Bill, later described to us by one of his crew as the quintessential English gentleman, was not only born of German parents but, amazingly, his parents had not taken British citizenship, and remained German nationals. Bill had managed to keep his background utterly secret. This meant that a highly regarded and decorated RAF officer who gave his life for his country fighting Germany was actually the son of German parents.

Another surprise was finding an eyewitness who had actually seen Bill's Lancaster crash in Germany and was able to fill in that part of the story. Slowly we were able to piece together part of Bill's life, and what we found was a story of quiet courage, steely determination and utter selflessness. There were many questions to be answered, and my parents could have answered some when they were alive. If only I had asked. As it is, while many answers have been found, some questions remain and probably always will.

While this is Bill's story, it also reflects the experiences of the thousands of brave young men of Bomber Command who went through similar months of training and all too often met a similar fate.

CHAPTER ONE
STANDING ALONE

Bombed, battered and burned by the Luftwaffe, by early summer 1941 London was a changed city. Its population slept lightly now, used to broken nights filled with wailing sirens and the blast of exploding bombs. On 10 May, London had endured the worst bombing raid ever. The scale of the destruction had been devastating, with some 700 acres going up in billowing clouds of smoke and flames. Some of London's greatest buildings had suffered: the Chamber of the House of Commons had been destroyed and Westminster Abbey and the British Museum badly damaged. Now across the city the skeletal remains of shattered buildings thrust up, stretching pitifully skyward from heaps of rubble. Any breath of wind stirred up swirls of gritty debris, powdering nearby streets in a film of dust.

On this June morning, a light but persistent rain fell, washing through the dusty air. In the skies, the puffy white shapes of barrage balloons could be seen, offering an illusion of protection. On the once busy Euston Road, the traffic was light, strict petrol rationing ensuring that very few private cars ventured out. Bikes, buses and taxis moved easily through the streets. In contrast, the pavements were crowded with people walking briskly along, intent on getting to work. Long, patient queues formed at all the bus stops, and a steady stream of people made their way out of Euston underground station.

Among the crowd emerging from the station was a fresh-faced man; he stopped for a minute to get his bearings. Then, glancing around, he raised his umbrella and walked swiftly down the street. Avoiding the puddles, he crossed the road and continued on past the shabby shops that lined Euston Road until he came to a stop in front of a dingy building.

The ground floor had once been a shop, but now a large sign hanging above the door stated this was a Combined Services Recruiting Office. The windows were festooned with posters urging men to join up and serve their country and advertising all the different ways in which they could do this. Pushing open the door, the man found himself in a stuffy crowded room. At the far end stood three large tables with an officer sitting behind each one. Above their heads hung large placards stating the service – Army, Navy or RAF – they represented.

The man joined the queue in front of the table where an RAF officer sat. Finally, it was his turn. Sitting down, he quietly stated that he wanted to volunteer for aircrew and serve as a pilot. The officer looked at him slightly doubtfully for a minute, but after asking a few questions, handed over a form to be filled in. Carefully he completed the form and signed his name: William Alexander Meyer.

William Alexander Meyer, born Wilhelm-Axel Meyer-Braselmann, was then thirty-one years old and known as Bill. He was of average height and slim build with hazel eyes that gazed calmly out of an open face. He came from a wealthy background and, while quietly spoken, had an air of natural authority that fostered confidence and respect in others. His parents had been comfortably off when they arrived in England and since then Wilhelm Meyer senior had very successfully built up the family business. Considerably older than his wife, he had been delighted at Bill's birth and Bill had spent a happy childhood somewhat doted on by Emmy, his mother, and his grandmother, Laura, who had accompanied the family when they moved to England. However, Wilhelm senior intended his son to go into the family business, and he was brought up from a young age with a strong sense of duty and responsibility.

Bill was an only child and he was now the managing director of the family business, W. M. Meyer Ltd., having taken over the running of the firm on his father's unexpected death at the start of the war. As the firm was engaged in essential war work, supplying equipment to the armed forces, Bill was in a reserved occupation. He could have remained working in London in comparative safety for the rest of the war. However, that was not his way. He had wanted to volunteer immediately after war broke out but realised that his responsibilities to the family business and the contribution it made to the war effort came first. He would need to organise a team to run W. M. Meyer Ltd. By the spring of 1941 he was confident that such a team was in place. He was now determined to join up and equally determined not to let his German parentage prevent this.

Bill had come to the conclusion that joining the RAF as a pilot would be the most immediate way of getting into the war and, importantly, where his abilities would be most useful. Pilots were needed and he knew he had a 'feel' for handling machinery. However, the RAF had strict age limits. While the limit was thirty-two for aircrew, it was thirty-one for pilots. Bill, already thirty-one, realised he would have a difficult job to persuade the RAF to accept him for pilot training. Aware that he was too old to fly fighters, he knew that if accepted, he would almost certainly be posted to Bomber Command. He also knew of the extremely high casualties suffered by bomber crews and of the extra risk he would be running with his German background should he ever have to bail out over occupied Europe. It did not deter him.

Bill was told to report for a medical and an interview at the Euston Air Candidate Selection Board at Euston House in Eversholt Street on the morning of Wednesday, 11 June. He duly presented himself and, after his papers were checked, he was quickly despatched upstairs to sit exams in maths and English and undergo various aptitude tests. An initial medical followed. This included stringent sight checks and a peculiar hearing test that involved being blindfolded while the range of hearing was tested with a tuning fork. Having passed these hurdles, one remained: the all-important interview with the Selection Board. Quickly straightening his tie, Bill walked into the room. Behind a large wooden table sat five RAF officers. They greeted him politely and asked him to be seated before questioning him about his education and why he wanted to join up as a pilot. To Bill's relief, no questions touched on his family background and, needless to say, Bill did not mention it. He was both determined and persuasive and evidently he impressed the Board as, despite his age, he was immediately recommended for calling up as 'Pilot/Observer' in six weeks' time and for a commission after initial training.

At this time, Britain found herself standing isolated and alone against a triumphant Germany now in control of most of Europe. Following the declaration of war in September 1939, the next six months had been quiet with so little happening that it became known as the 'Phoney War'. This proved to be the quiet before the storm. In the following months, German forces rampaged across Europe in a breathtaking sweep that saw Norway, Belgium, Holland, Denmark and France flattened by the German *blitzkrieg*.

The collapse of France saw the British Expeditionary Force, there to support the French Army, driven back and trapped by the rapid German advance. Together with many French troops, the remains of the Force found themselves encircled in and around the small town of Dunkirk. In a desperate effort to recover men, if not their equipment, the Admiralty launched a makeshift rescue operation: 'Operation Dynamo'. Not only naval vessels but fishing boats, lifeboats and almost anything that could float were pressed into service to become famous as the 'little ships of Dunkirk'. This motley armada succeeded in evacuating some 338,000 troops between 26 May and 4 June 1940, with many of these troops then able to go on to fight in the North Africa campaign. Despite the disastrous defeat that led to this operation, the successful rescue was a tremendous morale booster. The Prime Minister, Winston Churchill, acclaimed this as a victory in itself, 'a miracle of deliverance'.[1] However, he also warned his people that, 'What

General Weygand called the Battle of France is over. I expect that the Battle of Britain is about to begin'.[2]

As Churchill had warned, a triumphant Hitler now ordered his generals to initiate plans for the invasion of Britain, with the first step being the establishment of air superiority over the Channel to prevent the RAF destroying the invading force. The Luftwaffe attacks commenced, and throughout the summer and during the early autumn of 1940, what became known as 'The Battle of Britain' raged, forcing Hitler to delay the invasion. Pressure mounted on RAF Fighter Command as the Luftwaffe sent over fighters and bombers by day and by night as it sought to overwhelm and destroy the RAF both on the ground and in the air.

By early September, the situation was becoming critical as the loss of experienced RAF pilots and the damage to airfields and radar installations mounted. Had this level of losses continued, they would have been unsustainable. Fortunately for Britain, Hitler intervened. On 24 August, the Luftwaffe dropped bombs on London. This was by accident but it provoked Churchill, who ordered that Berlin be bombed in retaliation. Furious at this, Hitler ordered the Luftwaffe to change tactics and launch a bombing campaign against cities and industry in an attempt to break the morale of the population and force Britain to come to terms. From early September, the Luftwaffe were forced to change their tactics, and although British cities now suffered, Hitler's decision gave the RAF a much-needed respite and a chance to repair and rebuild.

This was the start of the Blitz, when Londoners were bombed every day or night for fifty-seven days from 7 September 1940. Other cities were bombed sporadically but the heaviest raids were on London. This changed in November when the German High Command decided to broaden the focus of attacks and began heavy raids on other major cities. On 14 November, Coventry suffered the most concentrated attack of the war so far. For eleven hours wave after wave of bombers flew over Coventry dropping incendiaries and bombs that devastated the cathedral and ancient town centre. Such was the scale of the destruction wreaked by the Luftwaffe that a new word was coined, 'coventrated', meaning to totally devastate by heavy bombing. The impact of the raid was enormous and for a few days civilian morale wavered as people wandered around dazed and helpless. Fortunately, a visit from King George VI helped dispel the mood of despair.

Night after night, waves of German bombers dropped explosive and incendiary bombs, and night after night, Londoners listened to the crump of bombs exploding around them. The resulting fires sent flames blazing through the smoke-laden air, turning the dark night sky scarlet as buildings and whole streets burned. The air was filled with the crackle of fires and the roar of collapsing buildings.

The government had devised a means of basic protection in the form of Anderson shelters, and these had been distributed for construction in people's gardens. They consisted of sheets of corrugated metal bolted together and then covered in soil and sandbags. They were better than nothing at all but no protection against a direct hit. For Londoners, an alternative was to take refuge in the Underground stations. At 4 pm, people were allowed into the stations for the night and, clutching babies, blankets and sandwiches, they descended into the dark to settle down as best they could. Others made their way into designated shelters and when the air raid sirens sounded, people automatically rushed into the nearest one.

Each morning people awoke tired and sore having spent the night huddled together sleeping on underground platforms, sometimes even between the rails while the current was turned off or, alternatively, crammed into fetid, overcrowded shelters. They emerged to find plumes of smoke rising through the gritty air. The smell of cordite lingered, mingling with that of burst gas mains and burning timber as people stumbled through the choking dust to pick their way through rubble-strewn streets to get to work, or to return home to see if it was still standing.

The offices of the business W. M. Meyer Ltd. were situated in Southwark, one of the most heavily bombed areas in London as

German bombers targeted the industrial heartland and transport links of the capital. As Bill walked to work every day, he passed the facades of wrecked buildings and stepped around the piles of glass and masonry that littered the pavements. St George's Cathedral in Southwark, designed by Pugin, had been practically destroyed and a public shelter nearby flattened by a direct hit, killing sixty-eight people and injuring another 175.

In towns and cities throughout Britain, ordinary men, women and children found themselves on the front line as the Luftwaffe unleashed its bombs and brought the war right to their doors. Blackout regulations meant ensuring that all windows were covered. Strips of sticky tape were used to tape neat diamond crosses on windows to prevent bomb blasts sending lethal shards of glass flying everywhere. Underground trains had their windows covered, making seeing which station to get off at difficult. Streetlights remained unlit and cars could not use their headlights. Traffic lights were masked with a small slit for people to glimpse the red, amber and green sequence. Inevitably, this led to frequent accidents and road traffic deaths soared. Staple foods such as meat, butter and tea were already rationed, but food shortages were getting worse and more items were continually being added to the list of rationed products.

The German invasion of Yugoslavia and Greece was now complete, and Britain had suffered a string of defeats in North Africa and Crete. This, then, was the situation by the summer of 1941. With most of Europe overrun and civilians throughout towns in Britain suffering under the Blitz, these were the darkest days of the war. Recruiting posters stated that 'Pilots of the RAF [...] are chosen for their spirit and self-reliance, because of their desire for action and adventure'. They asked for 'Determined men. Men that know that they have a great cause to fight for'.[3] Bill was just such a man.

CHAPTER TWO
JOINING UP

A few weeks later, the expected letter arrived. On opening it, Bill found he was to report to No. 1 Air Crew Receiving Centre (ACRC) on 28 July 1941. There he was issued with his service number and became an aircrew cadet, an Aircraftsman Second Class, the lowest form of life in the RAF. Together with other new recruits he now faced a further barrage of medical and intelligence tests. These took place at No. 1 Aircrew Reception Centre, located in the splendid surroundings of Lord's Cricket Ground. There, in the refined and dignified setting of the Members' Pavilion, the volunteers underwent a decidedly undignified range of medical tests and vaccinations, including a close examination and tests for venereal disease.

Bill and the other cadets in his intake were allocated accommodation in what had been luxurious flats overlooking the Regent's Canal with elegant names such as Bentinck Close, Viceroy Court and St. James's. The elegance and luxury did not survive the arrival of the RAF. The rooms were stripped out and the windows were largely bricked up. Five or more beds were squashed into each room. Bill, so much older than the other recruits and from a privileged background, must have felt very out of place. Used to giving orders himself, he now found himself ordered around by fierce sergeants and subjected to military discipline that steamrollered individual identity into the raw manpower needed for melding into aircrew.

During the three weeks of induction, the aircrew cadets were detailed in groups of fifty. One of their first stops was the barbershop, where they all received a quick once-over with electric clippers. Thus shorn, they marched off to be issued with some essential items. These included uniforms, woollen long johns and hefty sheepskin boots, together with gas masks and other pieces of equipment. The RAF requisitioned all kinds of property; thus, uniforms were issued in a garage, sizing relying solely on the experienced eye of the tailors, whose quick decisions led to some strange results. The coarse stiff material used for uniforms made them very scratchy and uncomfortable. A white flash worn in the peak of the forage cap indicated cadet status.

By reputation, the RAF was less militaristic than the other services, and many cadets thought that drilling was part of Army rather than RAF training. They soon discovered otherwise. To their surprise and dismay, they found that most of their time was spent being shouted at by NCOs as they marched around the leafy streets of St John's Wood, while the rest was spent having RAF regulations drummed into them. On Sundays, church parade was compulsory. Another unwelcome surprise was a swift and thorough introduction to such domestic skills as polishing boots and floors. A session at the local swimming baths was also on the curriculum and everyone had to try and swim one length. Bill had no trouble with this but those who did received a crash course in swimming, the idea being that they should be able to survive ditching in the sea. The only indication they had that they were in the RAF was when they were introduced to the basics of aircraft recognition and signalling skills.

The RAF, making the most of all the local facilities, arranged for the cadets to take their meals in the Pavilion at London Zoo, just five minutes from the cricket ground. The most dangerous animals had been evacuated due to the bombing and the zoo itself closed to the public for the duration. Now feeding time at the zoo continued, but for men rather than animals. Although the dining rooms there had been stripped out, they were far too small for the large numbers sent there. As the men approached the Pavilion, they were met with a sickening smell of stale cooking mingled with pungent animal smells coming from the cages of the remaining animals. Once in, it was every man for himself. Grabbing some cutlery, they queued to be served from giant industrial catering cauldrons and then struggled to find a seat. To try to speed things up, cutlery was not sent back for washing but just dipped in buckets of greasy warm water in the dining room and left ready for the next person.[1] No time for Health and Safety nonsense then.

Having survived this robust introduction, the group were ready for the next stage, which was a posting to an Initial Training Wing. Bill was sent to Initial Training Wing No.1 based at Babbacombe in Devon on the 'English Riviera'.

Sitting atop red sandstone cliffs, Babbacombe was known as a quieter, more traditional seaside resort than its lively neighbour Torquay. Families came there to play on the sandy beaches and to admire the spectacular views from the clifftop promenade. The beach itself was reached by steep paths running through the green woodland of the neighbouring downs. The famous funicular, the Cliff Railway, in operation since 1926, provided an alternative and easier means of reaching the beach. Long-established clubs offered residents a choice of genteel sporting activities, such as bowling, cricket or sailing. There was also a little theatre at the end of the downs where concerts and summer shows provided entertainment for holidaymakers and residents alike.

When war broke out, this peaceful existence vanished. The Cliff Railway closed and guns were placed on the top of it. Guns were also placed on shelters and some hotels to provide protection from the Luftwaffe. Most of the hotels and boarding houses in the area were requisitioned by the military to house the cadets, and the little theatre was used for military lectures.

No. 1 Initial Training Unit had been formed at Babbacombe in June 1940. Here cadets would find themselves living in billets with names such as The Sefton, Oswalds, Trecarn, Foxlands and Palermo, gracious names associated with carefree summer holidays rather than the rigours of RAF training. RAF Headquarters were at the Norcliffe Hotel, high up on the clifftop with spectacular views overlooking Lyme Bay. This hotel managed to survive the worst the RAF could do to it and is still a hotel today.

These courses lasted from ten to twelve weeks, and Bill's course started on 9 August 1941. Arriving by train, Bill and the other cadets marched to their commandeered hotel and settled in. Many had been hopeful that the days of square-bashing would now be over. Again they were to be disappointed. The surroundings were far more pleasant but the regime was just as arduous and the endless drills and parades continued. Most of the time a twelve-hour day was the norm, often seven days a week. For the unlucky ones, lights-out was at 9 pm in some billets. Any spare time had to be spent preparing for an exacting morning inspection when eagle-eyed sergeants would come round and scrutinise kit and bed space. Every fold of bedding had to be correct and buttons and boots had to positively dazzle.

On their first morning the cadets were given a grading test in elementary maths. Then most of the days were spent in lectures covering the theory of flight, meteorology and the basics of wireless, navigation and Morse code. There were classes on aircraft identification; the ability to distinguish quickly and accurately between friend and foe would often mean the difference between life and death. To teach identification, models of aircraft were hung from a ceiling and painted black, just as an aircraft would appear when approaching from a distance. They were also taught how to strip down and put together a machine gun blindfolded, a skill only the gunners might possibly need in the skies over Germany.

The RAF wanted their recruits to be fit and ensured that they had plenty of physical exercise. To their dismay, they found that square-bashing, lengthy route marches and exercise sessions in the public parks were the order of the day. Frequent formal inspections, such as those before church parade, ensured the cadets were kept constantly on their toes. One of the few escapes from the classroom and the endless drills came in the form of navigation exercises. These were popular, as they involved going out in RAF launches in Torbay. Once out on the water it felt more like a holiday as the cadets looked around at the palm-lined cliffs and beaches of the 'English Riviera'.

There was little time off and Bill, older than most, tended to spend the time catching up with letters and reading. However, many of the cadets headed down to the pubs to meet up with local girls. On warm summer days they seized any opportunity that arose to swim and relax on the sheltered sandy beaches. There was also the not-to-be-missed chance of meeting girls at Saturday evening dances in Torquay. These were popular despite involving a long walk back afterwards, as the buses stopped running quite early. Occasionally the little theatre reverted to its original purpose as members of ENSA, the Entertainments National Service Association, which provided entertainments for the forces, put on performances.

During the course, the volunteers were constantly assessed and tested. At the end of the course those who passed were then informed – there was no choice in the matter – what 'trade' they would pursue: pilot, engineer, navigator, bomb aimer, gunner or wireless operator. Bill was delighted when he received confirmation that he would be trained, as originally recommended, as a pilot. He was now issued with a full set of flying gear. It included three layers of gloves: a silk pair, a woollen pair and huge leather gauntlets that fitted over the lot. Then three flying suits of varying thickness were issued. The thickest was a padded affair of duvet-like material in a vague human shape with zip pockets. Two flying helmets, one warmer and one lighter, fur-lined boots and goggles completed this daunting outfit.

As the course came to an end, there was much discussion among the cadets as to where they would be sent next, and wild rumours started flying around. Finally, one cadet could bear the uncertainty no longer. In his eagerness to find out, he broke into the Commanding Officer's office one night, searched it, and returned with evidence that they were all being sent abroad in forty-eight hours. This caused much excitement and a scramble to sort out belongings. To their intense frustration, however, they found themselves still in Babbacombe three weeks later.[2] It was not until early October that their orders came through. Crowding around the notice board, pushing and jostling, the cadets tried to find their names on the list. Running down the list, Bill found his posting: he was being sent to the USA for flying training.

CHAPTER THREE
A JOURNEY TO THE USA

At the outbreak of the war, the RAF realised that it would be impossible to train all the aircrew that would be needed in the UK. The Empire Air Training Scheme (also known as the British Commonwealth Air Training Plan) was set up to train British and Dominion nationals in Canada, Rhodesia, South Africa and Australia. Although the USA was not yet in the war, British and US Air Force officers started exploring the possibility of training RAF pilots there since enemy aircraft and bad weather would not interfere with training. The passing of the Lend-Lease Act in March 1941 enabled the USA to provide assistance in the form of equipment and supplies to the Allies and allowed President Roosevelt to give final approval for a scheme known as the All Through Training Scheme, or ATTS. In May 1941, this scheme established six British Flying Training Schools in the USA, using civilian airfields and instructors.

Another agreement followed in June 1941 for the setting-up of an additional training programme, the Arnold Scheme (named after Henry H. Arnold, the Commander General of the US Army Air Corps). In this scheme, RAF training would take place under the United States Army Air Corps using the Corps' own schools in the SEACTC (Southeast Air Corps Training Centre) region of the USA. A third scheme, the Towers scheme (after Vice-Admiral John H. Towers of the US Navy), commenced in July 1941; this scheme also included Fleet Air Arm pilots. In all, some 13,673 pilots were trained in the United States under these schemes.[1]

Bill was still unaware of his final destination, knowing only that it would be somewhere in the USA. Before they were sent abroad, the cadets were allowed to go on leave. Worried about leaving his mother to face the bombing alone in London, Bill persuaded her to move to Cornwall. He drove her down there and settled her into the luxurious surroundings of the Grenville Hotel in Bude. The hotel was an imposing castellated building looking down on the estuary and Summerleaze beach. There they walked along the long sandy beaches talking of what the future might bring. It was all too brief a break and soon Bill had to return to London before reporting for duty.

Fresh after their leave, Bill and the other cadets now set out on the first leg of their long journey. This was to be by train. They scrambled into the carriages, piling their equipment as best they could into luggage racks and under seats. The train rattled its way through the countryside through occasional anonymous towns and villages. The stations they passed through revealed nothing, all names having been removed at the beginning of the war in case of invasion. The men dozed, those nearest the windows waking from time to time to rub at the steamed-up glass and try to spot some identifiable landmark. Occasionally, the train stopped at nameless little places where women volunteers handed out welcome meals or mugs of tea to the cadets. Night fell and with it the rain – it beat down, further blurring the view from the windows. Finally came another stop and shouts from the sergeants: they had arrived at their destination. This turned out to be Wilmslow in Cheshire. It was 3 am and chilly rain poured down relentlessly. The cadets, already tired and stiff from the hours on the train, found there was no transport to meet them and so, shouldering their kit, they marched the two miles in the pitch-black to the transit camp, arriving cold and wet and miserable.

Their temporary base was the Personnel Despatch Centre, Wilmslow. RAF Wilmslow, like many other places, had been hurriedly thrown up in 1940. It was a soulless place. Long rows of wooden huts were interspersed with parade grounds and large hangars that were used for training. An outer fence of barbed wire surrounded it. Thousands of men had passed through the camp on their way to Canada, the USA and Africa, and the thousands of heavy RAF boots had turned the entrance to each hut into a muddy swamp. The exhausted cadets stumbled into their huts, hardly noticing the filthy mud-spattered blankets covering the bunks, and just fell into bed and slept.

Unfortunately for them the Station Commander was a stickler for correct appearances and promptly issued an order stating that '…particular attention is to be paid to their general turn-out and their hair'. Despite making some efforts to comply, the quagmire around their huts meant it was a losing battle. To reinforce his point, the Commander informed them that '12 hours before departure there should be a full dress parade and inspection'.[2] This was not well received.

Life in the transit facility was boring. Orders were issued then countermanded and men were marched around aimlessly. Rumours as to where they were being sent spread like wildfire, and hopes were raised only to be dashed again. There was a general feeling of being in limbo as they waited to find out their final destination. Much of the time was spent joining various queues to receive yet more items of equipment and various papers. On reaching the head of one such queue, the cadets were told to select a civilian suit from a bunch hanging on a rack. A collective groan went up as they saw the hideous old-fashioned double-breasted design and odd shapes of these ill-fitting garments. Bill, always immaculately dressed in civilian life, looked at them in dismay. They were also issued with an overcoat, a trilby hat, shoes, a Woolworth's tie and, for no apparent reason, a beret. The next item to be issued was a cheap fibre suitcase in which to put all this finery. There was much debate as to whether these would withstand the first shower of rain.

In the evenings, the cadets were allowed out of camp briefly but there was little to do. There were two small cinemas but these were soon sold out, leaving a visit to one of the local pubs as the only alternative. After ten days, orders finally came through for their departure. Such was the relief that no one complained about their departure time, which was scheduled for 3 am.

On 14 October 1941, Bill and his fellow cadets, now brandishing their dubious suitcases as well as kitbags, again walked in the dark to the siding and boarded the waiting troop train. Despite the cramped uncomfortable conditions, exhaustion ensured sleep came quickly. The train rumbled its way north, clattering through isolated stations before arriving at Carlisle at 8.45 am the next morning. Gathering their kit, the men clambered down onto the platform before gratefully drinking the hot tea offered by volunteers.

After a short break, they boarded another train that lumbered slowly on, passing through Gretna Green before taking them through the striking red sandstone buildings of Dumfries, Robert Burns' hometown. From there the track climbed up over the moors through Kilmarnock, the home of Johnny Walker whisky, before finally entering the majestic glass-covered concourse of Glasgow Central Station.

In no mood to admire the station's splendid architecture, the men shouldered their gear and left the train, making their way down the platform to the NAAFI canteen, eager to get their hands on steaming mugs of hot tea and cigarettes. The station was filled with noise and bustle. Whistles blew, escaping steam hissed up around engines that were ready to depart, catching under the station's glazed and sooty roof. This glass roof let in no light; the panes had been painted black to hide the station from German bombers. Edging their way through other groups of servicemen, the men trudged along the platforms in search of their next train.

The piercing shriek of the guard's whistle, and a jolt as the engine moved off, started them on the last stage of their rail journey. Shrouded in steam, the train wound out through the sprawling southwest suburbs to the edges of the Firth of Clyde. Here, famous shipyards such as Scott Lithgow and John Brown were working at full capacity, building and repairing ships and submarines for the Navy. Late in the evening, the men reached their destination, Gourock, situated on the point where the Firth of Clyde turns south towards the sea.

Gourock had flourished as a tourist destination in the nineteenth century and a station had been built at the pier head for the convenience of holidaymakers taking the paddle steamers to the seaside towns on the other side of the Clyde. Now the pleasure craft were gone, and liners converted to troop ships lay at anchor while merchant convoys assembled offshore. Disembarking from the train, Bill caught the first glimpse of the ship that would take them to America.

The *Pasteur* towered over the pier at Gourock, her single funnel standing high above the sleek lines of her hull. She was one of the most luxurious liners of the time, and one of the fastest, having been designed by the French for the France–South America run. Her beautiful lines reflected her speed and the determination of her French owners to take the Blue Riband of the Atlantic, an award for the fastest Atlantic crossing by a passenger liner, away from Britain. She was launched on 15 February 1938 and christened *Pasteur* by Louis Pasteur's godmother, Madame Pasteur Valléry-Radot. The French Government was so proud of her that a stamp was issued bearing her image. Completed in August 1939, she was capable of 25 knots. Her inaugural cruise, due to take place in September 1939, had to be cancelled after war was declared.

In June 1940, she sailed on her maiden voyage carrying part of the gold reserves of France, some 213 tons, to Canada for safekeeping. However, on her arrival, France having surrendered, the grateful Allies promptly seized both the gold and the liner. The *Pasteur* was now painted camouflage grey and converted into a DEMS, a Defensively Equipped Merchant Ship. The title was impressive but misleading; the defensive equipment consisted of one gun positioned on the stern. A better defence was her speed, and it served her well in the dangerous Atlantic runs.

For Bill, the sight brought back nostalgic memories of happy times lazing in the sun on cruises in the Mediterranean. While the *Pasteur's* looks were admired, she was regarded with mixed feelings. She had an infamous reputation for rolling and corkscrewing. There was a rumour that she had a kink in her keel, but it's more likely that a rather flat bottom accounted for her instability. She had not been built for the North Atlantic. Despite wartime censorship, rumours were rife that the conditions were so bad on board that first Canadian and then New Zealand airmen had refused to sail in her.

On boarding, the cadets set about finding their lodgings. Among them was twenty-year-old Ken Gilderdale. He was dismayed to find that their accommodation was on E deck, down in the bowels of the ship. Trudging down narrow staircases, he finally reached it and entered a large and very crowded room. The air was already thick with the smell of unwashed bodies, sweat and cigarettes. There was no fresh air; the portholes were tightly shut, as they were close to the waterline.

Accommodation was arranged in three layers. Those in the top tier lay in hammocks, swinging to and fro and bumping each other constantly. Unlike sailors, the aircrew cadets had no idea how to sling a hammock and spent most of their first night wide awake swinging around bent double. Below them, and occasionally brushed by the hammocks swinging above, slept another layer of cadets on thin mattresses on top of the mess tables. Finally came the bottom layer, on mattresses placed on the floor beneath the tables. Ken chose one of those mattresses and it turned out to be a good choice. The smell was not quite so strong and there was less danger of being bumped into. It also offered another significant benefit. The table above acted as protection when, inevitably, the cadet above was violently seasick. Sanitary arrangements were primitive in the extreme. There were just a handful of saltwater showers and only intermittent hot water supplying the few basins. The ship's lavatories were firmly bolted shut. In their place was a long room in which the lavatory consisted of a trough made from a stripped pine tree trunk to sit upon, cheek to cheek in every sense with fellow cadets. At times, there would be forty ashen-faced men sitting there in abject misery.

On the morning of Friday 17 October, heavy vibrations ran through the hull of the *Pasteur* as the great engines began to turn; the rattle of chains signified that the anchors were being lifted and then very slowly she started to move. The submarine nets that protected the upper Clyde opened and she made her way past the rugged Argyllshire mountains and the islands of Bute and Arran before arriving at the mouth of the Clyde and anchoring there. Around midnight, the thud of the engines was heard again as the *Pasteur* gradually got under way and headed out to sea. The next morning, she met up with her convoy, consisting of an aircraft carrier, five destroyers and two armed merchantmen. As the wind reached gale force, the destroyers could be seen rolling and pitching as enormous waves crashed over their bows. There was an ominous swell running. Most of the men had never been at sea before and were already overcome with seasickness.

On Monday afternoon, there was some excitement as a ship was sighted off the port side and an Albacore aircraft was launched from the aircraft carrier to investigate, but it proved to be a false alarm.[3] By now the weather had deteriorated even further. Huge waves slammed into the ship and she rolled to and fro with tremendous shudders and groans as she struggled to right herself. There were also constant course changes to deter submarine attacks and occasionally a tremendous vibration ran through the ship as an extra-large wave crashed into her. Confined below deck because of the bad weather, the cadets were left to their own devices. They could wear what they liked and, if still on their feet, fill in time by playing poker or going to the ship's cinema. The food served up was almost inedible. Few could face it – the relentless juddering, rolling motion saw to that. After a miserable few days, the weather improved as the ship approached the USA. Their naval escort left them on Friday and the *Pasteur* then made a dash for Halifax at top speed to outrun any lurking German U-boats.

It was with some relief that Bill and his fellow cadets left the ship. Arriving at Halifax was like entering a different world. Looking around, they saw lights blazing from buildings and roads illuminated by street lights in contrast to the near total darkness of England in the blackout. Their train, its huge locomotive wafting plumes of smoke into the night sky, was waiting. Settling on board, they peered out, catching tantalising glimpses of cinemas, restaurants and shops as the train made its way through the town. The headlights of the many cars picked out people on the streets going about their business or shopping, carefree and relaxed. It was a glimpse of normal life, a world away from the deprivations and hardships of wartime Britain. As night fell, the train wound through snow-covered forests gleaming in the moonlight, past the log cabins of sleepy villages until, some six hours later, it pulled into Moncton, a small town on the Petitcodiac River in New Brunswick. It had been named after Lieutenant Colonel Robert Monckton, a British officer who had captured the nearby Fort of Beausejour in 1755.

On arrival, yet another unwelcome shock awaited the tired cadets. They tumbled out into the cold night to discover that they faced a chilly march out of the town and through the forest to their camp. As they crunched through the snow, the wind sent down scatters of snowflakes from the laden branches; the damp flakes settled on shoulders and crept insidiously down collars and into cuffs. For an hour they tramped, mostly in silence, before the sound of hammering came through the cold night air and lights began to be seen flickering through the trees. It was 6 am before they arrived at the Royal Canadian Air Force Transit Camp at Moncton.[4] To their dismay, the cadets could now see what the hammering was about; the camp was still under construction. Through the trees appeared half-completed buildings with men working furiously on them. Some dug drains and others laid water pipes and hammered roofs into place. After the sea voyage, a train journey and a cold march through the forest, everyone wanted nothing more than hot showers, warmth and food. What they got were cold, unheated, incomplete buildings, blankets, buckets and a suggestion they use the woods for their toilets and walk into town to eat in the town diners. Mercifully, at least breakfast had been arranged, 'consisting of eggs, bacon, bread and butter (as much butter as you liked) and tea with plentiful supply of sugar'.[5] No one wasted a moment – they fell to with glee. Later, on venturing into town, the cadets found the shops filled with cigarettes, chocolates, oranges and all sorts of items either rationed or unobtainable now in Britain. Main Street was lined with diners whose menus offered huge T-bone steaks, eggs and ham; the cadets looked on in awe before rushing in and placing their orders.

In all the sources drawn on in this account, the descriptions of the food found in the USA have been amazingly detailed. Meals are described with a relish that we, used to the plenty of the modern supermarket, can only wonder at. It brings home how desperate the situation in Britain was at the time. Food rationing in Britain in 1941 entitled a person to one egg per week if available, and often it was not. Bacon, sugar, tea and jam were also rationed. Coffee was very difficult to obtain and tea leaves were reused as many times as possible. Today, Moncton's website describes it as 'Canada's most courteous city'.[6] The cadets certainly found it so in 1941. The people of Moncton were both kind-hearted and generous and invited them to their homes for some home cooking and relaxation. The lucky ones were offered the chance of a good night's sleep in a real bed again. Those not so fortunate ended up in the unfinished huts with no heating. The day after their arrival, the cadets all had their photographs taken for identity cards. Ken Gilderdale spent his free time at the cinema before enjoying a supper of ham, eggs, bread, butter, tea and coconut cream tart with ice cream. Bananas had ceased to be imported to Britain in 1939 so that when he sampled a new delight, the banana split, the next day, he made a special note of it in his diary. The standard of living amazed the cadets, as even in this small town, neon signs lit up the streets and everyone seemed to have cars and fridges.

On the third day, 29 October 1941, the cadets were divided into groups of fifty, told their destinations and ordered onto various trains. Bill Meyer, Ken Gilderdale and Richard Hough were part of the contingent headed for No. 2 British Flying School, at the Polaris Flight Academy in California. The Polaris Flight Academy was a civilian flying school that had been contracted to train military cadets. This was fortunate, as Richard Hough was warned, 'The ones belonging to the Army Air Corps are run like West Point and the few survivors are never the same men again'.[7] In fact, the numbers eliminated on the courses run by the Army Air Corps were around 40-50% compared with a rate of approximately 25% in those run by civilians. At 9 pm, Bill's train departed for Montreal and he found to his delight that they were travelling in luxury for a change. Everyone settled down in comfortable first-class seats or wandered off to the observation car or a club car where they could smoke and gamble. The train ran through the night following the course of the St Lawrence River and they reached Montreal at 7 pm the following day. On arrival, they found a coach waiting to whisk them off on a two-hour tour of the city. Then it was time to board another train bound for Toronto, Detroit and Chicago. The USA was still a neutral country so, in order to avoid any embarrassment at the Canadian/USA border, the cadets were told to change into their civilian outfits, trilbys and all, for the border crossing. This order was swiftly reversed after the crossing, possibly because of the dire sight they presented in their ill-fitting suits.

In Chicago, the cadets were allowed out on the town for a few hours. Beforehand, an officer warned them that as they were the first contingent to visit the USA in uniform, they had to be sure to make a good impression and with that in mind to go and smarten up. On arrival, the magnificent columns, marble floors and vaulted ceiling of Chicago Union Station were left unnoticed as the men rushed out in search of bars and restaurants. Their uniforms created some surprise but a warm welcome. Ken Gilderdale ended up in a bar where, when it was discovered that they were RAF cadets, the pianist played *The White Cliffs of Dover*[8] especially for them. It was a nostalgic reminder of home.

Back at the station, the cadets made their way to the train that would take them to Los Angeles; this was the famous *Challenger*. Bill walked to the head of the train where he was met with an awe-inspiring sight. Towering above him stood an enormous articulated locomotive. Black smoke already poured from the funnel and steam wreathed around its fourteen wheels. Above the iconic single central light on the front of the engine was a large bell, while below it the cowcatcher stood ready to brush aside any obstacles. The on-board facilities were equally impressive. The *Challenger* had originally been designed as a deluxe train and the men now enjoyed the comforts of Pullman coaches equipped with relaxing chair seats and tables for fine dining.[9] A heavy snowfall during the night delayed the train for a couple of hours, but comfortable, warm and with plentiful supplies of food and drink, the cadets could not have cared less. The train ran throughout the night, coursing across the plains of Nebraska, and the next morning found them amidst the rugged and splendid scenery of the western edge of the Rocky Mountains. It wound on through tunnels, emerging between the rocky walls of canyons, past cliffs, snow-capped peaks and verdant forests before arriving in Salt Lake City. There they were treated to a quick thirty-five minute tour of the city.

Once back on the train, they settled in for the final night of their journey as the train carried them across the vast Nevada Desert and through the bright lights of Las Vegas before pulling into Los Angeles Union Station on Monday 3 November. There they emerged rumpled and yawning in the soft, warm Californian air. Heaving their packs and suitcases onto the platform, they changed trains for the last time. The train that they now boarded was 'a snorting old Wild West train'.[10] It wound its way slowly north through Los Angeles and then out through the grasslands of Antelope Valley, so named after the herds of Pronghorn antelope that used to graze there. Finally, the train drew into their destination: Lancaster, California.

CHAPTER FOUR
POLARIS FLIGHT ACADEMY

The small town of Lancaster is located in the wide Antelope Valley about 80 miles north of Los Angeles. The town was founded in the late 1870s when the Southern Pacific Railroad Company came through the valley forging a link between Los Angeles and San Francisco. Standing at an elevation of 2,380 feet, it basks in the sunshine of the blue Californian sky. The rugged peaks of the San Gabriel range lie to the southwest and those of the Tehachapi Mountains to the northwest, while the plains of the great Mojave Desert stretch away to the east. The weird shapes of giant cacti rise up out of the scrubby grassland, and the gnarled and twisting branches of Joshua trees dot the landscape. These spiky trees were named by early Mormon settlers who felt the stretching branches recalled Joshua's raised arms as he led the Israelites into the Promised Land. In spring, the dusty grassland comes alive as wildflowers and poppies, California's state flower, carpet the desert in vast swathes of brilliant colour. At night, in the clear desert air, the glow of the distant lights of Los Angeles suffuses the southern sky, hinting at the excitements of Hollywood not too far away.

Eight miles to the west of Lancaster lay the aptly named War Eagle Field, the home of the Polaris Flight Academy. When No. 2 British Flying Training School (BFTS) had been set up in June 1941, it was originally based at Grand Central Air Terminal in

Glendale under the auspices of Major C.C. Moseley, who had been a pilot in the First World War. However, the foggy conditions at Glendale, situated on the outskirts of Los Angeles, had meant that flying training often had to be done at an auxiliary field at Newhall, some 40 miles away. After a couple of months, the school moved to War Eagle Field, where the clear desert air was better suited for flying despite the high winds that swept off the mountains.

No. 2 BFTS was a curious mix; a military training school for pilots run by civilian instructors with the cadets under the charge of three British officers. The aim was to take in batches of fifty trainees every five weeks and turn them into qualified pilots by the end of a twenty-week course. Each course had a cadet course commander who was responsible to the Commanding Officer for the cadets on his course. Under the Course Commander, the course was divided into two groups, each with a squad commander and deputy. They all wore marked armlets and were considered as cadet captains or NCOs. Their seniority was marked by certain privileges, such as not having to book in and out of camp and enjoying more spacious accommodation.

After their lengthy journey, everyone was delighted with the accommodation that awaited them at the Polaris Flight Academy. They found brand-new four-room bungalows with bathrooms, each surrounded by carefully tended lawns and flowerbeds. Photographs taken at the time show immaculate white-painted buildings, with overhanging roofs to provide protection from the sun. The control tower, a three-storey building with outside staircases, proclaimed it to be 'War Eagle Field', while above the main door was painted the legend 'Polaris Flight Academy'.

The hybrid nature of the establishment was the cause of some very British concern regarding discipline. The commanding officer, Squadron Leader Whitlock, was worried that 'Familiarity… was not going to help in the preservation of discipline and morale'. Squadron Leader Whitlock considered that while a certain amount of informality led to useful discussion between instructors and pupils, too much fraternisation was to be discouraged and '…such foregatherings should stop before they reach the point where Christian names are employed and instructors and pupils drink together on every "open post" night'.[1]

While Bill was there, a flying school magazine, *Salute*, started up. The first edition appeared on 14 March 1942. This has proved to be an invaluable record of both daily life and the mishaps of the cadets. As ever, what initially impressed everyone was the food. While in England they lived on powdered eggs, sausages and endless Spam, here there was an abundant supply of milk, cream, butter, bacon, eggs, honey and jam for breakfast, and steaks, salad and fruit for lunch. However, the initial delight at such plenty seems to have soon worn off and after a month complaints were heard. A Course Messing representative asked, "Why the hell do Englishmen have to eat hot cakes for breakfast, and how can a fellow do slow rolls with his belly full of half-cooked bacon floating about in a pool of syrup?"[2]

The day started early with *reveille* at 5.45 am, followed by bed-making and a substantial breakfast. Some cadets had thought they might not be required to use their newly acquired domestic skills in this more relaxed environment; once again, they were to be disappointed. After breakfast, it was time to clean and polish everything in sight until the Flight Sergeant was satisfied. Flying and ground training started at 7 am. At ground school, the cadets were taught technical subjects such as navigation by cultured academics from the University of Southern California. While half of the school was thus engaged, the other half was flying. The flying side of things was decidedly less cultured. A motley bunch of tough ex-crop-dusters and stunt flyers from nearby Hollywood had been assembled, and it was their task to instil basic flying skills into the cadets. Ken Gilderdale recalls their teaching technique was not for the faint-hearted. Patience was in short supply, while cursing and swearing were not.

The cadets were introduced to their training aircraft, the Stearman PT (for Primary Trainer) 13. The PT 13 came into service as the basic trainer for the USAF in 1936 and continued in this role throughout World War II. It was a simple and rugged biplane with an open cockpit designed to teach students to fly by 'feel', with only the most basic instrumentation to monitor performance. Unusually, it was flown from the rear cockpit with the instructor in the front watching the student through a mirror. Forward visibility from either position was limited and these tail-wheeled aircraft had to be taxied in S-shaped curves to give a clear view of what was ahead. These creations of struts and canvas were painted a startling bright yellow. As one instructor explained encouragingly, "That colour stands out when they're looking for the goddam wreck."[3] Despite being a forgiving and responsive aircraft to fly, it became known as the 'Yellow Peril' due to its somewhat tricky ground-handling characteristics. On landing, it was all too easy for a cadet to either bounce along the runway or to ground loop it.

A ground loop occurs when, having landed on the runway, instead of just going straight ahead, the airplane does a complete spin through 180 degrees on its wheels, something easily done on tail-wheel aircraft. Many ground loops were recorded in the Operations Reports. There was another feature the students hated, a one-way voice tube intercom system called a Gosport tube, through which the instructor bellowed at the student, while the cringing student could only listen and suffer. Even worse was '… having to endure the vivid red face of Mr. Logan (Senior Flying Instructor) glaring at them through the mirror during a check flight'.[4]

Finally, six months after joining up, Bill had his first flying lesson. On 6 November, his logbook records an hour's 'air experience' in a Stearman with his instructor Mr H.T. Riley. The first couple of weeks of the course were spent learning basic flying skills. Such phrases as 'Watch the airspeed' and 'Centre the needle' would have rung in his ears as turns, spins and stalls were practised repeatedly. Stalls in the Stearman were both gentle and predictable. Take-offs and, much more demanding, landings had to be mastered before the first solo flight. As the author of a poem, one G.A.W., put it in *Salute*:

> 'If only, when you'd had your flight
> You didn't have to land…'

The cadet pilots found landing a challenge, and the strong crosswinds experienced at Lancaster only added to the difficulties. All too often, the wind could catch a wing like a sail and the aircraft would then career off the side of the runway.

After the cadet had some ten to twelve flying hours, the instructor would decide the time had come for the first solo flight. This is a thrilling and eagerly anticipated milestone for any student pilot but one which can cause a few butterflies in the stomach. Often, instructors would give no warning but would hop out of the aircraft after a landing and tell the student to just get on with it.

On 26 November, it was Bill's turn to solo. Alone in the cockpit, Bill checked and rechecked his instruments. Carefully lining the aircraft up, he opened the throttle and started moving down the runway till it was time to get airborne. Any pilot will know the tremendous exhilaration and pride of being alone in the sky for the first time. The sense of freedom as the aircraft responds to your touch, man and machine functioning as one in the open skies with the earth left far behind. It is a magical, never-to-be-forgotten moment. Another never-to-be-forgotten moment follows shortly after, often viewed with considerably less enthusiasm. The first solo landing. No instructor now to remind you of the right airspeed or that you are still too high… only your own judgement and the checks that have been drummed into you.

Richard Hough found it completely terrifying. He recalled three tremendous bounces as he touched down that left him with his eyes tight shut and a sense of amazement and gratitude that the aircraft was still in one piece.[5] Possibly Bill had a similar experience. His logbook reveals a flight with his instructor the day after his first solo to practise take-offs and landings.

Despite being something of a landmark, a successful first solo flight was just one of the hurdles to be surmounted. The

Primary Course continued with days spent practising various manoeuvres, lazy 8s, loops, rolls, slow rolls, chandelles, half-rolls and more spins and stalls. Bill learnt manoeuvres such as the Immelmann turn, which was invented by a German WW I flying ace. Immelmanns are basically an interrupted loop with a half-roll at the top. It is a good way to gain altitude over an enemy while turning towards him.

His flying was going well and on 2 January Bill was sent on his first solo cross-country, a simple navigation exercise north to Mojave then south to Palmdale and back to Lancaster. The cadets were under constant pressure, and failure to show the required aptitude, becoming sick while flying aerobatics, showing lack of coordination, flying illegally, or failing a test meant instant elimination from the course. The elimination rate was high. Every page of the Operations Book shows the entry, 'One (two or even three) eliminee (s) departed for Canada'.[6] Often, it was just a lack of aptitude or for failing a test, but there were also misdemeanours, such as the cadet who was reported for low flying and who damaged his landing gear on some high-tension cables. While unlucky to have been reported, he was lucky not to have been electrocuted.

By mid-January, Bill had progressed to the next stage of training, the Basic Course, and a new and more complex aircraft, the Vultee BT 13-B. He also had a new instructor, Mr G.D. Hathaway. The Vultee was a more powerful and less forgiving aircraft. It was equipped with radio and had landing flaps and a two-position variable pitch propeller. It also had blind flying instruments to teach the cadets the basics of flying at night or in bad weather. Student and instructor sat once again in tandem but now in the luxury of a closed cockpit. This aircraft's most unusual characteristic gave rise to its memorable nickname – 'The Vibrator' – so called due to the vibrations caused when it approached its stall speed.

On this part of the course, the cadets were introduced to formation flying and allowed to leave the immediate surroundings of Lancaster and range farther afield, practising their navigation on cross-country flights. Bill also spent some hours in the Link Trainer, a very basic type of flight simulator that looks like a large wooden box, bearing a slight resemblance to a cockpit. Inside is a pilot's seat with flight controls and instrumentation. It is mounted on a universal joint on a turntable, allowing movement in three axes. This movement is provided by a series of air-driven bellows that judder, puff and shunt the device around in response to the pilot's controls. An instructor sits at a separate desk with a duplicate set of basic instruments and a mechanical device known as 'the crab' that follows the route flown by the student on a map leaving a trace. The instructor can also create different navigation scenarios and routes and spring them on the unwary student. The trace left by 'the crab' would often be the subject of some heated discussion.

On 23 February, Bill passed his check flight for this part of the course and at the beginning of March moved on to the Advanced Course and yet another new aircraft. The North American AT-6, known to the Commonwealth Air Forces as the Harvard AT-6, was a single-engine two-place advanced trainer. The AT-6 was one of the most widely used and successful training aircraft for allied pilots in World War II. It continued to be used in a training role in the USA for over twenty years. In comparison to the Vultee and the Stearman, the AT-6 was a much more sophisticated aircraft. It had a retractable undercarriage and something of the performance and handling of a combat aircraft. This performance made it much more fun to fly but also much less forgiving of any mistakes and it needed careful handling, especially at low speeds. On first stepping into the cockpit, Bill was faced with a daunting array of switches, warning lights, dials and levers, and yet another new set of procedures and drills to be learnt until they became automatic.

First came familiarisation flights, circuits and bumps – landings and take-offs, and then it was on to the more serious stuff. At this point, the cadets discovered the Harvard was not as well mannered as their previous aircraft. It required a delicate touch to maintain the proper attitude for both take-off and landing. The narrow landing gear made it easy to ground loop. There was a tendency to swerve on landing – either way – and this swing had to be caught promptly before it got out of control, or the result could be a written-off aircraft. The previous aircraft the cadets had flown gave plenty of warning of an incipient stall and, when it happened, it was in a relatively slow and controlled manner. The Harvard had a vicious stall and, if this was clumsily corrected, a nasty habit of going into a secondary stall in the opposite direction. Learning spin and stall recovery required strong nerves, a strong stomach and plenty of altitude.

No longer complete novices, the cadets were now sent on longer cross-country exercises. On 19 March on one such exercise, Bill followed the iconic Route 66 west to the town of Needles where the three states of California, Arizona and Nevada meet. Then on 20 April Bill, together with Ken Gilderdale and several other cadets, flew across the arid desert to Yuma on the Mexican border some 120 miles away. They took a commemorative photo which shows the cadets looking rather pleased with themselves, their instructors, kneeling in front, decidedly less so.

There were plenty of fascinating places to fly to. To the northeast lay the Mojave Desert with its snow-capped mountains, spectacular rock formations and valley floors shimmering silently in the heat. The northern part, known as Death Valley, is a uniquely harsh environment; it is the lowest, hottest, driest place in North America. The highest temperature ever recorded on Earth was recorded there, 134 degrees Fahrenheit (56C) on 10 July 1913. The lowest point in the western hemisphere, 282 feet below sea level, is on the salt flats there at Badwater. It is here that one of the cadets ended up on a navigation exercise to Pasadena. He made a fundamental navigation error and flew a reverse compass bearing, going in exactly the opposite direction to where he was aiming. Finally, he ran out of fuel and landed on the road in the middle of Death Valley. He was very lucky as, after several frightening hours, a car finally picked him up, hot, thirsty and very relieved. However, as they came to the end of their course, the cadets became more confident and adventurous and trips often went well beyond where the instructors intended; Richard Hough reports on surreptitious trips as far afield as Mexico.

The cadets were decidedly accident-prone, both in their training and their recreation. The Operations Record Book records their many disasters, often ground looping incidents. One cadet wrote, tongue in check, that 'one of the unwritten manuals on flying states that no one may call himself a pilot until he has at least one of these extremely difficult manoeuvres to his credit'.[7] Perhaps this is why the Commanding Officer, Squadron Leader T.G. Whitlock, wrote rather defensively in his report on the school that, 'Some mention must be made, however, of the very high winds prevailing at LANCASTER'.[8] Mastering landing techniques proved a trial for the cadets. Some of the more notable and embarrassing mishaps of the cadets were also recorded in *Salute*, including this puzzling statement: 'MEYER tried to perform "forward rolls" on the landing strip at night when he thought no one would see him'.[9] Obviously, this was some kind of fairly drastic mistake on landing, although what exactly happened remains unclear. However, for five days in a row in March, Bill was practising night take-offs and landings, presumably as a result of this mishap.

The Operational Record mentions several incidents where a cadet managed to 'Turn his ship on its back' causing varying degrees of damage. One cadet's landing attempt resulted in a terse 'Aircraft written off. Minor superficial damage to cadet'.[10] Another cadet, going solo for the first time and keen to return to Mother Earth, managed a truly exceptional spot landing. Completely unaware, he managed to land his PT-13 on top of another PT-13. Both cadets were unhurt but the unfortunate instructor in the landed-on aircraft was badly cut. This might account for a comment in *Salute*:

'On moving to Basic [training] several members had the shock of having the same instructor there as on Primary. Few were pleased about this, but the sentiments were mutual. It is said that some instructors concerned have threatened to have breakdowns if they have the same students on A.T's.'[11]

Due no doubt to the restricted vision from the cockpit on the ground, aircraft collisions were frequent when taxiing. However, one cadet taxied into a car, to the detriment of both aircraft and car. Nor was their recreation time uneventful. One cadet broke his wrist wrestling. Several others managed to break their arms in various ways, while a car crash injured four, including the original 'A' Course Commander, John Tyrell.

Despite the high number of incidents, there was only one fatality. On 13 February, the weather deteriorated and snow flurries and high winds brought flying to a halt. As a landing Harvard taxied in, L.A.C. Maier Ben Himmelstaub walked out towards it. He was killed when he walked into the spinning propeller. This seems especially tragic, as L.A.C. Himmelstaub was a Pole who had managed to escape and make his way to Britain before volunteering. His parents had been rounded up in the Warsaw Ghetto and sent to Bergen-Belsen concentration camp. Because he had no family in Britain, he was buried in Lancaster. There he has not been forgotten. In February 2007, a ceremony was organised by Lancaster residents and a memorial dedicated in his honour. At the ceremony, a representative from the War Graves Commission unveiled a new headstone.

Bill was chosen to take over as Course Commander of 'A' Course on 5 February 1942, and *Salute* reported he did a 'creditable job with a difficult assignment'.[12] The difficulties included ensuring that the reluctant trainees fulfilled their allotted domestic duties in order to make their bungalows ready for inspection. Another important task as far as the cadets were concerned was for their Course Commander to find compelling reasons for them to avoid their physical training sessions. Sometimes this worked and sometimes not – fitness was taken seriously. There was dismay when several cases of mumps and chickenpox appeared. Fears mounted that an epidemic would rage through the school. Fortunately, this did not happen. All in all, though, both mechanics and doctors were kept busy.

Life was not all work, however. Just down the road lay the Antelope Valley Country Club and Dude Ranch, enticing the trainees with its cocktail lounge and promises of 'unsurpassed food'.[13] The bright lights of Hollywood were only 50 miles away, and the cadet's pay, at $2.25 a day, was about four times what they had been receiving in England, and it went much further too. Weekend passes were granted on average once a fortnight and for a few days before the cadets graduated. At the end of the Primary and Basic stages of training, they were given seven to ten days' leave. Time enough to explore this land of plenty.

To the north there was the possibility of skiing in the crisp powder that lies on the snowy granite peaks of the Sierra Nevada. Then there was the vast wilderness of Yosemite National Park, with its giant sequoias and the stunning cobalt-blue waters of Lake Tahoe to be explored. To the east lay the sophisticated attractions of Los Angeles, including colourful and vibrant Chinatown with its five-tier Golden Pagoda, or Venice Beach with its piers and attractions. The Pacific Highway offered other possibilities as it wound along the spectacular California coastline, passing through places with names full of sunlight – Malibu, Big Sur, and Monterey – before reaching San Francisco. There stood the famous Golden Gate Bridge, glowing rusty orange against the waters of the bay, the colour chosen specially to make it stand out from the fogs that frequently roll in from the sea.

The cadets also had their instructors to thank for several extra days' holiday. These civilian instructors demanded various extra days off for US holidays, much to the British Commander's concern. The Operations Record notes:

> 20–23/11/41 Leave. This included Thanksgiving Day; the long "weekend" was granted as a result of the Instructors requiring leave.
>
> 1–2 January 1942 Leave – on request of school for New Year.

Thanksgiving was a new experience; turkey with cranberry sauce and all the trimmings was served to the cadets, who appreciated both that and the extra time off. The New Year leave was only for one day – on 2 January, Bill was out practising rolls, spins, loops and Immelmans before his first solo cross-country.

Sport was popular but it had proved difficult to provide a range of sports facilities at the airfield. There were attempts made to hack out a soccer pitch, but the resulting field was condemned as too dangerous to use. Sometimes the cadets were able to use the facilities at the Lancaster High School. Polaris teams played regularly in the Los Angeles Soccer League and were very popular with the American crowds. Ken Gilderdale was in the football team and recalled playing in the Loyola Stadium in Los Angeles on the afternoon of 7 December 1941, the day Pearl Harbour was attacked. He loved football and was one of the stars of the team as the flying school magazine noted: 'Gilderdale, centre forward, was the highest goal scorer and played very well throughout the season'.[14] The team also visited San Francisco at Christmas 1941, winning games against both the San Francisco Bay League Champions and a special all-star team. There were also two cricket elevens and a full fixture list for each of them for the season.

As in Moncton, local people were kind and welcoming, often inviting these young men to their houses. One particularly memorable event took place on Christmas Day, 1941. The British film colony in Hollywood, headed by the British film star Ronald Colman, organised a party for the cadets in the luxurious surroundings of the Beverley Hills Golf Club.

The 1930s and early 1940s are often referred to as Hollywood's 'Golden Age'. People welcomed the opportunity films provided to escape from the hardships of the Depression for a few hours and forget themselves in the glamorous world of the movies. In the 1930s, the cult of stardom had reached new heights. During the '40s, the US government was keen to encourage the movie industry, seeing films as an essential means of boosting morale and also as a valuable propaganda tool. The stars of the day were worshipped from afar; their glamour and sophistication both dazzled and enthralled their audiences. They existed in a glittering world far removed from the humdrum existence of everyday life, and now the cadets were being invited to meet some of them.

The three British officers and around eighty cadets attended, Richard Hough and Bill among them. The cadets arrived to find the stars they had so revered on cinema screens back home now lined up in the flesh, waiting to welcome them. Excitedly, they tumbled off their coach to be met by most of the big names of Hollywood. The men wore black tie while the women shimmered in fabulous evening dresses, sequins sparkling against glistening satin and diamonds flashing and dazzling in the candlelight. Richard Hough describes it as the 'only party I have ever been to at which I have known *everyone*'.[15] That was because some of the most famous film stars of the day, such as Myrna Loy, Basil Rathbone, Maureen O'Sullivan and Olivia de Havilland, were present. At first, it was all a little overwhelming, but any initial shyness vanished as 'Liquor flowed like Niagara!'[16] There was dancing to one of the Big Bands of the period; the great concert pianist Arthur Rubinstein played dance tunes on the piano; other stars sang and the cadets concentrated on enjoying themselves. Some cadets enjoyed themselves so much that they did not even make it as far as the buffet supper later. They regretted this afterwards, as a spectacular array of gourmet dishes awaited the ever-hungry men. By 2 am, the party was quietening down, largely because so many of the cadets had had such a good time they were now barely capable of remaining upright, let alone dancing. Some of the stars gave more impromptu performances, and Arthur Rubinstein was persuaded to play the haunting *Moonlight Sonata*. The evening finally ended around 4.30 am. As the trainees emerged star-struck into the moonlight, they found the lights of Los Angeles twinkling below them. They must have felt a little like Cinderella after the ball. It had been quite a party.

On 15 April, Bill had his final check flight, this time with Squadron Leader Greaves. He passed, being awarded an 'Average' grade for his flying. His last flight at Lancaster was on 22 April when he practised aerobatics. The cadets then faced their 'Wings' written examination on 15 May 1942. Of the fifty-four who started the course, fourteen had been eliminated for various reasons, an elimination rate of some 25%. Not all the course passed this written exam. Richard Hough commented that most of those who failed this final exam were '…the older men – those grizzled middle-aged fellows of twenty-three and twenty-four'. By this reckoning, Bill, now thirty-two, must have appeared more like a grandfather. Despite his great age, Bill passed his 'Wings'. However, some ten cadets who did not were re-examined a couple of weeks later. A novel method of improving results was employed for the resit. The instructors sat among the candidates during the examination, thus ensuring a 100% pass rate.[17]

The graduation parade for No. 5 Course took place on 29 April. Photos show Bill standing in front of his course as the cadets were awarded their 'Wings' and sergeant's chevrons. The Academy also presented each man with a memento certifying that he had graduated from Polaris. This was in the form of a wallet and bronze plaque engraved with the Polaris logo and their names. Ten of the forty cadets who graduated were specifically recommended for commissions. Bill was one of those recommended.

On 30 April, No. 5 Course left Polaris and once again wound their way across the USA on various trains till they arrived back at Moncton. While in California, the war must have seemed very distant as the cadets enjoyed the relaxed Californian lifestyle and the attention and hospitality accorded them there. At Moncton, they were rapidly reacquainted with normal military life.

The course embarked on the *Duchess of York* around 20 May for the trip home. The *York,* built in 1928 and converted into a troopship in 1940, provided a much more comfortable passage than the voyage out. The weather was warm and the seas calm and, as graduates, the whole course was comfortably installed in passenger cabins for this crossing. There were a number of abortive U-boat attacks, but the ship arrived safely in Liverpool eight days later.

CHAPTER FIVE
ADVANCED TRAINING

In 1941, Western Approaches Command Headquarters had moved to Liverpool to plan the Battle of the Atlantic. Now Liverpool played a vital role both as a naval base and as the hub of the Atlantic trade convoys. The Germans were well aware of its importance and, as a prime target for the Luftwaffe, Liverpool had suffered more attacks than any other British port outside London.

The Navy, Air Force and Royal Marines worked together there to combat the U-boat menace and ensure that Britain continued to receive the millions of tons of food supplies and equipment without which she could not survive and fight. With European ports under German control, almost all of Britain's supplies had to come across the Atlantic. The ships carrying these essential goods ran the gauntlet of the German U-boat fleet and it became a cat-and-mouse game as the Germans sought to cut this vital lifeline.

When the men disembarked, the harsh realities of wartime Britain confronted them as they saw the scale of bomb damage in Liverpool. Although the docks were the main targets, the sheer scale of destruction in the heart of the city and areas on both sides of the Mersey was extraordinary. All around, the blackened, jagged shells of buildings reached up from heaps of rubble, and buckled lampposts stood on pavements strewn with debris. It was a stark contrast to the comfortable normality of the USA.

The airmen gazed silently at the destruction around them before boarding their train.

After this sobering arrival, they were sent to the limbo of No. 3 Personnel Reception Centre in Bournemouth, a clearing house from where they would be posted. At this point, the paths of Bill, Richard and Ken diverged. Richard went on to fly Hurricanes and Typhoons while Ken first became an instructor before flying Lancasters with 150 Squadron. They both survived the war.

After his leave, Bill was told to report to a Pilots Advanced Flying Unit, (P) AFU for short. The aim of Advanced Training Units was to bring pilots up to the standard necessary for operational training to begin. The pace of life now quickened, no more weekends off but ten-hour days, seven days a week, with twenty-four hours off once a fortnight. Flying in England was very different from flying in California. In California, navigation had been easy thanks to the fine weather and the open desert, with easily recognisable landmarks in the form of small towns and large mountains. There were also long straight roads and railway lines to follow. The network of villages, fields and winding roads of England was much more confusing. Before and after the war, pilots uncertain of their position might fly low enough to read road signs but now, due to the threat of invasion, all the signposts had been removed. No more sunny Californian skies either – the skies would often be murky with cloud, wind and rain hampering visibility.

Bill had been posted to (P) AFU No. 3, based at RAF South Cerney in the heart of the Cotswolds. On 30 June 1942, he left London to drive up there. The village lies to the southeast of Cirencester, just off the old Roman Ermin Way (now the A419). The airfield had been built by the RAF in 1936/37 and was located to the north of the village.

On joining No. 29 Course at South Cerney, Bill was introduced to the RAF's trainer, the Airspeed Oxford, known to trainee pilots as the 'Ox-Box'. The Oxford had been developed from the 1934 Airspeed Envoy and came into service in 1937. It was a twin-engine monoplane advanced trainer and was used by the RAF to prepare complete aircrews for Bomber Command. While only able to carry three people at a time, it could be used to train pilots, navigators, bomb aimers, gunners and radio operators. Constructed mainly of wood with a retractable undercarriage, it was known to be difficult to land and easy to ground loop.

Once again, there was a series of tests to be passed: solo flying, navigation and a progress test. Bill was relieved when he passed these tests. He was now able to go on cross-country flights, sometimes alone and sometimes acting as navigator for another pilot. The village had several lakes nearby and one of these, surrounded by woods, was used for practising low flying.

Surprisingly, there had been little night flying carried out in America, so this now formed an important part of the course. Flying and landing at night required new skills; depth perception, visual clues and runway perspective all appear different in the dark. It was something that took getting used to, and the latter part of the course was focused on night cross-countries, landings and overshoots. At South Cerney, as at many other RAF bases, the runway was lit by a flare path made from gooseneck flares. These devices resembled watering cans filled with paraffin with rags stuffed into the spouts which, when lit, resulted in a dull, smoky orange flickering light. They were then lined up on the left side of the runway in use.

Flying day and night, Bill practised formation flying and fighter affiliation as well as taking part in mock dogfights, where cameras were used instead of guns to record accuracy. On the 21 July, he was promoted to Pilot Officer.

The conversion to twin-engined aircraft did not always go smoothly. The Operations Record Book for July 1942 makes startling reading. In the thirty-one days of July 1942, there were no fewer than twenty-one accidents. Fortunately, it was mainly the aircraft that bore the brunt of these crashes. However, there were three fatal accidents during this month, including one where the record states both instructor and pupil were 'Fatally injured in crash'. On the 3rd, 4th, 9th and 16th there were two accidents each day. Some were the result of mechanical breakdowns, sometimes quite spectacular ones. Sergeant G.F. Disbury must have been more than somewhat dismayed when, as the ORB reports, 'Engine and mountings fell out of aircraft when in flight'.[1] The record shows that he made a successful landing and was uninjured. Often basic mistakes were made. Undershooting, overshooting and heavy landings provided plenty of work for the ground engineers. One pupil grabbed his undercarriage lever instead of the flap lever after landing, resulting in an abrupt collapse onto the ground but, surprisingly, only slight damage. It was not only the pupils who had problems. An instructor, too keen to get safely up in the air, raised the undercarriage before the aircraft was airborne, resulting in serious damage to the aircraft but no harm to himself or his pupil.

While the airmen found this series of accidents worrying, they found the lectures they were given on the fundamentals of first aid even worse. The emphasis was largely on the dangers of shock and the importance of treating it. However, ten basic types of injury scenarios were described in question-and-answer format. These varied from simple and compound fractures to head injuries, broken backs and abdominal wounds. The aircrew were informed that in the case of 'A wound of the abdomen (your stomach) with intestines pushing their way through' the casualty would, unsurprisingly, '...complain of pain in the stomach'. They were further informed that '...when you cut away the clothing you will resist the temptation to push the strange things you see there back to his abdominal cavity, and will apply a shell dressing only'.[2] Instructions were given on how to inject morphine from pre-loaded syringes, known as 'Tubunic Ampoules'. The lecture finished with the traditional warnings of the dangers of venereal diseases. Usually by this point, several men had fainted while the rest were desperate to get back to straightforward flying training.

On 6 August, Bill finished his training on Oxfords and was given a couple of days' leave before being posted to an Operational Training Unit, OTU for short. At OTUs, airmen formed up into crews. They learnt to work together, master operational techniques and practise navigation before flying on operations.

OTU training had recently undergone changes under Bomber Command's new leader, Air Marshal Arthur T. Harris.

During 1941, Bomber Command had suffered increasing losses. The operational role of the RAF was expanding as the policy of strategic bombing assumed an ever-more important role in the conduct of the war. Replacement crews were urgently needed. The RAF was faced with two alternatives to alleviate the shortfall in manpower. One was to recruit and train more aircrew. This would take up both time and resources, as more schools, training aircraft and instructors would be required. The alternative was to cut the training time for the aircrew they already had, thus turning out qualified personnel at a quicker pace. This was the chosen option so that in April 1941 the OTU courses were reduced from twelve to six weeks. The downside of this policy quickly became clear. The accident rate rose immediately as inadequately trained aircrew failed to cope with conditions on operations. After a rapid rethink, in January 1942, Bomber Command increased the length of the course to eight, ten or twelve weeks. The actual length of each course was largely dependent on the time of year, with shorter courses in the summer when weather conditions and light allowed for longer flying hours.

Towards the end of 1941, Sir Charles Portal, Chief of the Air Staff, had become increasingly concerned at Bomber Command's performance and the mounting losses it was suffering under its chief, Air Marshal Sir Richard Peirse. Feeling that a shake-up was required, in February 1942, Portal recalled Air Marshal Arthur T. Harris from Washington where he had been heading the RAF delegation and appointed him as Commander-in-Chief of Bomber Command.

'Bomber' Harris, as he became known, had joined the Royal Flying Corps and fought in World War I before commanding various Bomber Squadrons during the interwar years. In the 1930s, he had been the Deputy Director of Operations and Intelligence, and later Director of Plans at the Air Ministry, a role that involved inter-service planning. In November 1940, he had been appointed Deputy Chief of the Air Staff based at the Air

Ministry in London. Here, he instilled a 'can-do' attitude in his staff and made sure that they knew that their job was to support the operational units at all times. This was not always popular with Ministry staff but much appreciated by the men and women in his command.

On 14 February 1942, a week before Harris's appointment, the Air Ministry had issued the Area Bombing Directive. This directive ordered the bombing campaign to 'be focused on the morale of the enemy civilian population and in particular the industrial workers'.[3] Harris's task was to turn Bomber Command into an efficient and effective force capable of inflicting severe damage on Germany's industrial capacity. At this time, the Command was the only means available of striking directly at Nazi Germany. This point was made forcefully by Harris in a memorandum that Churchill asked him to prepare for the War Cabinet in August 1942: 'To sum up, Bomber Command provides our only offensive action yet pressed home directly against Germany'.[4] These important facts are often forgotten in the post-war debates on the rights and wrongs of the bombing campaign and Harris's conduct of it.

Early in the war, Harris, standing on the roof of the Air Ministry, had watched bombs dropping on London and famously commented, "They have sown the wind, and so they shall reap the whirlwind."[5] He now set about organising this harvest. Harris was well aware that the Command had to compete with both Fighter and Coastal Commands for the limited resources available. Most of the aircraft used by Bomber Command at this time – the Bristol Blenheim, the Armstrong Whitworth Whitley and Vickers Wellington – had not been designed for long-range bombing and were incapable of carrying the bomb loads now required. The first Lancasters were only just being delivered to a few squadrons and none were operational yet. Harris started by speeding up the production and delivery of what became known as the 'Heavies' – Stirlings, Halifaxes and Lancasters. These were the larger four-engine aircraft that could fly higher and carry larger bomb loads.

Harris also took the decision that there would be only one pilot per bomber, rather than two, which previously had been the norm. The heavy loss of aircraft, each with two pilots, was unacceptable. This decision had the effect of both reducing the shortage of pilots and allowing men to focus on their specific role in the crew. In March 1942, aircrew duties were redefined. Before that time, the term observer denoted a role that combined navigation and bomb aiming. However, the increasing complexity of both aircraft and systems called for greater specialisation, and this position was replaced by the separate roles of navigator and bomb aimer. The radio operator and two air gunners also became specialists in their respective fields, with no cross-training. A new position, that of flight engineer, was initiated to assist the single pilot by managing the four engines of the new heavy bombers: 'These changes had the effect of allowing each member of the crew to specialise, and it therefore permitted him to receive much more training than had previously been the case.'[6] More accurate navigation would prevent wasted time and effort over enemy territory and only with experience could a pilot react and fly his aircraft to the limits and beyond. Both could mean the difference between life and death.

Bill was due to report to his next posting on 11 August and so, after a hectic couple of days in London, he caught the overnight train north and reported to No.19 Operational Training Unit based at RAF Kinloss in the far north of Scotland on the Moray Firth. RAF Kinloss had been established in 1938 as the RAF expanded to meet training requirements in preparation for the coming war. It was built on land requisitioned from both local farms and the Kinloss Estate, to the northeast of the village of Kinloss. It opened on 1 April 1939. The accommodation was extremely basic and the weather often terrible. Icy winds swept across the station, often bringing heavy rain, and it was cold even in what passes for the Scottish summer. It was not the best spot for aircrew training and the accident record was atrocious.

Early in the war, there were concerns that the station could be attacked and so efforts were made to camouflage the airfield. One such effort was to paint the outlines of buildings on the grass. This artwork was not a complete success. Rather than confusing the Luftwaffe, it amused them; a German aircraft photographed the attempts at camouflage and mockingly published them in a magazine.

Food rationing caused shortages everywhere, but it seems to have been worse here. At one point, things got so bad that an enterprising Station Commander ordered an aircraft to drop a small bomb in nearby Burghead Bay. This produced excellent results and masses of stunned fish were collected by the air/sea rescue launch. Fish dishes of all kinds appeared on the menu for the next few days, providing a much appreciated supplement to normal rations.[7] It was a far cry from the warmth and plenty of California but there were a few compensations. In summer, the light lingered so long that it was possible to read outside at midnight and towards winter the skies were sometimes suffused with the glorious glowing and swirling Northern Lights, the Aurora Borealis.

Even up in the far and windswept north, there were constant reminders of the war. One came in the form of 'plots' – enemy aircraft on patrols. When this happened, the OTU flights were usually recalled. The operational records detail numerous instances of flying training being cancelled while this threat was dealt with. In the first week of September 1942 alone, this happened three times. A harsher reminder was the number of accidents as trainee crews were pushed beyond their limits by the bad weather and the worn-out aircraft handed down from operational squadrons.

The RAF Kinloss Squadron History relates how many trainees were caught out when they ditched in Findhorn Bay. This was '...a Catch 22 situation. If you ended up in the bay when the tide was out the dinghy was useless as the bay was a quagmire, and when the tide was in it occasionally flooded the airfield. One crew were completely caught out when they landed and saw the water. Thinking they had overshot the runway, they made a distress call and climbed into the dinghies, only to see the fire trucks drive right up beside them'.[8] It took a while to live that down. However, it was forgotten when an Anson managed to land directly on top of a Whitley that was about to take off from Kinloss at night. The Whitley veered off course and the startled wireless operator reported that a wheel had suddenly appeared beside him. Amazingly enough, all the crew were unhurt but had to put up with the ground crew's lewd remarks when they found the 'mating couple' the next day.

Bill was part of Course 45, which commenced with enough airmen to make up fourteen crews on completion of training. The course began with a couple of weeks of ground school before continuing with flying training. Trainees were divided into four 'Flights'. Bill joined 'C' Flight which was based at a satellite airfield nearby. This was at Forres, one of Scotland's oldest towns and an ancient Royal Burgh Town.

The airfield was a mile to the west of the town and known colloquially as Balnageith after a nearby farm. Today, a memorial cairn marks the place where so many airmen were trained for Bomber Command. There is also a memorial plaque in Forres itself that commemorates a tragic accident that happened in November 1940 when a Whitley from Balnageith crashed into the centre of Forres, killing all the crew but, miraculously, no one on the ground. At Balnageith, the runways were grass covered with a steel mesh to prevent the aircraft from bogging down. The usual paraffin-filled watering cans, the goose-necked flares, were laid out to form a flare path providing the runway lighting. In the distance to the north of the field ran the Inverness to London railway where the London-bound trains passed.

RAF Kinloss used both Avro Ansons and Armstrong Whitworth Whitleys for training. Bill was trained on the Whitley, a twin-engined bomber. The Whitley had been introduced in 1936 and was the RAF's first heavy bomber. It was a sturdy slab-sided aircraft with somewhat mediocre performance and a reluctance to do what it was told, which is why it earned its unfortunate nickname of the 'Flying Coffin'. It had a characteristic nose-down attitude in flight due to the wings being set at a large angle of incidence to compensate for having no flaps. By mid-1942, it had been phased out of front line operations as its low speed made it increasingly vulnerable. The Whitley was both larger than and twice as heavy as the Oxford Airspeed. Engine failures were frequent and as these new pilots had little twin-engine experience they had difficulty coping with the loss of an engine on this heavy twin-engine aircraft. In a twin-engined aircraft, when one engine fails there is not only a loss of power to contend with but the drag increases considerably due to the asymmetric forces that yaw the aircraft in the direction of the failed engine. Fast reactions are needed to cope with the yaw, and a sharp eye must be kept on the airspeed.

The Operational Record for September 1942 gives an example of the terrible loss rate suffered during training. On 3 September, the first loss of the month occurred when a Whitley crashed on take-off at Forres. There were no survivors. On 10 September, another Whitley crashed 5 miles south of the airfield following an engine failure. On 14 September, two Whitleys crashed. In one case, the crew became lost on a night cross-country. Both radio and lights had failed and after two attempts to get below the cloud over the sea, they took the difficult decision to abandon the aircraft and parachuted down. The ORB comments that 'it was considered that the crew put up a very good show'.[9] The crew in the other Whitley were not so lucky. In poor visibility, it crashed in the sea off Aberdeen with no survivors. On 22 September, there was only one survivor when another Whitley crashed downwind at Forres on coming in to land. On the 26th, engine failures meant two more Whitleys had to make forced landings. One landed in the sea near Loch Ryan while another made a wheels-up landing near West Freugh. Both crews survived. A total of seven aircraft and fourteen lives were lost in one month alone.

'Friendly' searchlights were an additional hazard when flying near towns such as Edinburgh. There were frequent occurrences of aircraft being picked up by these searchlights and being fired upon by their own side. This happened despite the relevant authorities always being notified when training was going to be carried out.

Up until this point, aircrew had concentrated on learning their individual skills. That was to change at the OTU when the novice crew formed up. Crews were formed by a most unlikely and anarchical process more akin to an "Excuse me" at a dance than a formal military procedure. The whole course, with all the various 'trades' – pilots, navigators, engineers, wireless operators, bomb aimers and gunners – were herded into a hangar and told to sort themselves into crews. Considering how strictly controlled and regimented the rest of their training was, it seems amazing that, at this late stage, they should be allowed such freedom of choice. Usually, the pilots started the procedure by picking a navigator, and the two of them would then circulate, talking and summing up members of the other 'trades' until they had collected the rest of the crew. In practice, this laid-back approach to crewing usually worked extremely well. Some people had precise ideas as to whom they would like to fly with – there were some teetotal crews, for example. Sometimes people who had met during training or who shared a common interest or background got together, and at other times a face just seemed to fit. The disparate backgrounds, both social and geographical, were unimportant; each man would become part of that single entity, the crew.

A natural leader himself, Bill had given much thought to the individual qualities that he looked for in each member of his crew. Far older than most aircrew, he knew the importance not only of sharp wits and keenness but also the value of maturity, experience and reliability, and his choice of crew was to prove inspired. Every member of his crew was hand-picked.

Bill chose for his navigator Neil McCorkindale, a tall, thin twenty-one-year-old Scot from Galashiels with a dry sense of humour. He was a quiet man, well educated thanks to the rigorous Scottish education system. He was a librarian by profession. Neil, who became known to the crew as 'Mac' or 'Corky', had also trained in the USA. Having safely crossed the Atlantic and got as far as New York, Mac and his fellow cadet navigators had travelled by train to Miami. Not just any old train either – this was the streamlined and flamboyant *Silver Meteor*. The locomotive and coaches were decked out in a vibrant paint scheme of orange, yellow, green and silver, representing the Sunshine State that was its final destination.

Neil attended the Pan American School of Navigation at Coral Gables in Miami. The school was based in the University of Miami with flying from the interestingly named Dinner Quay. Mac was part of Course 42/2 and spent some fifteen weeks learning to navigate there. When the time came to get out of the classroom and into the air, he found himself practising navigation on board one of Pan Am's now obsolete Commodore Flying Boats. The comfortable interiors had been ripped out and converted into a flying classroom equipped with ten large worktables. A continuing problem was the lack of practical flying training due to lack of aircraft. When he qualified, Mac had only twenty-three hours' daytime flying and barely twenty-seven hours' night flying. However, he graduated with very high marks on his navigation course, including an outstanding 98.5% for 'navigation plotting problems'. Quick-thinking and meticulous, Mac could always be relied upon to have a good idea of their position. This was an enormous asset when the most common response to a pilot enquiring, "Where are we?" was "Somewhere between our base and the target." Alan Hart states that, 'Corky [Mac] never lost us and he was always able to steer us clear of the heavily defended areas that were highlighted in the briefings'.[10]

Not only was Mac a brilliant navigator but he also possessed another outstanding talent, one that made him very popular and much in demand in the mess and at squadron weddings. He was a great piano player, one of those gifted people who can just hear a tune once and play it back by ear. On nights off or after a sortie was cancelled, the mess would fill up, and men, pints in hand, would thump the tables and demand a tune from Mac. Then, sitting at the piano in a fug of tobacco smoke and beer fumes, Mac would bang out request after request while men clustered round bellowing out songs old and new and the war was briefly forgotten.

Stafford Sinclair, aged twenty-nine, was invited to join the crew as the wireless operator or 'Sparks' as they were known. He already had a lot of experience, having been a wireless operator in the merchant navy for several years. He was promptly nicknamed 'Sinc' by the crew. Good-looking and fun-loving, Sinc was an inveterate smoker and partygoer. He was seldom to be found without a cigarette in his hands, even in formal photographs. He was the oldest man in the crew after Bill and was someone the younger members of the crew felt they could confide in. A wireless operator had to read and send messages in Morse code, and Sinc turned out to be a very fast 'Sparks' indeed, well able to 'key' at a higher rate than the twenty-five words per minute that was the RAF requirement. Wireless operators also had to learn semaphore, though whatever use this could be inside an aircraft is difficult to imagine.

The flight engineer, Wilson Hunter, was also twenty-nine years old and came from Sunderland. He became known as 'Geordie' for obvious reasons. Short, stocky and tough, Geordie had been a mechanic in civilian life and was thoroughly familiar with engines and their quirks. He had a natural 'feel' for engines and a real love of them. He cosseted his engines and complained loudly and bitterly if he felt they were being maltreated in any way. The four mighty Merlins were always perfectly adjusted so that they ran in synch – at the same speed so there would be no annoying vibration or 'beat'. His ear would be the first to detect any sign of distress from them. Easy-going and confident, Geordie always kept his head in every emergency.

Donald Willbee, the bomb aimer, came from the province of Ontario in Canada and had a soft Canadian drawl. A tall, slim man, he had been a bank teller in civilian life, a job requiring accuracy and being good with numbers, useful skills for his position. He was a somewhat laid-back character and off-duty he was a bit of a dreamer. His family had emigrated from Scotland and he would spend every leave in Scotland immersing himself in all things Scottish. He was generally known as 'Wilkie'.

The final member of the crew to be chosen at this time was the rear gunner, Thomas Johnson. Thomas had only just qualified from the Air Gunnery School at RAF Morpeth on 7 August and come straight to RAF Kinloss. In the RAF in those days, it was unusual to see anything but white faces among ground crew and even more so among flight crew. Thomas Johnson was of mixed-race and had a somewhat unusual job in civilian life, having worked in a circus as a prize-fighter, despite being a very small man. He also had an unusual background. His mother had been a missionary working in Nigeria and his father a Nigerian Ibo chief whom she had tried to convert. Whether or not she succeeded, she brought him back to England, and Thomas was born in Liverpool. They took her family name to avoid prejudice. His nickname was 'Darkie'. Today, this would sound racist and politically incorrect, but it must be understood that in the context of the time it was just another affectionate nickname. He was very young, just eighteen years old, but he had been absolutely determined to join the RAF as aircrew. It says much about his character that he succeeded. Bill must have felt sympathy for an outsider, being one himself due to his German background. He saw a keenness and spirit that appealed to him. He must also have realised that the fast reactions and aggression essential for prize-fighting were just what an air gunner would need.

It was now time to meld this bunch of individuals into a team and to develop the interdependence and trust that would enable them to act cohesively. Training consisted of a mixture of cross-country flights, bombing practice and air firing. Bill did some of his training on a Link Trainer and also gave Don Willbee some three hours of instruction in the Link as a safeguard should he ever become incapacitated on a sortie. For the first time, on 28 September, Bill's logbook refers to 'Self' and 'Crew'. On that day, the crew started flying together. Now, like pieces of a jigsaw, all the things they had learnt individually would start to come together.

Cross-country flights offered navigators some much needed practice; there are several reports in the September/October Operations Records of crews becoming lost and having to land away from their base. After a short briefing, they would take off and set course. All the turning points on the route had to be spot-on and the timing had to be kept to. Often, the bomb aimer would assist by taking drift sights to check on the effects of wind. The wireless operator would also help the navigator by getting bearings from radio stations with the Direction Finding Loop. The longest flights, around six and a half hours, were at night to duplicate operational flying conditions.

Bombing practice usually took place at the Tain Bombing Range on the Dornoch Firth. The bomb aimer could then practise his timed runs to targets usually at height, but sometimes at low level. Mishaps were not uncommon. One aircraft 'lost' its practice bombs on a day cross-country. The record ingeniously states, 'They were considered to have fallen in the sea'.[11] Just as well that they were over the wilds of Scotland. On another occasion, a crew mistook a lighthouse at Stack Skerry for their aiming point and duly bombed it. Fortunately, their accuracy left much to be desired, and the unfortunate lighthouse and its keeper remained unscathed.

The course passed out on 19 October 1942, having had approximately seventy hours' flying time, half of it night flying. Of the fourteen possible crews at the start of the course, eleven completed their training. Five of these crews were sent for conversion training onto Lancasters. Bill and his crew were delighted to be one of the crews chosen to fly this latest and most successful heavy bomber in the Command. This final training would be done at a Heavy Conversion Unit known as an HCU. This was the last step in preparing the crews for operational bombing missions.

CHAPTER SIX

AN INTRODUCTION TO THE LANCASTER

The crew's next posting was to an HCU in Lincolnshire. Their destination, RAF Swinderby, lay on the southeast side of the A46, the Fosse Way, built by the Romans some 2,000 years before. The Romans had drained the fens, leaving flat open countryside that was perfect for building runways on. So, in place of Roman camps, there were now seventy-three RAF bases dotted across the Lincolnshire Wolds. Lincolnshire itself became known as 'Bomber County' because of the number of RAF Bomber Command bases there.

When the station opened in 1940, it was allocated to Group 1. Polish-manned squadrons flying Fairey Battles were the first to operate out of it, but in the autumn of 1942, Swinderby had been selected to become an operational training station for No. 5 Group with the newly formed No. 1660 Heavy Conversion Unit based there. The unit flew Manchesters and Lancasters. Bill would get to know the 'feel' of a Lancaster there and would learn the best tactics to use, practising them incessantly until they became second nature.

Unlike the Halifax, the Lancaster carried two air gunners, one at the rear and one in the mid-upper turret; the crew would need an extra man. It was at Swinderby that Bill found the final member of the crew, Alan Hart, who joined them as their mid-upper gunner.

Alan was from Wales; he was only eighteen, dark haired and slightly built. He had just completed his training at No. 4 Gunnery School at RAF Morpeth in Northumberland. There he had learnt about firing, basic hydraulics, aircraft recognition and deflection shooting; the art of aiming ahead of a target to allow for the speed of travel. At the end of the course, he was given forty-eight hours' leave and told to then report to RAF Coningsby. He duly reported there on 16 November 1942, together with three other air gunners. On arrival, the four of them were promptly informed that they should be reporting at RAF Swinderby. After a long wait, a crew bus finally drove them over there.

On his arrival, Alan was immediately dispatched to have his first flight in an Avro Manchester. Coincidentally, Bill and the rest of the crew also had their first familiarisation flight in another Manchester that same day. For the next ten days, Bill and the crew flew with various other air gunners before first flying with Alan on 28 November. Alan recalls being very keen to be picked to join Bill's crew, as they were already known to be a 'hot' crew. He was absolutely delighted when he was then asked to join them; he had a feeling he would be safe with Bill.

Alan describes Bill as someone who never panicked, 'a quiet sort of man but he always seemed to know exactly what he was going to do. He was very much in charge and an excellent pilot. As we went through our tour I cannot remember him having to repeat any instructions in the aircraft'.[1] Alan felt that Bill's calm self-assurance inspired confidence, trust and obedience. He states that, 'If we happened to chatter a bit on the intercom then, when the time was right, he would say, "Okay, chaps, that's enough" and we would all stop and start to pay more attention to what we should be doing'.[2] As he was older than the rest of the crew, they came to rely on him. One of Bill's hobbies was driving sports cars and he always took his car to wherever he was based, much to the delight of his crews. Alan recalls: 'he was like a father figure but he never acted like a father figure. He had a sports car that we did all pile into on the odd Saturday nights when we went to one of the local pubs'.[3] Although Bill was the only officer among them, such things counted for little in the RAF. What was important was confidence, individual and mutual, and with that came the trust and cohesion that was the essence of a good team. This was what Bill took great pains to instil in his crew. He felt a deep sense of responsibility for their well-being and took a paternal interest in them, especially in the younger members who had never even been away from home before. He was determined they should both do their job well and have the best chance of survival.

A couple of weeks into the course, flying training started in Avro Manchesters, the smaller twin-engined predecessor to the Lancaster. Its Rolls-Royce Vulture engines were notoriously unreliable. Alan Hart comments wryly that they only 'went when they wanted to,'[4] and often they did not want to. Finally, on 28 November, Bill and his crew flew for the first time in the aircraft they would use on operations, the legendary Avro Lancaster.

The Lancaster has become an icon of the Second World War, and with good reason. It was undoubtedly the supreme heavy night bomber of the war. Designed to replace the Manchester, its designer, Roy Chadwick, added 12 feet to the wingspan and replaced the two troublesome Vulture engines with four Rolls-Royce Merlin V-12s. The result was a superb aircraft: the Avro Lancaster. It made its maiden flight in January 1941. The Lancaster was 69' 4" (21.11 m) long with a wingspan of 102' (31.09 m) and a height of 20' 6" (6.25 m). It proved to be strong, reliable and a delight to fly, although crew comfort was a secondary consideration. The whole aeroplane rattled and vibrated with the power of the four piston engines, but it was extremely manoeuvrable and could manage steep dives more appropriate to a fighter. Such manoeuvres demanded great physical strength, though; the controls were not power-assisted and it was a heavy aircraft.

The loads the Lancaster could carry became legendary. With an empty weight of 36,900 lb (16,738 kg), it could take off with a 33,100 lb (15,014 kg) load of fuel and bombs. Incredibly, this meant it could almost carry its own weight. Not only that, but it could suffer massive damage and an experienced pilot could still get home. However, there was a price to pay for this tremendous carrying capacity. Due to the enormous 33-foot long bomb bay, the huge main spar ran through the interior of the aircraft. To escape by parachute meant getting to a hatch in the front of the aircraft. The gunners used the rear door but it was dangerous because of the tail plane. Not only did aircrew have to locate their parachutes and put them on within seconds in the dark but also clamber over the main spar in all their gear. This was hard enough on the ground but in a damaged aircraft, in the dark, the increasing G-forces made it almost impossible. Many crews found themselves unable to leave a doomed aircraft because of this.

The Lancaster had virtually no defensive armour, relying mostly on a camouflage paint scheme to conceal itself. The upper surfaces were painted in dull green and brown tones and the underside was painted in a dull, sooty black paint so that it would absorb rather than reflect the light of searchlights and fighter flares. The front, mid and rear gun turrets were hydraulically powered and carried a total of eight .303 (7.7 mm) calibre machine guns for defence against enemy aircraft. This was not much protection against the better-armed German night fighters that they would come up against, including the Messerschmitt 109. The 109s were fitted with 20 mm cannon and machine guns, giving them both greater firepower and the ability to fire from a greater and therefore safer distance.

It is immensely sad that out of a total of 7,377 that were built, there is now only one Lancaster left in flying condition in Great Britain. This wonderful example, Lancaster PA 474, is owned by the RAF and is based at RAF Coningsby as part of the Battle of Britain Memorial Flight.

The Lancaster's cockpit looked rather like a glasshouse. Inside, the pilot sat high up on the left-hand side – visibility was excellent but it was a very exposed position. In view of this, a small armoured plate was fitted behind the pilot's head to offer some protection. He had to sit on his parachute which was placed behind his thighs. Pilots found this '…bloody uncomfortable but very comforting'.[5] It made movement awkward. Behind the pilot, the navigator sat sideways in a small curtained-off compartment. This was to prevent the light that he needed to work by from giving away their position to enemy fighters. The navigator was a vital member of the crew, responsible for tracking the aircraft's progress, reporting headings and distance and estimating the effects of weather and adjusting the course accordingly. He was expected to know where the aircraft was at all times and was constantly replotting its position. No easy task with only basic navigation aids to help him, often less than accurate meteorology reports and a pilot throwing the aircraft all over the sky when evasive manoeuvres became necessary. He had to route the aircraft clear of known searchlight and flak battery belts. This job required both concentration and quick thinking; a good navigator was a huge asset to a crew.

Beside the pilot, on the right-hand side stood the flight engineer. He had a pull-down seat that could be raised to allow the bomb aimer to reach his position. The engineer assisted the pilot on take-off and landing by handling the throttles and watching the engine instruments. As mentioned, the Lancaster had no power-assisted operation whatsoever and the pilot had to use sheer brute force on the controls; sometimes the flight engineer's strength was needed as well. In flight, the engineer was constantly checking his panels to monitor oil, fuel and pressure gauges to assess engine performance and fuel consumption from the Lancaster's six wing tanks. Although flight engineers were often expected to be able to fly the aircraft 'straight and level', they had no formal pilot training. When things were quiet, some pilots would encourage their engineers to take the controls and get in some practice. They must have hoped their skills would never be put to the test. However, there were instances of flight engineers who managed not only to fly their aircraft back but to land them safely when their skipper had been injured or killed. In view of Don Willbee's (bomb aimer) time on the Link Trainer, it appears that he was the one designated to take over should it become necessary.

The bomb aimer's compartment was in the front of the aircraft slightly below the level of the main cockpit. In order to guide the aircraft onto the target, the bomb aimer would have to lie on his stomach and look through the bombsight that rested on the large Perspex blister. In this uncomfortable and vulnerable position, he had to calculate with the aid of his bomb sight when to release the bomb load. This involved taking into account wind speed and direction over the target, the aircraft's height and speed, and the type of bomb carried, as each type had different aerodynamics. The data was fed to the gyroscopic bombsight that would project an illuminated cross onto the glass sight. The bomb aimer then had to get the aiming point in the centre of the cross. He also had to set the order and timing of the bomb release, as the bombs had to be dropped in the correct sequence to maintain the aircraft's balance.

At the rear of the cockpit section, just in front of the main spar, was the wireless operator's station. It was behind the navigator's section but it faced forward. Radio silence was in force when on operations to avoid detection by the enemy. The wireless operator kept listening out on the Bomber Command frequency for coded instructions that were sent out roughly every thirty minutes. These might be weather reports, the occasional message to abort or to jam an enemy frequency. The W/O was also expected to have some understanding of the navigator's equipment and the aircraft's electrical and intercom systems. It was his duty to provide any first aid that was needed. He could also be up in the astrodome keeping a lookout if there were enemy fighters about. The astrodome was a dome-shaped piece of Perspex that protruded above the aircraft's fuselage so that the navigator could take the star shots needed for astro-navigation.

The mid-upper gunner and rear gunner completed the crew. The mid-upper gunner's seat consisted of a strip of canvas slung beneath the turret and was attached once the gunner had clambered into position; there he perched for hours on end. The air gunners, particularly the rear gunner, had the coldest and loneliest positions in the aircraft. Far from the rest of the crew, the rear gunner had to crawl into his turret before closing its doors. It was so cramped that his parachute had to be left outside. Night fighters would usually attack from the rear and their first target was the hapless rear gunner. Air gunners had to stay alert and scan the night skies looking for enemy fighters for as long as ten hours. They could not afford to let their attention slip for a moment despite the discomfort they suffered sitting almost immobile in their icy cramped metal and Perspex turrets. It was their vigilance that would warn crews of impending attack, and their instructions to take evasive action were followed instantly and unquestioningly by their skippers.

By way of safety equipment, Lancasters had dinghies on board in case of ditching. There were emergency packs and first aid equipment and, as a last resort means of communication, homing pigeons were also carried in watertight containers on each sortie, the idea being they could be released with a message giving the crew's approximate position in the event of a crash. Amazingly, this unlikely form of emergency communication saved many lives when planes were forced to ditch.

On 30 November 1942, Bill was to fly a Lancaster for the first time, spending two hours on a familiarisation flight with Flight Lieutenant Gilpin, doing circuits and landings. Taxiing was difficult, as the Lancaster's nose obscured the view ahead. Perched high above the ground, pilots had to zigzag along the perimeter track in order to be able to see ahead, but once in the air the visibility was excellent. To taxi, alternate bursts of power from the outer port and starboard engines were used to swing the aircraft right or left. This needed careful judgement, as use of the brakes had to be rationed. The brakes were pressure-operated – the starboard inner engine operated the pump's motor but the pressure could soon be exhausted. Not only that, but if the brakes were overused, the brake drums would overheat, causing damage to the tyres. Once in the air, the controls were light and responsive and Bill quickly became used to the Lancaster's slight tendency to float down the runway on landing.

That afternoon, Bill and the crew flew again, alone this time. After an early lunch, they collected their equipment and jumped aboard the crew bus. Rattling along the perimeter track, they peered out at other aircraft until the bus halted at the dispersal pan where Lancaster R5856 awaited. The Lancaster made an imposing sight as she loomed over them with her ground crew around her. After completing his checks, Bill climbed the steps at the rear and made his way over the main spar to the front of the aircraft, where he gently lowered himself into the pilot's seat, adjusted the seat harness and settled down. The rest of the crew followed, finding their places and checking their equipment. There was some banter over the intercom while they prepared and then, checklist completed, Bill taxied to the holding point and at 13.45 they were airborne. Bill was getting accustomed to the brute strength that was needed on the take-off run. Due to the torque from the engines, the aircraft wanted to go to the right until the tail came off the ground when the airflow over the rudders made them fully responsive.

As well as getting to know the Lancaster, Bill's crew were getting to know each other and learning to work together. The emphasis at this stage was on training in the air so that the crew gained confidence in each other. Despite the foggy weather, the following week the crew managed to do some training flights. Each man was very aware that their lives depended on each other. This interdependence created a strong bond that transcended any differences in rank.

The crew started practising at the bombing range and the gunnery targets at Wainfleet near Skegness. One exercise involved firing at drogues, cone-shaped devices that were towed behind other aircraft. Each pilot's bullets were greased with a different colour so that hits could be counted. On another day, the target was laid out on the bombing range in the form of the outline of a ship. After several near misses with the 10 lb practice bombs, the bomb aimer, Don Willbee, got a direct hit on the canvas target. This was worth celebrating, so on their return Bill told them to pile into his car and they set off for a lively night at the pub.

The gunners honed their skills in fighter affiliation exercises. An area would be set aside for the exercise and, once inside the designated area, the crews would have to look out for fighters, generally Spitfires, 'attacking' them. The Spitfire pilots were typically experienced pilots resting from operations and they were adept at sneaking up on the trainee aircrews. They enjoyed creeping up from underneath the bomber, its most vulnerable point, and then suddenly popping up feet away from the rear turret and giving the rear gunner an almighty fright.

Another part of this course consisted of survival and evasion training in case they were shot down over enemy territory. The crews were bundled into trucks, driven into the countryside and dropped off miles from anywhere with no money and no food. They then had to find their own way back to base without being seen by anyone, especially police, soldiers or service police. Different approaches were taken to this exercise. Some crews really got into the spirit, crawling along ditches and hiding in woods, emerging cold, wet and muddy near their bases, if they could find them – many did not. Others took a different approach. The more cunning and lazy managed to hide some money on them. Thus equipped, they headed off for a comfortable day in the nearest café or pub and then caught a bus or train back to near their bases, slapped on a bit of mud and reported back.

On completion of the course, Bill had some eight hours' daylight and five hours' night flying experience on Lancasters. This was minimal training and in the spring of 1943, after complaints from squadrons, Bomber Command realised that the Conversion Unit crews were 'turned out with insufficient experience in the Lancaster... They have in fact to do some 10–15 hours in the Operational Squadrons before they can be considered trained'.[6] This was exactly what Bill and his crew would have to do with the squadron they were now assigned to.

CHAPTER SEVEN
IX SQUADRON

The squadron that Bill and his crew were to join was an illustrious one. RAF IX (B) Squadron has the distinction of being the oldest dedicated Bomber Squadron in the RAF. The squadron was initially formed at St Omer in France in 1914 to absorb the Wireless Flight of the Royal Flying Corps. There the squadron took part in the Somme and Arras offensives. After being disbanded a couple of times, it was reformed in April 1924 and equipped with Vickers Vimy bombers. It started the war in Group 3 but in August 1942 the squadron became part of Group 5, a group that included some of the finest squadrons of Bomber Command.

The squadron badge is intriguing and rather appealing; it features a small green bat with outspread wings. This badge was approved by King Edward VIII in 1936 and was based on a device used previously. The green bat represents both their night flying ability and, charmingly, the colour painted on their original aircraft, the BE2C biplanes. The squadron motto is '*Per noctem volamus*' or 'Throughout the night we fly', an appropriate motto for their role in the Second World War. There is also an unofficial squadron motto, one that accurately reflects the heartfelt feelings of many members of the squadron past and present: 'There's always bloody something!'

At the beginning of the war, the squadron was equipped with Wellingtons but Lancasters replaced these in 1942. The squadron was responsible for some of the most famous attacks of the war, including the sinking of the German battleship *Tirpitz*. After several bombing raids, the *Tirpitz* was finally sunk on 12 November 1944. Two squadrons were tasked with this mission and both scored hits with Tallboy bombs. There was considerable debate as to exactly whose bomb finally sunk her, but recent research concluded that the decisive bomb was delivered by Dougie Tweedle of IX Squadron. In 2014, the squadron celebrated its centenary in great style at the airfield in St Omer where it formed up. In recent times, the squadron has taken part in Operation Herrick in Afghanistan and Operation Shader in Syria. The latest addition to its long list of battle honours has recently been awarded (2020) for service in Afghanistan. Having flown the Tornado for many years, 2019 saw the end of the Tornado era with IX Squadron reforming at RAF Lossiemouth, flying Eurofighter Typhoons and continuing its role as a leading squadron.

In late 1942, the squadron was based at RAF Waddington, 5 miles south of Lincoln. It was one of the oldest RAF airfields, having been in use since 1916. Here, unlike the newer airfields, there were more permanent buildings with heated barrack blocks and comfortable messes for officers and men. The Officers' Mess was particularly splendid. In winter, a welcoming fire blazed in a large fireplace that was surrounded by shabby, soft, comfortable chairs where men would flop down and relax.

Bill and his crew became operational at a time when a new directive had just been issued for bomber operations. In January 1943, the Prime Minister, Winston Churchill, and US President, Franklin Roosevelt, held a conference in Casablanca that resulted in the Casablanca Directive. This laid out plans for an Allied strategic bombing campaign designed to destroy German military, industrial and economic systems while simultaneously undermining the will of the German people to fight. To implement these plans, what would become known as the Battle of the Ruhr was about to begin.

On 10 December 1942, Bill drove the short distance to RAF Waddington. It would be another month before the crew became operational. In mid-December, winter set in, the weather turning cold and misty, and for the rest of the month there were no major raids. Before being passed as ready for operations, a final series of exercises had to be undertaken. The time was spent carrying out bombing exercises, practising air firing and flying in formation at altitude and at low level. Mac had the chance to sharpen his skills on navigation exercises and finally there was a command 'Bullseye' exercise. A 'Bullseye' exercise was practising evasion techniques against searchlights and night fighters over a city. Bill was pitted against the searchlights of Sheffield for his 'Bullseye' exercise.

They only flew at night on two occasions, one being a navigation exercise on Christmas Eve that routed them over York, Cromer and Cambridge, all almost invisible in the blackout. Then the weather closed in again. Early Christmas morning, a little snow fell and a blanket of chilly fog swept across the airfield, deadening sounds. Hoar frost glistened and iced the skeletal shapes of trees and fences. Airmen venturing out of their barracks and messes caught an occasional glimpse of a snow-clad Lancaster looming out of the mist, but most of the field had vanished, hidden in the stillness and intense cold that gripped the countryside.

That morning, there was a carol service for those who wished to attend, followed by Christmas lunch. RAF tradition dictated that officers served the 'other ranks' their Christmas lunch and so Bill made his way to the Airmen's Mess. In the mess, a transformation had taken place. Paper chains and streamers hung on the walls; tables had been covered with cloths and beside each place setting stood a small Christmas menu. The men made their way in, squeezing themselves into chairs and benches until everyone was seated. Then the amateur waiters appeared, weighed down by enormous dishes of turkey, roast potatoes, Brussels sprouts and stuffing. Tucking in with relish, the men soon demolished the turkey, and the feast was completed with traditional Christmas pudding, followed by cheese, pickle, biscuits, mince pies and, best of all, plenty of beer.

By the time the pudding was finished, a fog of cigarette smoke hung over the tables. A dance band started playing and soon requests were being shouted out. Someone started singing and others joined in, first with carols then favourite songs, the songs growing steadily filthier as the afternoon wore on and pints disappeared ever faster. For one day, the war was forgotten.

Snow fell heavily in the first week of January, curtailing both operational and training flights. It was not until 8 January that Bill could fly on his familiarisation flight. Before novice crews started operating, the pilot was taken on an operation with another experienced crew to gain some combat experience. Six Lancasters of IX Squadron were briefed for the operation that night, and Bill was to act as flight engineer for no less a person than his Squadron Commanding Officer, Wing Commander J.M. Southwell DFC in Lancaster WS 4253–W, 'WS' being IX Squadron's code, 4253 the aircraft registration number and 'W' its assigned squadron identifier. Wing Commander Southwell was a very popular commander, relaxed enough to be one of the boys but still able to maintain good discipline. He believed in flying with his men and, unlike some commanders, he always chose the more dangerous operations to go on. Bill could not have asked for a better person to show him the ropes.

For Bill, like all aircrew on their first operation, there was a sense of tremendous excitement tinged with apprehension. As he heard the target for that night, his stomach tightened. It was to be Duisburg in the Ruhr Valley. Duisburg was a major logistical centre at the confluence of the Rhine and Ruhr rivers; there were key chemical, iron and steel works located there. The whole Ruhr area was known with black RAF humour as 'Happy Valley'. This was Germany's industrial heartland and the Germans threw everything they had into defending it. A seething cauldron of searchlights and flak awaited those who ventured over the Ruhr, and German fighters were always in close attendance, waiting to pounce.

The pre-operation routine now took over: pre-flight meal, getting kitted up and then the bus to their dispersal. To prevent bombing attacks damaging aircraft, the Lancasters were kept in individual bays known as 'dispersals'. These were located off the perimeter track, the peri-track for short, which led round the outskirts of the airfield. In the fading light, the huge black shapes of the Lancasters reared up, standing out in sharp contrast against the snow-covered airfield. After tramping around the aircraft doing the pre-flight checks, Bill stood, thoughtfully drawing on his pipe and mentally running through the flight engineer's tasks and the emergency procedures. Once all were settled in and ready, Wing Commander Southwell gave the thumbs-up to the ground crew. The ground crew attached the starter trolley to each engine in turn and then Southwell pressed each starter button in sequence. Bill stood beside him, his eyes on the instruments as, one by one, the four great Merlins coughed and roared into life. The noise was overwhelming; the fuselage shook and rattled as vibrations ran through it. As the engines were opened up to full power on take-off, Bill's hand was right behind Southwell's on the throttles, ready to take over. Fully laden with fuel and bombs, the Lancaster needed some firm handling to get her into the air; it was a two-handed job. It was the engineer's job to ensure that, as the engines were opened up to full power, the throttles stayed fully open and friction nuts were tightened to prevent an inadvertent loss of power. As they rose slowly into the air, the tight knot of apprehension in Bill's stomach eased. There was a sense of relief that the waiting was over; this was what he had spent eighteen months training for.

As they approached their target, Bill saw for the first of many times the inferno that was 'Happy Valley'. Thick cloud covered the valley and swathes of searchlights played across the cloud base, turning it into a beautiful but deadly floor of light against which the Lancasters were silhouetted. What looked like solid sheets of flak sparked and burst above the cloud. As they approached, above the thrumming of the engines could be heard flak shells bursting close by, their fragments pattering against the fuselage. Explosions nearby rocked the aircraft; standing there, Bill hung on as best he could. Meanwhile, Flight Sergeant Rogers in the Wireless compartment was busily stuffing 'Nickels' (propaganda leaflets) out of the flare tube. On the intercom Bill listened intently to the patter as the bomb aimer gave final instructions to his pilot on the run in. W/C Southwell steadied the aircraft and waited impatiently to hear the expected 'Bombs Gone'. It did not come – there had been a 'hang-up'. The bomb load consisted of a 4,000lb 'Cookie' and the rest were incendiaries. These incendiaries were loaded into SBCs (Small Bomb Containers), basically aluminium boxes with a release mechanism that was triggered electronically, allowing the bottom to open and release the bombs. After he had pressed the release buttons, F/O Higginson, the bomb aimer, noticed that one red light remained. This meant that part of the load had not released. Repeated efforts failed to free them so finally Southwell ordered the bomb door to be closed. There was no choice but to return with these incendiaries on board, not a recommended procedure. The extra weight affected speed and climbing ability, and there was always the possibility of them being set off by a shell or piece of flak.

As they headed for home, the flak seemed thicker than ever. Bill wondered how you ever got used to it. Routing over Belgium and the north of France, they crossed the Channel to face another enemy: the weather. The skies were filled with lowering clouds and visibility was deteriorating by the minute; it would be a race against time to get back before the base was closed in. However, Wing Commander Southwell was a man who liked to sleep in his own bed. He just managed to slip in to Waddington, landing at 21.09. He was the only one of the squadron to get in; the rest had to divert to other airfields. This had been a bad night for the squadron. Out of the six aircraft dispatched, one aircraft took a direct hit that killed the rear gunner, and another failed to return. It was a harsh introduction to the realities of life and death in Bomber Command.

At Waddington, Bill's crew had been waiting and wondering. It was not unknown for crews to lose their skippers on these first familiarisation flights. As the bombers started to land, they went over to the Ops room and checked. Grins lit up their faces as they saw Lancaster W-4253 and Bill were safely home; they were still a crew.

Having satisfied his CO that he was ready to fly on operations, Bill was now attached to 1506 Beam Approach Training Flight at Waddington in addition to being available for operational flying. Standard Beam Approach, or SBA as it was known, was an early form of instrument landing system introduced to enable pilots to land in bad visibility. It was based on a pre-war German system, the Lorenz system.

Originally known as the Standard Blind Approach System, the name was changed to Standard Beam Approach, as it was felt that the term 'blind' had singularly unfortunate connotations for a system designed to help you find – and land – at an airfield. It had been introduced despite concerns from Bomber Command, who stated that, 'in all probability only a few pilots in the Command could be relied on to make an approach and landing under IFR conditions'.[1] IFR stood for instrument flight rules: i.e. flying blind on instruments alone. These concerns were not groundless.

SBA was a system that employed radio beacons emitting signals aligned with the centreline of the runway. The signals were first picked up by the pilot at the outer marker of the airfield. He listened and flew according to what the tones indicated. If he was left of track he would hear dots and if right of track dashes and if on the centre line they merged into a continuous tone. There was also a visual display in the cockpit in the form of a left/right needle indicator. It sounds a simple procedure but it took skill and above all, practice, to use it. The kind of precision flying required was extremely difficult to achieve when returning from operations exhausted, short of fuel and possibly damaged, but in fog and bad weather it provided a lifeline, the only chance of getting down safely. Much of the SBA training was spent practising hunched-up in the Link Trainer. Although the sensation of flying in a Link Trainer was limited, as it lurched about in a way no aircraft did, it was a useful means of practising radio navigation. Bill did some training in an Oxford, but most of it was done in this cramped and uncomfortable device.

CHAPTER EIGHT
FIRST OPS

The winter of 1943 was bitter. During January, icy winds blasted across the Lincolnshire fens, bringing with them heavy snowfalls. Snow blurred the edges of buildings and out on the dispersals the aircraft appeared like giant white sculptures materialising out of the frosty air. The temperature continually dropped below zero degrees centigrade. Despite the blizzard conditions, runways were swept clear of snow and operations continued whenever possible. Off-duty airmen of all ranks were dragged from their beds to assist with shovelling snow off the runways and the dispersals. However on 10, 11 and 12 January, the snow brought all flying to a halt.

On 16 January, Bill awoke early; a clear white light filtered through the frost-coated windows, reflecting the snow outside. Rising, he dressed hurriedly. At breakfast, the talk was of operations being resumed that day and who might be on the Battle Order. After breakfast, he stepped out of the warm mess to find the wind whipping flurries of snow through the air, the bitter cold catching in the throat. Snow was still lying a foot deep in places and the paths were treacherous with ice as Bill trudged off to check the Battle Order. His eyes ran down the list and stopped. There it was: 'P/O Meyer and crew'. Beside his name was the aircraft they would be flying in that night, Lancaster WS 4761 P-Peter. A thrill of satisfaction, nervous excitement and pride ran through him as he turned away.

Preparations for operations started in the morning around ten o'clock, as soon as the Squadron received its operational orders on the teleprinter from Group Headquarters. These orders specified the target, the number of aircraft required and the type of munitions to be carried. Then the crews would be chosen and their names and the aircraft that were to 'work' that night would be posted on the board. The crews would then start their checks.

Usually, crews did an air test to ensure all the various systems – mechanical, electrical, radio and armaments – were working. The gunners always wanted to check their guns and ammunition belts. The wireless operator too wanted to check his equipment. At this point, the crews did not know where they were going, but a quick word with the ground crews to see how much fuel had been ordered up enabled them to make a good guess. Unusually, Bill and his crew did not perform their own air test that morning, although Geordie, the flight engineer, made a point of going down to talk to the ground crew who worked on P-Peter. Every Lancaster had its own idiosyncrasies; it was as well to be aware of them.

Early in the afternoon, the crews assembled in the Aircrews' Briefing Room, crowding in to await the arrival of their commanding officer. Tobacco smoke hung thickly in the air as men nervously puffed away at cigarettes and pipes. On the far wall hung a large curtain. This covered the giant map of Europe and hid the all-important 'Target for Tonight'. Keyed-up and excited, the crew discussed where they might be going on this, their first sortie. They already knew from the fuel load that it was going to be a long flight.

Rookie crews were usually given a comparatively easy first operation, often mine-laying or sometimes dropping leaflets, but the fuel load indicated that this was unlikely to be one of those operations. As the Station Commander and Squadron Commander arrived, the men fell silent. The briefing started. Stepping up to the wall, the Commander pulled back the curtain and, with those inimitable words, announced, "The target for tonight is… Berlin." It was 'The Big City' itself. The route was mapped out with tapes and pins. Areas to be avoided were marked prominently on the maps. Flak batteries were crosshatched in red and searchlight batteries in green. The crew realised that this was going to be no easy introduction but straight in at the deep end. The Squadron Operational Record notes, 'The target, Berlin… was received with delight by the Squadron'.[1] A view that was probably not shared by some of the more experienced aircrew who knew exactly what they would be in for. The air defences surrounding Berlin were awesome. It was ringed with searchlights, anti-aircraft guns, decoy fires and decoy markers that spread across more than 37 miles. Alan Hart recalled, "Now that was a real target to be scared of but to us it was a big adventure." Bill, at the grand old age of thirty-three, was somewhat more thoughtful. He had some idea of what was in store.

The Senior Intelligence Officer explained what kind of target they were to bomb and its importance. Then other officers gave out information such as headings, timings, heights and the expected weather en route and at the target. Mac studied the route carefully, noting the dangerous areas where batteries of searchlights or flak guns awaited them. Bomber Command played a game of cat and mouse with the Germans. In addition to the main target there were diversionary raids on other targets. The routes were carefully planned to zigzag in such a way as to leave the Germans guessing for as long as possible as to which of several possible target destinations was the chosen one. Wireless operators were also briefed on the radio frequencies for that night. Stafford Sinclair wrote down the codes and the identification colours to be fired from the Very pistol and the emergency airfields available. Meanwhile Don Willbee noted the types of bombs and the heights en route and for the bomb drop.

This was the first time Berlin had been attacked for fourteen months and 201 aircraft were to be dispatched. It was also the first time that target indicators, marker flares for the bombers to aim at, were used by the Pathfinders. Berlin was well beyond the range of 'GEE' and 'Oboe', the basic navigation devices in use at the time. GEE was the first navigation aid to provide navigators with a means of quickly determining their position. The name GEE was the code name for a hyperbolic radio navigation system whereby a combination of three signals received by the aircraft was used to establish an electronic grid of latitude and longitude. It allowed an aircraft to locate its position by timing the delays between two sets of signals from stations in England; the signals being displayed on an oscilloscope. GEE was a line-of-sight system and thus accurate over home territory but much less so over Germany.

Oboe was a blind bombing targeting system based on radio transponder technology. The name came from the musical pulses it emitted. Once again, it was a line-of-sight system and had a range of roughly 300 miles, but within that limit it was very accurate. It was used mainly by Pathfinder Force, as only one aircraft could be controlled at a time. The Pathfinder squadrons formed an elite group, Group 8, and their crews received specialist training in navigation to enable them to accurately mark targets for the main force to bomb.

Before each operation, the crew had their special 'Ops. meal', usually bacon and eggs. This was a well-deserved perk for airmen on operations; civilians were rationed to a meagre one egg per week. After the meal, the long process of gearing-up started. This meant emptying their pockets of all their personal belongings to prevent anything that could possibly be of use falling into enemy hands should they be captured. Then they struggled into the heavy flying gear needed for protection against the cold. What they put on depended on their position in the crew. The wireless operator often roasted, as the heating outlet was in his compartment, but while the pilots' and navigators' positions had some heating, the gunners' positions had none and they endured freezing conditions in their lonely turrets with temperatures as low as minus 40 degrees. Aircrew were issued with shearling suits – the jacket was known as an 'Irving' jacket and was often worn on its own. The gunners were issued with electrically heated Sidcot suits. These consisted of an inner kapok liner and an outer suit that was electrically wired to be plugged in on the aircraft to provide heating. They had fur collars to keep out the drafts. Alan Hart felt it impeded his field of vision and, deciding that staying alive was more important than staying warm, he cut off his collar to allow him an unhindered view as he scanned the skies. Bill, in the warmer cockpit, usually flew in 'Battledress', the heavy blue/grey serge short jacket and trousers that could be buttoned together at the waist.

The next stop was the parachute section to be issued with a parachute and a Mae West, the inflatable lifejacket named after the famously curvaceous American actress. Girls from the WAAF (Women's Auxiliary Air Force) carefully packed the parachutes. If the parachute had to be used, and you got safely back, it was customary to reward the packer whose skills had saved your life. A small escape kit was issued. This held items such as a map printed on a silk handkerchief, Horlicks tablets, a water bottle, water purifying tablets, a small compass, barley sugar sweets, a needle and thread and a small amount of French or Dutch money. Each man received a flying ration of a bar of much-prized chocolate, boiled sweets and a flask of coffee. Having donned all their kit, the crew were ready for the crew transport to take them to their dispersal.

At the dispersal, Doctor Wright, the squadron's Medical Officer, visited them. He visited each dispersal, 'making his rounds in the old Blood Wagon or "mis-carriage" – as he sometimes called it! Doling out wakey wakey tablets and anti sicks'.[2] The wakey wakey tablets were the stimulant drug Benzedrine. It was used by crews on long operations to combat physical and mental exhaustion. However, there was a price to pay: the effects lasted and made sleep difficult when they did get back. It was also often saved up for what was considered to be an equally important purpose: to ensure they were able to make the most of any parties they went to on nights off.

The squadron were due to take off around 16.30. All day long the ground crews had worked in the bitter cold, preparing the aircraft, each dispersal a hive of activity as all the various specialist trades swarmed over the aircraft. Electricians, fitters, engineers, wireless specialists and riggers all got in each other's way, each intent on making sure the system they were responsible for functioned perfectly. At the bomb dump, well away from the main airfield and protected by high soil embankments, armourers had sorted out bomb loads for each aircraft. The loads were laid out on trolleys that were joined to form a 'train' that was pulled by a tractor. This volatile 'train' then snaked slowly along the peri-track, stopping at each dispersal. Then a segment would be carefully positioned under the bomb bay of each Lancaster and disconnected. Just as important as the technical preparations were simpler tasks such as cleaning and polishing the Plexiglas turrets over the gunners' positions. The smallest smear or piece of dirt could lead to misidentification with fatal results in the hostile skies over Germany. The last job of all, in winter, was to de-ice the aircraft before the crews arrived to make their final checks before boarding.

The crew were both excited and apprehensive, hiding their nerves in a constant stream of light banter. Bill had made a point of talking them through his previous trip to give them some idea what to expect. He had described the flak and searchlights over Duisberg and they had heard stories from other airmen, but until they experienced it themselves there was the nagging uncertainty of how they would react under combat conditions. This was deeply unsettling.

The last flickers of daylight faded gradually on the horizon as Bill and Geordie walked slowly around P-Peter doing the external pre-flight check. Pitot head covers removed, all cowlings, inspection panels and leading edges secured and tyres checked for creep. Then it was time for a quick last pee against a wheel – the ritual of 'watering' a wheel being thought to bring good luck. Stubs glowed as last cigarettes were swiftly inhaled and then extinguished. Bill carefully knocked out his pipe and put it away. Then, one by one, the crew climbed the awkward narrow ladder at the back of the plane and, encumbered by their gear, threaded their way through the narrow fuselage to their positions. In his little cubicle, Mac carefully spread out his navigation aids: charts, pencils, navigation slide rule, protractor, etc. Behind him, in the radio compartment, Sinc sorted out his radio codes and checked that the Very pistol was in position behind his seat. The gunners checked their guns and plugged their electrically heated suits into the aircraft. All busily checked and rechecked their equipment.

In the cockpit, Bill and Geordie ran through their list of pre-start-up checks then Bill called over the intercom to see that all the crew were ready; his calm voice was reassuring. In turn individual voices answered affirmatively. Starting with the starboard inner, Bill pushed the starter buttons and one by one the Lancaster's four mighty Merlin engines sparked and crackled into life. As Geordie adjusted the throttles and mixture, the checks continued: temperatures, pressures, altimeter... Finally, the chocks were pulled away. Bill advanced the throttles and slowly the great aircraft lumbered out onto the peri-track to join the other Lancasters zigzagging their way to the Control caravan that stood at the end of the runway. There they stopped, engines screaming, waiting in line to be given the green Aldis light, the signal that they could take off. Talking on the radio was forbidden, as the enemy could monitor this; the green light would be their final contact with their base until they returned. Soon it flashed for them and P-Peter taxied out and lined up on the runway. The engines were run up to full power, the aircraft bucking and straining against the brakes before Bill released them and they hurtled down the runway. Slowly the tail rose up and finally P-Peter lifted heavily off the ground and clawed her way up into the dusky sky.

Mac (Neil McCorkindale), the navigator, later wrote down his impressions of their first sortie to Berlin and sent them to his father. The narrative gives such a vivid feel both of the men's state of mind and the conditions they endured over Berlin that it is included here. It starts as they thunder down the runway and finishes over Berlin:

Geordie, the engineer, pushed hard against the throttles with his left hand and screwed them tight with his right. We were off the deck and tearing past the vague shapes of houses, fields, haystacks and woods which were earthbound in the dusk of this lovely autumn [actually winter] evening, in this lovely English countryside. Across the outer perimeter lights, banking to the left, ever climbing to get up and away from that Earth, that good Earth, where fires were burning in cottages, where clocks were ticking beside pictures on mantelpieces, where people were laughing at *Itma* [a radio comedy of the time]. We had thirty-five minutes to waste before setting course at Sheringham [64 nautical miles from Waddington] and climbed during that time to 15,000 feet, on various courses which took us over a wide area of England, from Lincolnshire to Oxfordshire, Bedfordshire, and then the rendezvous in Norfolk with its lonely searchlight shining vertically, a single gatepost to the field of War. Course was set for a point on the Danish coast north of Esbjerg and the crew settled down to this long haul across the grey North Sea, invisible in the haze below. It was a run of seventy minutes with a following wind of forty knots, the Navigator checked his met. forecast winds, with those he found from his general fixes. He adjusted the courses he would use in the later legs of the trip. The Gunners swung their turrets, cocked the guns, the bomb aimer fused the bombs, and the WOP listened for any messages that might come from Base. All on board were tensed, expectant, excited, thrilled perhaps, afraid undoubtedly, because it was their first operational flight and Berlin was a big target materially and psychologically. It hadn't been attacked for over a year and now with these two hundred Lancasters and Halifaxes we were on the way to open a new stage in the Air War. A confident, aggressive phase had started. Ten minutes to go before reaching the Danish coast and there hadn't been a sign of life outside that little world of seven men and a machine, that roaring death-carrying entity, vibrating, rushing through the dark night. "Searchlights ahead Skip." Wilkie's [Don Willbee, the bomb aimer] voice startled us, and something thumped inside – this was it, the enemy coast ahead. I went out to stand behind the engineer and see what German searchlights looked like, so vastly different from our own – menacing – seeking and searching not for raiding planes, but for us, for me, for the purple heather on the moor, and the burn with the waterfall at the top of the brae. Let not your heart be troubled neither let it be afraid. When we reached the coast which was faintly visible as a whole line caused by breakers. We changed course to take us over Denmark to a point on the Baltic coast. The searchlights groped hither and thither but there was no flak and we were on the look out for fighters, which might come up from Odense or from some other airfield on Jutland. In twenty minutes we had set course across the Baltic for D [a turning point] on the German coast and by this time we were coming over a layer of cloud about 10,000 feet below, a welcome blanket. Now there was much more activity – flashes ahead lighting the cloud – sparks in the far ahead where the Pathfinders were already over the coast flashing and crackling like those penny sparklers which we bought as boys and held out to frizzle and burn on a wire. They came much closer when we turned on the last course for Berlin – the big smoke. Various coloured lights could be seen all around, they meant nothing definite to us, but which mean a great deal. The gunners were swinging around continuously and the bomb aimer with 10 minutes to go was getting busy with his bomb sight setting on the new wind and heights, etc. All the while we maintained a weave – up and down, right and left, always changing course, but always going in the same direction, towards the flashing, burning, searing madness of light from hundreds of searchlights circling the huge city which was Berlin. Ahead some aircraft were coned by concentrations of 20 to 30 beams being pounded continuously by the guns. One would blow up in hundreds of fiery pieces and hundreds of pieces of crushed and broken bodies and somewhere broken hearts. How would we possibly get through that mess of light, those weaving needles? Little puffy clouds rushed past, the harmless aftermath of shell bursts. The flashes were intense; the vicious bursting of steel was vivid and blinding on every side. The red and green target markers were floating serenely, steadily down to their mark through the holocaust, and the bomb aimer started giving his instructions – bomb doors opens, left, left, steady, steady, steady, right, steady, hurry up, hurry up Wilkie [Don Willbee the bomb aimer], the unspoken plea from the rest of us, hurry let's get home. Oh how long, steady, steady. Bombs gone, bomb doors closed, another 50 seconds on a steady course to get our picture – the longest fifty seconds in the world. "Flak close behind, Skip," said Johnson in the tail. It was thumping underneath and the smell of cordite was sickly. Thump – thump.[3]

Many navigators found the view at the sharp end of a Lancaster over the target too much to take and remained closeted in their darkened compartment. Mac was made of sterner stuff and he took a good look at the skies over Berlin that night.

As they settled on track for home, the gunners were constantly scanning the skies for enemy aircraft. In the mid-upper turret, Alan Hart's heart suddenly pounded; he had spotted a Junkers 88. Warning the rest of the crew on the intercom, he held his breath as he tracked the German fighter, '… but he didn't see us so we didn't advertise our position there, and we all came back.'[4] This was normal practice, as bombers had very little chance of surviving an attack by a night fighter, so the best ploy was not to draw attention to yourself by firing on them but to try and remain unseen and get away. Some of the flak Mac mentions found its target. On their return, holes were found in the bomb doors and fuselage. Despite this, Bill's laconic comment in his logbook reads, 'Easy trip'.

The 'picture' mentioned in Mac's account was a photo taken after the bombs were dropped. The Lancaster carried a photoflash which had the equivalent of more than one million-candle power. It also had the explosive power of a 250lb bomb and was encased in a long aluminium cylinder carried in a tube in the middle of the fuselage. The photoflash was released at the same time as the bombs, and the camera timing adjusted to take the picture as it exploded. This enabled intelligence officers to plot how close to the target the bombs had landed; and to assess the damage. It also had another important function; it provided evidence that the crew had completed the operation, for without the photo, it would not be counted towards the thirty operations that constituted a tour of duty. The seconds waiting for the photo always seemed agonisingly long to crews with nerves already stretched by the flak and searchlights surrounding them.

Seven and a half hours after taking off, Bill heard, with some relief, the Morse code identifier for Waddington. Breaking radio silence for the first time as they approached, he asked permission to land and touched down at 23.53. It had been a long night. Tired but elated, the crew gathered up their gear and tumbled down the steps at the back, where their smiling ground crew waited. Relaxed now, they stood around lighting their cigarettes. Relief that they had come through their first operation showed on their faces as they chattered in the cold night air. The crew bus lumbered into view to take them to be debriefed; always the first thing that happened after operations. Hot mugs of tea or cocoa would be waiting and the Intelligence Officer and his assistants would question the crews as to how the trip had gone. They were interested in every detail – whether the timetable had been adhered to, whether they had seen the target indicators, if and when they had been attacked or if they had seen others attacked, etc.

Bill was pleased with the crew's performance on this their first sortie. They had managed to pick out the Spree, the river that runs through Berlin. His debrief reported in the squadron ORBS (Operational Record Book) states:

> BERLIN Station attacked. 20.20 hours 18,000 feet. Red flares seen at 19.45 at NEUWARP. No green flares but river and built up area observed. Own incendiaries seen and several other sticks some burning red. As left target number of fires seen to be steadily increasing. Believe small holes in bomb doors and fuselage. No major damage. Pilot states "Successful mission. Quite Satisfied".[5]

After the debriefing, they went for their post-operational meal, a breakfast often of bacon and eggs that was served to operational

William Meyer Portrait

Bill aged 19 on a cruise (left)
Bill on holiday (right)

Bill with his Wolseley sports car

Bill in 1938

Boulogne-sur-Mer 1938 The Meyer family on holiday. Bill second from right, his father, Mr Meyer senior next to Bill wearing a hat

'The Challenger' stopping en route across the USA, Bill is in the centre with his back towards the camera

War Eagle Field, California, home of the Polaris Flight Academy

Stearman taxiing out at War Eagle Field

Cadets and their instructors having flown to Yuma. Second from right Richard Hough, fourth from right Ken Gilderdale and Bill in the centre in sunglasses

Polaris Flight Academy 1942 'A' Flight Commander and Deputies, Bill is in the centre

Ken Gilderdale sitting in a Vultee BT-13 at Polaris 1942

Ken Gilderdale enjoying sitting in Lancaster PA474 of the Battle of Britain Memorial Flight in 2008

IX (B) Squadron, 'B' Flight with WS-Z Zola 1943. Bill front row third from right

*Bill and crew in front of Lancaster WS-U Uncle.
Left to right Geordie Hunter, Sinc Sinclair, Mac McCorkindale,
Bill, Donald Willbee, Alan Hart, Darkie Johnson*

U' Uncle nose art, the pawnbroker's sign - three glowing golden balls

*Geordie (Wilson Hunter) Flight Engineer (left), Mac/Corky (Neil McCorkindale)
Navigator (middle) and Sinc (Stafford Sinclair) Wireless Operator (right)*

Bill (William Meyer) with IX (B) Squadron (left), Don (Donald Willbe) Bomb Aimer (middle), Darkie (Thomas Johnson) Rear Gunner (right)

Al (Alan Hart) Mid-Upper Gunner (left), Alan Hart with Lancaster Plate 2008 (middle), Neil McCorkindale with his bike 1943 (right)

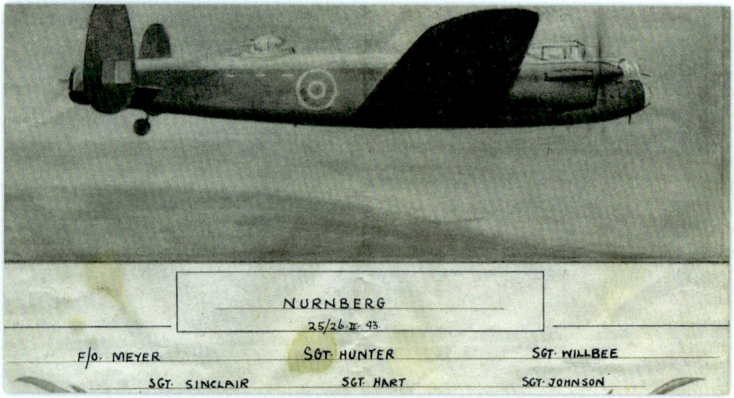

Card awarded to each member of the crew to commemorate outstanding bombing accuracy. Nuremberg on 25 February 1943

crews. As they ate, they mulled over the night's events. Having been so psyched up all day, it now took some time to unwind and relax before they walked back in the cold night air to their rooms to sleep.

It had been a baptism of fire. The BBC sent Richard Dimbleby to join a 106 Squadron Lancaster on this raid. He flew with Guy Gibson and his crew, and his words show how enormously impressive he found their courage and skill as they flew through flak and shell fire on their bombing run: 'Perhaps I am shooting a line for them but I think that somebody ought to. They and their magnificent Lancasters, and all the others like them, are taking the war right into Germany. They have been attacking, giving their lives in attack since the first day of the war.'[6]

However, Bomber Command did not consider this raid on Berlin to be a success. The forecast had been for good weather but the thick cloud en route and haze over the target made navigation difficult and bombing inaccurate. The Command decided to try again. The following night, another raid on Berlin was ordered. Eleven crews from IX Squadron were operating but, fortunately as it turned out, Bill's were not among them. The route planned was the same as that taken the night before and this time the Luftwaffe were waiting for them. The loss rate was a terrible 11.8%. The rate was much higher for IX Squadron; four of the eleven crews dispatched on that sortie did not return. Bomber Command did not attempt a similar raid until a new navigation aid, H2S mapping radar, was available.

This was the darkest, coldest time of the year; the time when the human spirit is at its lowest. The first flakes of snow floated slowly down as evening fell and by morning the landscape was again blanketed in white. During the next few days, freezing winds from Siberia sent temperatures plummeting. Ground crews still worked on their aircraft, bundled up against the cold but, of necessity, sometimes with bare hands that were left raw, seared by touching freezing metal. There was no flying for a couple of days.

Bill spent the next week completing his SBA training on the Link trainer with the occasional flight in an Oxford. It was not until 27 January that his name appeared on the Battle Order again with Düsseldorf as the target. Düsseldorf was a large commercial city and the administrative centre for the iron, steel, heavy engineering and armaments industries of the Ruhr, as well as an important engineering centre in itself.

After take-off, they flew to a holding beacon to form up into the bomber stream. There were 162 aircraft in all that streamed out over the North Sea. Perched in his mid-upper turret, Alan Hart suddenly spotted another Lancaster heading straight for them. "Dive, Skip," he shouted over the intercom. Bill responded instantly, shoving the controls full forward, sending the Lancaster into a steep dive. As the Lancaster plunged downwards, Alan instinctively ducked as the belly of a returning Lancaster passed just overhead. It was a near miss. Breathing heavily, Alan quickly checked before reporting that it was safe to climb again. Aircraft that developed problems and were forced to make early returns were meant to lose a set amount of altitude before turning to head back against the bomber stream. As in this case, the rule was not always adhered to, often with fatal results.

As they climbed, ice formed, slowly inching its way across the windscreen. Ice was a treacherous enemy, building up silently on wings and airframe surfaces destroying lift and increasing drag. Noticing his airspeed starting to bleed slowly away, Bill realised he would have to descend. As he did so, ice slowly flicked off the propeller blades, rattling unnervingly against the cockpit fuselage.

Nowadays, aircraft have inbuilt de-icing systems on vulnerable surfaces, but the Lancaster had only basic systems whereby de-icing fluid could be sprayed on the pilot's and bomb aimer's windows and also onto the propellers where centrifugal force distributed it. However, these systems were not very effective and, once icing took hold, the only remedy was to find less icy conditions at a different altitude, even if that meant facing other dangers such as flak. Ice was the nemesis of many a crew. Meteorology was in its infancy and it was simply not possible to forecast accurately the altitudes where icing would be a danger. Instructed to fly at certain heights, many inexperienced crews were killed when they stayed too long at these designated altitudes after encountering ice, its insidious build-up finally causing them to lose control of their aircraft.

Another IX Squadron aircraft became so heavily iced up that the pilot found he was struggling to maintain a mere 13,000 feet. Already uncomfortably low over the target, he then found that the 4,000lb 'Cookie' bomb had hung up. An attempted landing with it still on board would have been suicidal so they set about trying to jettison it. It took a nerve-racking hour twisting and turning and desperately trying every technique they could think of before they finally managed it.

Arriving overhead Düsseldorf, Bill found the visibility was good but the flak very heavy. After the bomb run, Mac gave a new track to follow and, as they turned away, they could see large explosions on the ground below as other aircraft dropped their bomb loads. In his freezing rear turret, Darkie shifted slightly in his seat as he continuously quartered the night sky. As he did, something just caught the corner of his eye. It was a night fighter and he saw, almost immediately, another one on a parallel course. Would the fighters spot them? On the intercom he warned the crew and waited, watching intently as they got closer. Better not to move the turret when you thought you saw something in case light glimmered on the Plexiglas and drew the night fighters' attention to you. Bill steadily held his course as the crew tensed expectantly – they all realised that they would not stand a chance against two fighters. For several long minutes there was only the crackle of static on their headsets before finally Darkie reported, with heartfelt relief in his voice, that the fighters had passed safely by. It had been such an anxious moment that Darkie made a specific note of it in his logbook.

German night fighters were organised in divisions, the *Nachtjagdgeschwader (NJG)*. A division contained three or four *Gruppen* of between thirty and fifty aircraft. Each *Gruppe* operated within a certain area that was based on a mapped-out grid of night fighter 'boxes', each approximately 32km long (north-south) and 20km wide (east-west), lying along the routes taken by the aircraft of Bomber Command. Each box, using ground radars, controlled one night fighter and directed him onto a single target. When close, the fighter picked up the target on his own *Lichtenstein* radar and attacked. This system enabled the Germans to patrol a vast area. However, it had the disadvantage that each fighter had to stay within its box and could not attack outside it, however tempting the target. This chain of boxes was known as the *Kammhuber* line after the man that designed it, General Josef Kammhuber.

It was in response to this chain that the concept of the bomber stream had been developed in 1942. This entailed all aircraft flying at the same speed on the same route to and from the target, with each aircraft having a specific height and time slot in the stream as a collision avoidance measure. As each controller could only direct six interceptions in an hour, the idea was to reduce the number of boxes the stream would pass through and thus reduce the chances of a successful German interception. The only disadvantage was an increased danger of collisions en route and over the target. In the dark, crews could not know who or what was around them, and the first indication they had of another aircraft nearby was usually the fright they got as the aircraft jumped around as it hit the slipstream of the aircraft ahead. Paradoxically, however, this also served to reassure crews that they were on the right track and in the thick of the stream, the safest place for avoiding enemy fighters.

This raid on Düsseldorf was the first occasion when Mosquitos, using the electronic aid Oboe, carried out 'ground marking' with flares; this was to become the standard form of target marking for the Pathfinders. It involved Pathfinder aircraft marking the aiming point for the main bomber force by dropping incendiary flares. Despite cloud over the target, the new system worked well and it was reported that the bombing was well concentrated over the southern part of the city.

On 21 January, the squadron had welcomed the arrival of the first of the new Mark III Lancasters, and the ground crews immediately went to work checking them over. The new Mark

III's used Merlin engines manufactured by Packard under licence from Rolls-Royce, but on paper there was little difference in their performance.

The arrival of the new Lancasters was a piece of luck for Bill and the crew. New and inexperienced crews usually got allocated the oldest, most beaten-up aircraft whose performance had suffered under the stresses of operational flying. Now they were to be allocated their own brand-new Lancaster. On 29th they first saw the Lancaster in which they would fly on almost all their operations for the rest of their 30-sortie tour. This was Lancaster ED 480 WS-U. She stood at the dispersal, majestic and immaculate. No dents, patches or ripples disfigured her skin; the cockpit and turrets gleamed in the dull winter sunlight. As they climbed the ladder and made their way through the fuselage – painted, as they all were, a bilious shade of green, known as 'cockpit green' – the paint was pristine. Looking around in delight, they were greeted with the smell of fresh paint rather than the stale smell of fuel, oils and sweat. After a preliminary air test, Bill took ED 480 WS-U up for a 'Height Climb' test to see what her operational ceiling was. The nominal service ceiling was 24,500 feet but a full load reduced this to 22,000 feet and individual aircraft varied in their performance. Afterwards, they tested the handling during fighter affiliation exercises.

RAF tradition dictated that a crew taking over a new aircraft were allowed (within reason) to choose some artwork that could be painted on the left side of the nose. Her designation in the squadron was 'U' and in the phonetic alphabet in use at the time 'U' was 'Uncle'. In those days, 'Uncle' was also a slang expression for a pawnbroker and so it was decided to have the three gold balls that symbolised a pawnbroker's shop proudly displayed on the side of the nose. Perhaps too the knowledge that their lives were 'in hock' to fate every time they flew on operations influenced their choice. Having decided, they knew just the right man to do the artwork. One of IX Squadron's ground crew had been a signwriter in civilian life. He was commissioned to paint their pawnbroker symbol for them and duly produced a stunning piece of nose art. To the rear of the bomb aimer's position, the letters 'UNCLE' appeared, while directly below the pilot's window hung the three dull gold balls, glowing out against the dirty grey/black background in 3D splendour.

Their first operation in 'Uncle' was to Hamburg on 30 January. It was to be the first time that Pathfinder aircraft employed a new radar navigation device, H2S. This had a ground-mapping capability used for both navigation and target identification.

As on so many winter nights, icing was a problem. As well as surface and propeller icing, it could also form in the engine carburettors. There was a critical temperature band when it was vital to adjust the temperature with carburettor heating to keep this icing at bay. Such conditions left the Merlin engines flat out, struggling for height. Three of the eleven IX Squadron crews who flew that night had to turn back when they encountered extremely severe icing conditions and were unable to maintain height.

Approaching Hamburg, Bill found broken cloud at 14,000 feet illuminated by searchlights, their intense fingers of light probing the skies, hunting their prey while their bright beams dazzled and destroyed night vision. Sheets of heavy flak rose up, bursting all around them. Lancasters were able to fly at heights above the light flak, unlike those unfortunates flying in Wellingtons, but they were vulnerable to the dangerous medium and heavy flak from 88mm and 128mm guns. Worst of all was radar-predicted flak aimed from batteries at individual aircraft and very accurate. That night, one crew failed to return. Another aircraft returning early due to icing crashed on landing but the crew escaped. Yet another came down over Yorkshire. There were no survivors.

CHAPTER NINE
UNCLE

The crew were next on the Battle Order on 2 February for a sortie to Cologne. All afternoon the rain sheeted down; by evening the temperature was dropping fast as an icy wind swept in off the North Sea. At their dispersal, the shivering crew did not linger and once the external checks were complete, they clambered aboard their new aircraft, WS-U. Eleven IX Squadron Lancasters were operating that night and 'Uncle' was airborne at 18.30. At his navigation station, Mac was attempting to tune the GEE set. To no avail; it was not working. GEE used the signals from multiple stations to allow the navigator to obtain a fix of his position. With a sigh, Mac now realised he would have to rely on dead reckoning alone; it would not be so accurate but he could cope, and they pressed on with the sortie. Another ten minutes passed; now Mac was watching the compass with growing concern. The readings were fluctuating wildly and making no sense. Without accurate readings, he would be unable to be sure of their heading and position. There was no choice; continuing on was impossible with an unreliable compass and GEE U/S (unserviceable). Reluctantly, he informed Bill and they turned back. This sortie would not count towards their thirty operational missions.

The next task was jettisoning the bomb load while they were still out over the North Sea. It was bad enough pounding down the runway on take-off with a full fuel and bomb load, but trying to land in that condition was an invitation to disaster. The 4,000lb High Capacity bomb that formed part of the load, known colloquially as a 'Cookie', was particularly sensitive. It had a thin casing to allow room for as much explosive as possible to be crammed in, and it looked more like an elongated oil drum than a bomb. Don opened the bomb doors to do a visual check before jettisoning the bomb load. He checked again carefully afterwards. To his relief, none had hung up. Despite the navigation problems, Mac got them safely back to Waddington where they landed at 21.48.

This operation on Cologne was something of an experimental raid, with Pathfinder aircraft using both Oboe and H2S to identify the target. Not only were the results disappointing, with the bombing being scattered, but a Stirling aircraft equipped with the new H2S device was shot down with disastrous long-term consequences for the Command. The Bomber Command diary states:

> The set was damaged but the German firm of Telefunken was able to reassemble it. This gave the Germans an early indication of the operational use of H2S and eventually led to the development of a device, "Naxos", which would enable German night fighters to home on to a bomber which was using its H2S set.[1]

The following night, only three aircraft from IX Squadron were on the Battle Order. Bill and the crew were one of them. It was Hamburg again and Alan Hart remembered this night clearly. They climbed out over the North Sea into icy skies with the temperature falling dramatically. As they approached the coast of Europe, flak ships opened up on them. German controllers had identified their target and as they reached Hamburg they were met with very heavy and uncomfortably accurate flak aimed straight up through the thick cloud that covered the town. Despite the ice and cloud cover, the fighters were waiting, although it was mainly the easier slower targets, the Stirlings, Halifaxes and Wellingtons, that they went after. Even with their electrically heated suits, Alan and Darkie shivered in their turrets as they strained to see out into the darkness around them.

As usual, the crew had their flasks of hot coffee with them. No one ever drank it until they were on their way home. On the return that night, Alan, frozen stiff with cold, finally decided to have a sip of coffee. With fingers made clumsy by the cold, he struggled to undo his thermos but found when he had '…the flask just didn't feel right and when I went to have a drink of it, it was all chips. I thought the glass in the flask had smashed so I didn't bother. When we got down, the flask was perfectly alright, and it was all liquid, so I can only gather that the coffee had frozen into these chips'.[2] The temperature in the aircraft, other than at the front where there was some heating, had fallen to around minus 48 degrees Fahrenheit (minus 44 Celsius) that night.

Operational sorties were interspersed with NFT, fighter affiliation exercises and bombing practice. NFT stood for night flying training but actually referred to air tests. There was no let up, and, weather permitting, if they were not flying operationally they would be doing some kind of training. The crews also carried out low-level formation flying exercises involving flying in a 'wing' of three or five aircraft, with one flying in the lead while the others formatted in a 'V' on him.

At other times they trained alone. One morning, they undertook some low-level flying north of Skegness. As they thundered along with the coast flashing past, the indicated airspeed read 160 knots (185 mph). Suddenly Bill turned inland and Geordie watched in some trepidation as Bill, aiming between two pylons, flew the mighty Lancaster under some high-tension cables. Alan gasped as the cables passed just over his head. The cables were only about 60 feet from the ground at their lowest point; no room for error there. There was more to come. In the distance, a goods train could be seen chugging along a railway embankment. As they approached and paralleled the embankment, the driver and fireman were startled and more than a little put out to find themselves eye to eye with a Lancaster bomber as it roared by. Turning, Bill brought them around for a second run alongside. This was too much for the men in the cab and the irate fireman started lobbing lumps of coal at the aircraft. Alan recalls that, from his perch in the upper turret, he was almost at eye level with the men in the engine cab as he warned, "Watch out, Skip, there's another lump coming."[3] This was not their skipper's usual style of flying and the startled crew were left wondering what on earth was going on and why Bill, normally so cautious and careful, should have taken such risks.

The reason may have been some special orders. Occasionally, pilots were briefed to fly certain manoeuvres without warning or involving the crew. Planning and training was going on at that time for the Dambusters raid. Group 5 was an elite group in Bomber Command and in March 1943, Wing Commander Guy Gibson formed 617 Squadron, from crews selected from 5 Group Squadrons. It was some of these crews that carried out the famous Dambuster raid on the Mohne, Eder and Sorpe dams on 16 May 1943.

Wilhelmshaven was the target on 10 February. However, once again the weather intervened and at 17.30 when the crews, including Bill's, were geared up and waiting for the crew transport, the sortie was cancelled. To no one's surprise, it was on again the following night. Wilhelmshaven was covered by cloud and the Pathfinders used a new method to mark the target. Using their H2S sets to pinpoint the target, they then marked it by the dropping of parachute flares. As these hung in the air, the method was called 'skymarking'. It was a success. Bill bombed from within cloud and his debrief report states:

> Both warning flares and T.I. [Target Indicator] markers in sights when bombs released. Bright red flash seen reflected on cloud believed 4000HC and a deep red glow was also observed.[4]

The 4000 HC was the 4,000lb High Capacity bomb commonly known as a 'Cookie'.

By now, the crew knew their roles and their aircraft and were operating well as a team. They were also discovering each other's little idiosyncrasies. Smoking was strictly forbidden on the aircraft for several very good reasons; the aircraft was filled with fuel, ammunition and oxygen, all highly combustible. However, Sinc was an inveterate smoker and, on the way home, his craving for nicotine often overcame him. As the aircraft descended on the return and they were able to come off oxygen, Alan recalls Sinc 'would sneak his crafty smoke'. Conveniently for Sinc, the Wireless Operator's compartment included the Very pistol port. This was where the Very pistol was first slotted in, then twisted and turned to lock it in, so the colours of the day or any recognition signal could be fired out of the top of the aircraft. This was a basic means of 'Identification Friend or Foe' or an emergency signal. However, Sinc found this port very useful for other purposes, and '… if he did not eject his fag end from the Very pistol port it would be orange peel that would bang against my turret'.[5] The fag ends caused a shower of sparks and Alan, sitting keyed up in the mid-upper turret surrounded by belts of ammunition, would get the fright of his life as sparks suddenly hit his turret or the orange peel cracked against the Plexiglass. Oranges were unobtainable to the public but, like eggs, were given out to aircrew. Alan rather wished they were not.

Their next sortie was to Bremen on 21 February. After a mid-afternoon briefing, they took off just before 19.00. However, they found the route was '…too well defended'[6] by flak batteries. Crews had to contend with flak defences in various forms. There were flak ships lying in wait off the coastlines and mobile flak units mounted on flatbed railway wagons that moved around. There were belts of flak batteries firing 88mm cannon that stretched across Holland and Germany, in places 20 kilometres thick. Colossal flak towers protected Berlin and other major cities. These were huge concrete structures with walls up to three and a half metres thick, almost impregnable to bombs and bristling with flak and anti-aircraft guns. Aircrew tried to give them a wide berth.

A flak barrage involved selecting and swamping an area of sky that the bomber stream was expected to pass through by throwing everything they had into this area or 'box' as it was known. Predicted flak was usually aimed at aircraft at the front of the bomber stream. It was radar-controlled; the height, direction and speed having been computed, the flak was then aimed at a predicted area. Flak was a constant nightmare for bomber crews who sometimes had to fly straight into what appeared to be a solid wall of yellow, red and black exploding flak shells as the Germans tried to gauge the height of the bomber stream and to set the shells to explode at the same height. When the shells exploded, they sent out shards of razor-sharp hot metal that could tear through the Lancasters' thin skins, and through anyone unfortunate enough to be in the way. When shells exploded close by, chunks of shrapnel would pepper the aircraft and the smell of cordite would percolate through it.

Alan Hart remembers that the flak was always at its worst during school holidays, which was when teenagers, sharp-eyed and keen, were helping man the flak batteries. This became a more permanent problem as, after the losses suffered by German troops at Stalingrad in early 1943, the authorities decided to replace the lost manpower by sending the troops that had been manning the flak batteries to the front. These troops were replaced by drafting these fifteen and sixteen-year-olds to man the flak batteries and fire-control radars.

Increasingly, the flak batteries were directed by radar and worked in conjunction with batteries of searchlights nearby. These batteries consisted of a blue master beam and three satellite beams. The master beam would sweep across the night sky and, when it illuminated a bomber, the satellite beams would then sweep round onto the unfortunate aircraft, 'coning' it in their blinding lights. Once coned, a pilot had to take swift and violent evasive action to get out of the light before more anti-aircraft and flak batteries homed in on him.

Arriving overhead, they found Bremen engulfed in a maelstrom. Flak burst all around them; its acrid smell filled the aircraft as shell fragments rattled against the fuselage. Thin cloud covered the target but the Pathfinder flares could be seen through it. Wilkie asked for the bomb bay doors to be opened, an uncomfortable moment as the lethal contents of the bomb bay were now exposed. One small shard of flak hitting any of that load and that would be end of them. On the bomb run, the rest of the crew tensed, willing Wilkie to get on with it and get rid of their deadly load. Seconds seemed like minutes until at last he reported "Bombs gone." As Bill and Geordie watched, they saw the huge flash under the cloud as their 4,000lb 'Cookie' exploded.

Bill turned and headed for home but found that the flak gunners had now accurately assessed the height of the bomber stream and were pouring a constant stream of shells into the sky. Darkie, perched in his turret, had an excellent view of exactly how close the flak was getting. Swallowing hard, he got on the intercom: "Flak's getting mighty close, Skip." The rest of the crew hung on to their seats as explosions rocked the aircraft, gritting their teeth as flak hammered into the fuselage sending judders rippling through the airframe. Geordie kept his eyes glued to the instruments, watching closely to detect the first signs of any serious damage. Bill wrestled with the controls, his arms aching from the sheer physical effort of trying to keep the aircraft on course and the constant corrections needed as the aircraft was tossed around by the exploding flak. The whole way back to the coast there was no let-up as a succession of batteries opened up on them and poured fresh waves of flak into the sky.

As they neared the coast of England, Bill was faced with a new worry. It had been cloudy and overcast when they took off and now thick fog had rolled in across the Lincolnshire Wolds, enveloping Waddington in its chilly grasp. Sinc's headset crackled into life as a warning came through on the radio: Waddington and the airfields to the south were now closed. It was a clear, starry night up above the cloud but below it the radio reported visibility dropping rapidly and the fog spreading. Mac set to work recalculating their route and double-checking the fuel figures while Geordie adjusted the fuel flows for maximum endurance.

They decided to try for Middleton St George near Darlington. There would be no problem locating the base; their GEE set was very accurate when navigating over England. In the wireless position, Sinc listened out intently for further weather reports. What he heard was discouraging; the fog was becoming denser and spreading north. They flew on up high above the thick white layer blanketing the countryside below. Soon they would have to leave the clear starlit sky and descend through the woolly mass below. Sinc reported that Middleton St George had lit up the gooseneck flares for them and Bill started the descent. As they descended, thick fog surrounded them; Bill knew he would have to use the Standard Beam Approach system to land. Peering out, he found he could barely see the navigation lights on the wingtips glowing hazily through the fog. He caught occasional tantalising glimpses of the orange glow of the flares below before the smothering fog closed in again. At the outer marker he listened intently, but instead of the dots and dashes of the SBA there was just the crackle of static; something was wrong. Fuel was now critical. They had run out of options; they had to get down. Dry-mouthed, Bill continued the descent. Beside him, Geordie stood tensely, watching the altimeter and calling out the heights, 600 feet, 500 feet, 400 feet… finally, a smoky orange glimmer could just be seen looming out of the mist. Focusing intently, Bill continued down as the flickering glow brightened and faded before finally resolving into a hazy line delineating the runway. It was midnight as 'Uncle' touched down at Middleton St George. It had been a long, hard night.

Middleton St George was the most northerly of Bomber Command's bases and survives today as Durham Tees Valley Airport. At the time, it was home to two Canadian squadrons. The following day, fog and low cloud persisted and they were unable to leave. They were now confronted with the problems that beset all crew who landed away – no change of clothes and no money, having had to empty their pockets before going on duty. They were given a little money to tide them over, to be docked from their pay, of course, but clothing was a matter of finding what they could scrounge off other aircrew, as they did not want to walk around in their flying gear. Inspecting 'Uncle' in daylight, they found shell fragments had pierced large holes in the underside of the aircraft and left shards of flak inside the bomb bay. Bill also discovered why he had not been able to use SBA (Standard Beam Approach); the aerial had been shot away.

That evening, the crew were allowed off-base and their friendly Canadian hosts took them down to the local pub. There they spent a boisterous and happy evening packed into a tiny bar. As word got around that they had diverted there after a raid, they found themselves being stood round after round of drinks. They left with heavy heads and a high opinion of Canadian hospitality.

The following morning, the fog had cleared and Bill and the crew flew the damaged Lancaster back to Waddington. The ground crew, known colloquially as 'erks', were less than pleased when they saw what had happened to their beautiful new Lancaster but immediately set to work patching the holes and repainting the fuselage. Working flat out, they managed to repair 'Uncle' by the next day and get her ready for another sortie to Hamburg that night. The briefing took place at 14.00 and the crew were already kitted up and out at their dispersal when word came through that the operation had been scrubbed. On the bus back there was much discussion among the crew as to where to go to celebrate this evening's reprieve; Bill decided to stay on base but the others thought there might be just enough time to catch the bus into Lincoln. Parachutes and kit were quickly returned and gear swiftly put away before they headed off for a boisterous night out in Lincoln.

On 25 February, 'Uncle' and her crew were sent to Nuremberg. There was some glee at this assignment; the ORB states ' …12 crews were briefed for an attack on the town of Nuremberg, so popular with the Nazi Party'.[7] Nuremberg was where the Nazi party held their annual pre-war rallies. Hitler addressed the enormous crowds of party faithful in the vast stadium there and they swore their personal allegiance to him. These rallies were tremendous propaganda events that served to enhance and reinforce the cult of personality surrounding Hitler. Nuremberg was also an important economic target, with factories producing engines for aircraft, submarines and tanks. It would be immensely satisfying to knock it about a bit.

Although twelve crews were briefed for the raid, the weather forecast was so bad that it was decided not to send two freshmen crews. It was not a very successful sortie due to the bad weather conditions and poor Pathfinder marking which was both late and inaccurate. The attack was ordered at a lower altitude than usual, between 10,000–12,000 feet, making them extremely vulnerable to the very heavy flak coming up over the target. Arriving overhead Nuremberg, Wilkie was ready, lying prone in the nose. Peering around, he could not spot any of the expected marker flares or target indicators so, getting on the intercom, he told Bill they would have to wait and stooge around until the Pathfinders arrived. A tense silence greeted this news as Bill turned onto the new heading. While they orbited, 'Uncle' was constantly buffeted by exploding shells, while occasional glimpses of other Lancasters were an unpleasant reminder that there were some 300 other aircraft also circling around in the same airspace. Bill and Geordie watched in dismay as a doomed Lancaster plunged past them, one wing gone and burning fiercely. They tensed, willing the crew to jump clear, but no parachutes appeared as they flew past.

Mac came up to the cockpit to act as an extra pair of eyes. Silhouettes of other Lancasters loomed out of the darkness, twisting and turning to avoid searchlights. Bill manoeuvred constantly to avoid collisions. As the minutes ticked away the tension mounted, and the Pathfinders were roundly cursed for their lateness. Bill noted at the debriefing that the target marking had been twenty-one minutes late. An extra twenty-one minutes spent circling in skies full of exploding flak trying to avoid other Lancasters. It had felt like an eternity.

After they had made their bomb run, Geordie carefully adjusted the fuel mixture and throttles to conserve as much fuel as possible. Nuremberg lay deep in the southeast of Germany. It would take around four hours to get back, and these twenty-one minutes had eaten into the fuel reserves. Huddled in his dark little cubicle, Mac constantly replotted their course, adjusting track and speed as necessary. After eight hours in the air, they landed at 03.30. When they entered the debriefing room, the waiting Intelligence Officers took one look at the drawn, exhausted faces and knew that it had not been a good night. Two IX Squadron aircraft failed to return from this operation. It seems likely that they were brought down by flak in the long minutes spent over the target. Another crew found themselves desperately short of fuel and jettisoned the containers that the incendiaries were released from. They landed with less than twenty minutes' fuel left.

Despite all the problems, this sortie earned the crew a small and charming reward. If your bomb plot photo showed you were on or very close to the aiming point, the successful crew would be given a little card with a drawing of a Lancaster on it and inscribed with the names of the crew, the date and the target. One was given to each member of the crew to put in their logbook to commemorate an operation well done. Bill and his crew all received this little memento of the Nuremberg raid. They would have preferred not to have had to hang around for twenty-one minutes to earn it.

The crew awoke the next morning to find they were 'working' again that night. Stifling their yawns, they started over again on the round of tests and briefings. The primary target that night was Cologne. It was a more successful raid as the Pathfinder marking was accurate. The crew actually saw their 4,000lb 'Cookie' explode over the target. The following day saw the squadron resting, but not for long. On the 28th, they would be operating again, to France for a change.

Early in 1943, Bomber Command started targeting the U-boat bases in France. The Casablanca Directive had focused on the progressive destruction and dislocation of the German military, industrial and economic systems. British and American Air Force Commanders were instructed to prioritise targets such as U-boat and aircraft construction, transportation, oil production and the armaments industry.[8] The convoys crisscrossing the Atlantic were Britain's lifeline, carrying vital supplies of raw materials, food, troops and equipment. Millions of tons of Allied shipping were being lost to German U-boat attacks and this level of loss was unsustainable. Disrupting the refitting and resupply of operational submarines was considered vital, it would reduce the number of U-boats and surface raiders loose in the Atlantic.

After raids on the submarine base at Lorient, attention was turned to the next target, St Nazaire on the mouth of the Loire. At St Nazaire, the Germans had constructed a large U-boat base with submarine pens, and also a huge dry dock. It had always been a prime target as it was the only facility in Axis Europe that was large enough to accommodate the *Tirpitz*, Germany's largest and much-feared battleship. In March 1942, a famous amphibious raid, Operation Chariot, had been launched to destroy the dry dock there. In this audacious operation, an old destroyer, *HMS Cambeltown,* laden with hidden delayed action explosives, had been rammed into the lock gates, and the resulting explosion the following day had put the dock out of action.

By 1942, the actual submarine pens had been reinforced with tremendously thick concrete covers that were impenetrable until the development of armour piercing Tallboy bombs in 1944. In 1943, the aim was to render the port unusable by destroying maintenance facilities and cutting power supplies and communications. To do this, Bomber Command dispatched 437 aircraft to bomb the port area. Eight IX Squadron crews, including Bill's, took part in the raid.

It was a clear night and the bombing was accurate. Many fires were started and the raid caused widespread destruction to the port area with half the town reported as having been destroyed. Fortunately, the population had been previously warned by leaflets dropped from aircraft and had largely fled into the countryside. Despite 'Uncle' suffering some flak damage, Bill considered it an 'Easy trip. Good prang'.

The crew had now completed eleven sorties in two months; they were no longer novices but there was still a long way to go to the completion of a tour.

CHAPTER TEN
THE BATTLE OF THE RUHR

On 1 March, the crews could tell from the heavy fuel loads that it was going to be a sortie deep into the heart of Germany. They stood as the CO entered the briefing room, before sitting down to hear their fate. Harry Yates, another Lancaster pilot, describes it: 'This was the moment when fear stirred in the pit of the stomach.'[1] Groans were heard as their worst fears were confirmed; it was the 'Big City', Berlin. It was going to be another long night.

As they took off, the last rays of light flickered over the horizon. Looking down, Darkie could see the countryside sliding by below them, serene and peaceful in the hazy twilight. Smoke drifted from cottage chimneys, swirling into the sky, and in the fields the dark shapes of cattle could be seen placidly grazing. But in the skies ahead, the mood was changing. As the sky darkened, the silhouettes of other Lancasters could be seen as the bomber stream converged before setting out over the North Sea. Soon the faint outlines of the enemy coast loomed out of the darkness, followed shortly by the first bursts of flak from ships lying offshore. Long before they reached the target, its formidable air defences could be seen. Searchlights sliced through the night sky, their dazzling light turning night into day. Closer now, Bill and Geordie saw the beams close on another Lancaster, coning it in brilliant white light. "They've been hit," Geordie murmured. As they watched, fire rippled over the fuselage, then a vast explosion turned the aircraft into a gigantic fireball, showering fiery fragments out across the sky. "Poor sods," someone muttered over the intercom. At such times, men were torn between pity for the other crew and a guilty sense of relief that it had not been them.

As they flew on, the brilliant red and green flares dropped by the Pathfinders were easy to spot as they floated gently down. Visibility was perfect. By the light of the firing guns, Bill recognised some of the broad, tree-lined avenues stretching beneath him and the dark line of the River Spree running through the heart of Berlin. Memories of happy times spent there with his family flashed through his mind. He flew on, struggling to stay on course as a shell exploded immediately below them, tossing the Lancaster up in the air and peppering the underside with fragments. Thankfully, the bomb doors had not yet been opened. Approaching on the bomb run, Wilkie was relieved to find the bomb doors functioned properly despite the battering they had received. "Left… left… hold it…" Now he had the red target indicators in his bomb sight and, pressing the release, he quickly reported, "Bombs gone." Then after a quick check to see there were no 'hang-ups', it was, "Bomb doors closed." Bill pulled up on the controls and, as they turned away, they saw bright yellow explosions erupting against the brilliant red glow of the fires burning below.

Bill had just got 'Uncle' established on the new course when Alan's voice came urgently over the intercom: "ME 110 ahead off starboard beam." The ME 110 was flying in the opposite direction, towards Berlin. Subconsciously bracing themselves for an attack, they watched intently for the first sign they had been spotted. Was he turning slightly? Alan shouted, "Corkscrew Starboard." Bill threw the Lancaster into a steep turn to starboard, initiating a stomach-churning dive, the altimeter spinning, dropping a thousand feet in seconds. Then a brutal heave on the controls to pull the Lancaster into a climbing turn to port, all the time watching closely as the airspeed bled away. At the top of the climb, Bill repeated the manoeuvre, wrenching the controls viciously as he went through the standard defensive tactic known as a 'corkscrew'. Alan and Darkie quartered the night sky for any further signs of the fighter but none were seen. Seconds ticked away. Finally, they were sure that the ME 110 had flown on, seeking easier prey. As heart rates slowly returned to normal, Mac's voice was heard over the intercom calmly giving Bill a new course to steer. In the cockpit, by the light of the faintly luminous instrument dials, he settled to the task of getting safely home.

Around half an hour later, when they were now some 100 miles away, Darkie's voice came softly over the intercom: "Fires are burning well, Skip."

Bill felt this was a good trip, writing in his logbook in the idiom of the time, 'Good Prang. Solo stooge over Emden on return'. Emden being a small town almost on the German/Dutch border. The return routing meant a long five-hour flight back to Waddington where they landed at 03.10. Stiff and exhausted after eight hours in the thunderous bone-shaking clamour of 'Uncle', it now took time to detach themselves from her. Oxygen masks and headsets had to be disconnected and equipment gathered up before squeezing back through the narrow fuselage and climbing down the rickety ladder to set foot on solid ground once more. They found the ground crew shaking their heads at the state of the bomb bay doors, which were once again peppered with holes where flak had found them. They had landed safely, though. Another returning IX Squadron crew had suffered more severe damage and their aircraft crashed near the airfield, killing three members of the crew and seriously injuring the rest.

Bomber Command considered this raid a success despite the bombing being widely spread out. Fortuitously, on this raid, some bombs destroyed the Telefunken factory where the captured H2S set was being reassembled but, by a cruel trick of fate, this very same night a Halifax crashed in Holland with an almost intact set for the Germans to resume working on.[2]

Aircrew would have been unaware that Bomber Command was about to launch a major offensive, a five-month campaign that became known as the 'Battle of the Ruhr'. This was in line with the policy decided at the Casablanca Conference and intended to disrupt and destroy production in the industrial heartland of Germany, the cities and towns of the Ruhr Valley. The steel mills, coking plants and synthetic oil works there supplied vital materials for the wartime economy. These materials were distributed by rail to industrial manufacturers throughout the Ruhr Valley. The most important of these was the massive Krupps armaments works in Essen.

Krupps' industrial capacity covered every facet of armament production from mining and steel works to tanks, guns and submarines. With good reason, they were known as the 'Armourers to the Reich'. The Battle of the Ruhr began on 5 March with an attack on Essen. Coincidentally, it was also the night that Bomber Command's 100,000th sortie of the war was flown. 'Uncle' and her crew were one of 442 aircraft dispatched to 'Happy Valley' that night to try to put the armourers out of business.

As they crossed the coast, the flak batteries opened up. Bill was constantly weaving, giving the gunners a chance to see below the aircraft, the most vulnerable spot where a fighter might creep up unseen. Soon the searchlights that heralded the approach to 'Happy Valley' came into view. The flak was getting heavier all the time.

Arriving overhead, Bill saw the fires burning below. Brilliant yellow flashes punctuated the red glow as 'Cookies' from other aircraft exploded. The sky felt crowded now as the bomber stream closed in on the target. Below them, other Lancasters could be seen silhouetted against the fires raging on the ground while still more were glimpsed above them with their bomb doors open, a worrying sight. This was yet another hazard, as Bob Lasham, who flew with IX and 97 Squadrons, remembers: 'We were "bombed" one night, incendiaries which didn't burn but we lost an engine'.[3] They could only hope these bombs would miss them on their way down. The thud of exploding shells seemed closer now, the red flashes indicating how close the bursts were. With relief, they saw the green and red target indicators drifting down through the smoke. The smell of cordite filtered into the aircraft as Bill fought to keep the Lancaster lined up for their bombing run.

Explosions below lit up the clouds, and dense columns of thick oily black smoke boiled up into the air. Finally, they were lined up. They waited tensely for the magic words "Bombs gone." Now they had to run the gauntlet of the searchlights again, Bill flinging the aircraft around the sky in an effort to avoid their penetrating beams and, all the time, the vicious puffs of exploding anti-aircraft shells followed them. It was a terrible night, so much so that Mac, who usually did not comment in his logbook, made a note of the tremendously concentrated defences they had faced.

The industrial haze that often persisted had hampered earlier raids on targets in the Ruhr, but on this night Pathfinder Mosquitos, using Oboe, successfully blind marked the target. Bombs hit fifty-seven separate buildings within the Krupps works. Bill was pleased too. His logbook reads, 'Wizard prang. Concentrated fires. Landed Skellingthorpe'. It is unclear why he landed there. Perhaps there was a temporary problem at Waddington. Skellingthorpe was only some 7 miles from Waddington and the Operational Record Book records him as returning to Waddington that night.

On 9 March, the target was Munich. As the birthplace of the National Socialist Party and its spiritual home, it was another very popular target. Wilkie was unfit to fly and F/L Higginson DFM replaced him as bomb aimer on this occasion. Wilkie must have been glad he missed this sortie, as things went badly wrong before they had even taken off. 'Uncle' was standing fully loaded on the dispersal with the bomb doors open, as some final adjustments had just been made. Bill, who had been doing his inspection, had been just about to walk under the bomb bay when, without warning, 'the Cookie groaned and fell out'.[4] The 'Cookie' with its 4,000 lbs of high explosive designed to detonate immediately on impact just crashed to the ground in front of them. The crew had been standing around having their final cigarettes but, after a split second's stunned silence, cigarettes were dropped as they all turned and fled. Amazingly, it did not explode. Somewhat shaken and with F/L Higginson cursing his luck, they flew in one of the spare aircraft that night. Squadrons always had a spare aircraft or two ready in case there were last-minute problems.

As well as bombs, they dropped 'nickels', propaganda leaflets, over the target. Icing was once more a problem as was heavy flak. They had to bomb from a comparatively low level – 11,600 feet – but despite this, they remained unscathed. Bill reported seeing a 'Terrific explosion emitting a large sheet of flame followed by large pall of smoke to 3-4,000 feet'. It was a successful raid that damaged many factories. These included part of the BMW factory where the aero-engines were manufactured; Krauss, a manufacturer of locomotives and armoured cars; and J. Rathgeber, maker of railway wagons.[5] The large explosion that Bill saw was a gasholder blowing up at the town gas works, which were badly damaged that night.

On the morning of the 11th, Bill did an air test on 'Uncle' before a sortie to Stuttgart. This was fairly uneventful unlike the next night, the 12th, when they were sent back again to Essen, one of the most heavily defended cities in the Third Reich. Bomber Command was intent on having another go at destroying the powerful industrial combine that was the Krupps works. The route out took them over Holland before they turned south towards Essen. Moonlight lit up the clear night sky, glinting softly on the bomber stream: perfect conditions for night fighter attacks. Crews hated it, feeling horribly exposed in the bright light. Alan and Darkie, the gunners, swung their guns around, incessantly quartering the skies for the enemy. From miles away, Bill could see the searchlights spinning their lethal web through the haze over 'Happy Valley'. The Germans had put up a smokescreen over Essen and the resulting haze was now lit up by the red and yellow bursts of exploding flak. Around them, master searchlights locked bombers in their blue glare, the victims twisting and diving desperately, trying to escape the volleys of flak that followed. Many were unsuccessful.

In the distance, red and green target indicators could be seen floating serenely down through the mayhem of bursting shells and smoke from fires that were already spreading throughout Essen. 'Uncle' lurched sharply as another Lancaster whipped past underneath them, seemingly close enough to touch. The smokescreen over the northwest of the town obscured the target.

As Wilkie made the final adjustments to the bombsight and armed the bombs, Bill fought to keep the Lancaster straight and level as they approached. Then, after completing the bombing run, the crew felt the aircraft buck as 'Uncle' lifted after the bombs were dropped. Once rid of the bombs, the Lancaster would fly faster, picking up another 20 to 30 miles an hour, and every mile an hour counted in getting away from the target. Below, Bill could see the hot glow of the fires as he waited those tantalisingly long seconds for the photoflash before he could bank and turn for home.

Flak filled the sky and Bill turned and twisted, trying to avoid the forest of searchlights. A blue beam swept across 'Uncle', filling the cockpit with blinding light. It froze, locking them in its bluish glare. Immediately, others converged, coning the aircraft in their yellow-white light and turning night into day in the cockpit. At once Bill rammed the control column forward, throwing the Lancaster into a vicious, steep diving turn to port. As he did, he lowered his seat to lessen the glare, concentrating fiercely on his instruments. With engines screaming, the aircraft plunged down, the whole airframe shaking under the pressure. The altimeter unwound sharply and the speed raced up. 280 mph… 290 mph… now Bill corkscrewed to starboard. As they dropped, the crew held their breath and, hearts pounding, hung on as best they could. Down they plunged and suddenly the beam was gone and merciful darkness enveloped them. Slowly, Bill eased back on the controls and levelled out before checking on his crew on the intercom. Geordie picked himself up off the floor and, grumbling, immediately checked on the state of his beloved engines. Chaos reigned in Mac's navigation area – maps, pencils, slide rules and the rest of his equipment had flown in all directions. Recovering quickly, he gave Bill a course to steer and set about sorting himself out. They had been lucky; most crews did not escape once coned.

As they picked their way through the explosions and searchlights, they kept a sharp lookout for the night fighters that always waited just outside the searchlight belt to pick off bombers at the edge of the stream. All the Lancasters of IX Squadron got safely back that night, but twenty-three aircraft belonging to other squadrons did not return. 'Uncle's ground crew found, once again, that there was plenty of work for them to do, patching up the many flak holes in her fuselage.

This was a highly successful raid and when Photographic Reconnaissance Unit aircraft flew over the area a few days later, they reported 30% more damage than on the previous raid. Bill reported that, 'one long factory appeared to be surrounded by fires'.[6] This was probably one of the Krupps works. These works employed some 80,000 people, manufacturing shells, tanks, guns, as well as locomotive and U-boat engines. An unusually detailed account of this raid appeared in the *Daily Telegraph* at the time. It gives an idea of the odds faced by RAF crews over Essen with its description of the defences as consisting of 300 heavy guns of 3.7 in. calibre and over, 600 light guns of 40 mm. calibre, 200 searchlights, squadrons of night fighters in the air and some 50,000 troops manning the defences on the ground. Bill described the inferno that night with typical understatement, writing in his logbook that it was a 'Tough trip. Huge searchlight concentration'. It was so bad that Mac felt compelled to add a terse note in his logbook too: 'Very concentrated'.[7]

The next week saw a lull in Bomber Command operations. Not that the men were able to relax; they were kept busy doing training of one sort or another almost every day. It was possibly during this week that a photo was taken in the Officers' Mess at Waddington. It is dated on the back as having been taken in March 1943. It shows a group of men in front of the fireplace, relaxing with drinks. It looks as though they have just come back from flying training or have been stood down after a cancelled operation, as several of them are wearing flying boots. They look tired but relaxed as they chat, drinks in hand with beer bottles lined up on the mantelpiece. To one side, one man stands out, quiet and serious-looking. It is Bill. He has a scarf still wrapped around his neck and he is the only one who is aware that the photo is being taken. He is looking directly at the camera and his eyes reflect exactly the same steadfast, watchful gaze as in his formal portrait photo.

A big raid was cancelled due to weather during that week and the squadron undertook just one operation when two Lancasters were dispatched on a 'gardening' sortie. RAF ingenuity came to the fore when it came to inventing code words for targets, types of operations and radio calls. Someone with a truly British sense of humour decided that minelaying should be referred to as 'gardening' and, naturally, the mines themselves were 'vegetables', such as Trefoil and Spinach. German cities were known as different kinds of fish, thus Berlin was 'Whitebait', Leipzig was 'Haddock', and Pforzheim was 'Yellowfin'. Sometimes the code was wickedly apt. If crews, returning to base after a mission, heard on the radio a warning of a 'Bog Rat', they would know a German fighter was lurking around the circuit hoping to catch returning crews with their guard down. When a pilot had to order his crew to abandon the aircraft, the unfortunate crew might hear the command, 'Abracadabra, Abracadabra, Jump, Jump, Jump…' A fitting command as the Lancaster was so difficult to move around in that it would need an element of magic for a crew to escape from a stricken aircraft.

After a week of not 'working', 'Uncle' and her crew were detailed for a raid on St Nazaire on 22 March. The forecast for conditions over the target was good, just a little cloud and haze. However, there would be a full moon, making the bombers clearly visible to prowling night fighters. Conditions over England were expected to deteriorate overnight with fog closing in on many bases. In the event, this happened earlier than expected and, although the plan was for 633 aircraft to operate, the 276 aircraft of Group 3 were recalled due to the deteriorating conditions, leaving 357 aircraft actually dispatched.[8]

'Uncle' was airborne at 19.00 hours and flew south across England towards the coast. Crossing the Channel into enemy airspace, Sinc could hear wireless traffic, clear evidence that enemy fighter patrols were about. As they approached the target, Bill could see that a smokescreen had been put up over St Nazaire to mislead the bombers. However, this had one benefit; it made it more difficult for searchlights and flak batteries to find them.

Any bombing operation over France carried the risk of injuring French civilians, and orders were framed to minimise this danger. The orders this night were '...if the markers were late for any reason, main force crews were not to bomb anything but markers before 21.45. If markers were not seen on arrival, aircraft of Main Force were to stand off and make a second run after 21.45'.[9] The aiming points were the submarine pens and the dock area to the north of the Bassin de Penhouet, and they were to bomb from 12,000 feet. Arriving over St Nazaire, the flak was heavy, bursting around them, filling the air with puffs of black smoke. Despite the smokescreen, Bill and Wilkie could clearly see the concentration of Red Target Indicators put down by the Pathfinders. They commenced the bombing run, Don's voice calling times and directions: "20 seconds... 10 seconds... Right, right... steady..." and finally, to everyone's relief, at 21.42, "Bombs gone."

Immediately after the target photo, Mac's voice came over the intercom giving Bill the course to steer. Maintaining his height, Bill started gently weaving to enable the gunners to check beneath them. Alan and Darkie had a routine. Unlike the rear turret, the mid-upper turret had a full 360-degree view and range of fire. Perched in his turret, Alan could see which way Darkie's guns were facing and would look in the opposite direction. Suddenly, over the intercom, came a sudden, urgent shout from Darkie: "Corkscrew Port, GO!" Immediately, Bill flung the aircraft into a steep left-hand diving turn until the wings were almost vertical while the airspeed raced up. "ME 109 on the port quarter," Darkie yelled. He had spotted the ME 109 600 yards away, slightly above them. Alan spun his guns round. The ME 109 was now 400 yards away and they both opened fire. A few seconds later, one of Alan's guns jammed. Cursing furiously, he continued firing with his one operational gun. The ME 109 came on until it was within 200 yards of them and then broke away, passing slightly below them to starboard. As the fighter broke away, Alan watched intently, giving a running commentary as it made a wide orbit to starboard, manoeuvring into position for a second attack from slightly above them on the starboard quarter. While the ME 109 manoeuvred, Bill continued throwing 'Uncle' through the sky so that the ME 109 was brought into position astern, where it was clearly silhouetted against the moon. Soon it attacked again. Darkie yelled, "Corkscrew Starboard." Bill flung the aircraft into another gut-wrenching dive. The guns chattered and tracer arced across the sky as Alan and Darkie brought their guns to bear. The ME 109 continued closing until, within 300 yards of them, it suddenly broke off the attack. As the ME 109 turned away, smoke could be seen pouring out on one side. It had been hit. As they watched, the aircraft plunged down with smoke streaming from the fuselage until it disappeared through a layer of cloud, diving headfirst towards the sea. They noted the time of the attack – 21.56 hours.[10]

Pulling with all his strength, Bill now heaved back on the control column and slowly, by degrees, 'Uncle' responded, levelling out then starting to climb. Hundreds of feet had been lost in the corkscrews but sharp eyes and quick reactions had saved them. The crew had practised corkscrews until it had become second nature and, despite the violence of the manoeuvre, the gunners 'knew how the a/c was going to react, in other words, even being thrown about the sky we knew where to look for it'. Alan felt that once 'in your gunsight... and given the right deflection then he [the ME 109] was going to have a nasty surprise'.[11] The gunners had got him silhouetted nicely against the moon – not a good position to be in.

As they climbed, they could see the sky above them etched with the contrails of other returning aircraft. They shone brightly in the moonlight, high above them. Despite their beauty, aircrew dreaded these condensation trails. They provided enemy fighters with a pointer to their prey. Back on track, they reached the English coast to find that now, as so often, they faced their other enemy: the weather. Fog was blowing in from the North Sea, heavy, impenetrable and spreading. It was going to be touch and go as to whether they could get home. As they flew north, Wilkie heard that Waddington had closed. They would have to find a diversion airfield. Conditions were now deteriorating fast, and base after base was closing as the fog thickened. Tension mounted as the needles on the fuel gauges fell and Geordie warned that fuel was getting critical. Mac advised Bill to try and land at Chipping Warden near Banbury. As they descended, the milky mist enveloped them, wrapping them in a claustrophobic white world. On the approach, Bill peered tensely out, relief flooding through him as he managed to spot the faint glimmer of runway flares shimmering through the mist. Turning slightly, he lined them up with the runway and landed. It was 00.45 hours. Another exhausting night.

The following morning, they had to wait until lunchtime before the fog cleared and they could return to Waddington. The ME 109 had to be claimed as a 'probable' rather than a kill, as they had not actually seen it hit the water. However, Alan recalls that they all had no doubt that they had shot it down. There are entries in Alan, Mac and Bill's logbooks and all reflect the same quiet satisfaction; Bill noted, 'Attacked by ME 109 twice. Beaten off'. It turned out that they had had another success that night. When 'Uncle's bomb photo was developed, it showed them to be directly over the aiming point. Such pinpoint accuracy merited a mention in the squadron monthly report. This report noted that it was one of only three aircraft out of the seventy-six aircraft dispatched by Group 5 to show the aiming point. They were now recognised as one of the best crews on the squadron.

CHAPTER ELEVEN
REST AND RECREATION

Aircrew led a strange kind of Jekyll and Hyde existence. One night seeing other aircraft explode in flaming balls of fire around them, hoping they would not suffer the same fate, and then the following night at the local pub downing pints and singing along around the piano. With the future so uncertain, aircrew were determined to make the most of the present.

Crews regularly worked two nights running, and usually – but not always – were stood down on the third night even if operations were on. Men made use of this when making dates with girls. They would tell them, "I can't get off tomorrow… and I may not be able to get the next night off, but if I am not here on the third night then I won't be coming back…"[1] It was apparently a very successful chat-up line.

On nights when the Squadron was not operating and the crews were 'stood down', they could spend the evening in the mess or, more often, head off to a local pub or to Lincoln. The bus stop was conveniently just outside the main gate.

There were pubs like the Horse and Jockey in Waddington village, an old sixteenth-century coaching inn that was popular with aircrew. In Lincoln, there were dances at the Assembly Rooms or variety shows at the Theatre Royal. Another favourite there was the Saracen's Head. These places provided an all-important chance to meet local girls or perhaps one of the many

WAAFs stationed at Waddington. However, in Lincoln, you had to be careful not to miss the last bus. Alan found this out the hard way. Enjoying himself in the Saracen's Head one night, he forgot the time. When he glanced down at his watch, he saw it was time for the bus to leave. Hastily abandoning the rest of his pint, he rushed out of the Saracen's Head, running for all he was worth around the corner to the Broadgate. He was just in time to catch a fleeting glimpse of the bus disappearing into the distance and realised with a groan that he now faced a 10-mile walk back to Waddington. Not only was it bitterly cold but wartime blackout restrictions ensured it was pitch-black and there were no road signs. After slogging along frosty roads in the deserted countryside, it was a very sober, half-frozen and footsore Alan who arrived back at base some three hours later.

Saturday night dances in the mess provided another opportunity to let off steam. Cheap RAF drinks loosened any lingering inhibitions, and mess evenings often turned into wild parties with increasingly riotous games such as 'Carrier Landings' where a long table was wetted and the contestants ran, jumped and slid along the table, trying to get to the other end without skidding off, those who succeeded being rewarded with a pint. Commanding officers understood the need for such boisterous occasions and sometimes participated themselves. The atmosphere of those mess nights is perfectly evoked by Patrick Bishop with his description of W/C John Voyce as '...a popular and notable courageous officer in 635 Squadron, in black tie and braces leading a chorus of a mess favourite entitled *Please Don't Burn Our Shithouse Down*.[2]

Aircrew were supposedly given 6/7 days off every six weeks, though it could be cancelled at the last minute. The logbooks of Bill and his crew suggest that they had a week off at the end of March. Rail travel was not officially restricted in wartime, although there were posters asking people to consider 'Is Your Journey Really Necessary?' Priority was given to moving troops, equipment and food, and passengers had to accept delays and crowded trains. Most crews went home for their leave, often having to spend long hours waiting at stations to do so.

Although leave was eagerly awaited, when it arrived it presented difficulties. The week away brought to mind a pre-war world and all the people who were part of it. Now only a small nucleus remained at home, mainly mothers and grandparents. Other friends and relatives were scattered far and wide, either in the services or working away from home. Some were listed as missing in action, while others were gone forever. The brief immersion in another world seemed almost unreal – questions had to be parried; no one wanted families to know just how terrible those nights over Germany really were. Thoughts constantly turned to the squadron, what was going on – the squadron was their home now and leave seemed a brief dream-like interlude. Despite this, men often felt a bittersweet nostalgia when they returned to duty.

One of the perks that aircrew had was a small petrol allowance. This enabled Bill to run his car, and he drove down to London to spend his leave. That March, he had something to celebrate. On 16 March, he had received a promotion and was now an acting Flight Lieutenant. Although most of the time had to be spent at the office of the family business, it was relaxing to live a civilian life for a few days. Even though London was a shadow of its old pre-war self, it nonetheless provided comforts and amusements unknown on an RAF base.

London buses now ran with netting over their windows to protect passengers from glass in the event of bomb blast. Sandbags were piled against important buildings and there were buckets of sand at the ready to put out fires. Trenches had been dug in the parks to grow vegetables. In the blackout, the West End was full of people fumbling their way around in the dark, relying on the lights from glowing cigarettes or from small torches pointed carefully downwards. There were cinemas that showed the latest newsreels and at the 'pictures' a full programme with both an 'A' and a 'B' film. There was the theatre too. In the spring of 1943, Joan Greenwood and Margaret Lockwood were playing at the Cambridge Theatre in *Heartbreak House* in costumes designed by Cecil Beaton. Alternatively, there was Coral Browne in *My Sister Eileen* at the Savoy Theatre.

Food rationing affected everyone. Chefs in London's restaurants did their best with the little that was available. In 1942, the Government decreed that restaurants could charge a maximum of 5 shillings (25p) for a meal. It was illegal to serve both meat and fish at a single sitting. Often, the main ingredient of a meal was Spam. Spam was ubiquitous. Packaged in tins, this pressed ham/pork meat was dressed up in many guises in sandwiches, in vol-au-vents, even as Chinese food. Its one great advantage was that it was not rationed as meat was. One of London's premier restaurants, The White Tower, in Percy Street, served a creation known as 'Spam à la Grecque'. It was very difficult to avoid it in some form or other.

When they were granted leave, Alan headed home to Wales while Geordie and Mac travelled north. Often, Don Willbee did too, spending the time investigating his roots and visiting the places that his family had come from. He had a passion for all things Scottish and particularly for the skirl of the bagpipes. On one leave in Scotland, he decided there and then that he was going to learn to play them. He was totally undeterred by advice that the pipes were not a 'learn it yourself' instrument. However, he did at least realise that the full set of bagpipes might be a little ambitious and so he bought a book of instructions and a chanter to practise on. On his return, it quickly became obvious that a great deal of practice would be needed. Don shared a hut with Geordie, Alan and Darkie, and his efforts with the chanter filled it with an ear-splitting cacophony of squawks and drones as he attempted to master it. As he had been warned, this proved difficult and he had little success. His roommates were less than delighted with his new hobby and told him so forcefully and frequently. To their profound relief, his new hobby did not last very long.

However, some of the things that were picked up on leave were even less desirable than the bagpipes. On one occasion, some of the crew returned to their hut to find Don sitting stark naked on the bed painting his private parts with gentian violet. Having had an extremely successful and thoroughly enjoyable leave, he was now paying the price in the form of a dose of crabs. Needless to say, he was the subject of unmerciful teasing ever after along the lines of, "What's the colour of the day today then?"

Sinc, a gregarious soul who loved a party, tried to catch up with as many friends and family as he could on his periods of leave. Whenever he went home, his mother would throw a party and invite all the family and friends round to celebrate. Sometimes the party would be interrupted by an air raid but they would then continue in the shelter. Sinc was engaged to a pretty girl called Eileen. Like food, clothing was rationed; clothing coupons were issued that had to be used for any purchase from hats to shoes. By 1943, the allowance had been reduced to forty-eight coupons per person per year. There was a precise tariff for each item of clothing, e.g. a cardigan or jumper 'cost' five coupons, pyjamas or a nightie, six coupons. This did not go far and Eileen's family and friends must have given her some coupons, as a photo shows her as a radiant bride in a long bridal gown and veil. It is touching evidence of the close bond that often developed between members of a crew that eighteen months after their tour ended, Sinc chose Darkie to be his best man when he married Eileen on 18 December 1944.

CHAPTER TWELVE

THE SQUADRON MOVES

In the crew's absence, 'Uncle' had been to Berlin on 27 March with F/O Van Note and his crew. Fortunately, they had brought her back unscathed. The first thing Bill did on returning was to take 'Uncle' for a NFT on 2 April. Then it was back to work again.

When the C/O pulled back the curtain covering the board on the 3rd, Essen was revealed as the target. Mutters and groans filled the hut as the crews contemplated yet another trip to this heavily defended target. Thirteen IX Squadron Lancasters were on the Battle Order but owing to technical problems only twelve actually took off. There is a recording made of an unknown Lancaster crew on this Essen raid. The crew comment in almost conversational tones, warning each other of searchlights and describing the flak bursts with almost surreal calmness. "You could light your fag on any of those," comments the pilot on the closeness of one flak burst. Looking out, the navigator exclaims, "By God, I have never seen anything like this before." The rasping breathing of the crew in their oxygen masks and the thump of flak exploding nearby bring home the horrors crews faced on every sortie.[1]

Even Bill, whose comments in his logbook are always understated, wrote of this night, 'Tough trip. Huge searchlight concentration'. Alan too made a note in his logbook of the terrible flak they encountered. Others also commented, amazed they had survived. Don Charlwood, an Australian Lancaster pilot on his twenty-eighth operation, wrote, 'The worst raid ever... the flak was more intense than anything we have seen.'[2] Eric Brown, a rear gunner in a Halifax, reported, 'Usual Happy Valley reception. Large concentration of lights. A/A fire very heavy. Essen well lit up. A Good prang.'[3] That night at the debriefing, returning crews were heard repeatedly expressing their amazement that they had made it back in the face of such defences. They were the lucky ones. On the board, the letters FTR (Failed to Return) appeared against the names of Squadron Leader G.W.J. Jarrett and Sergeant W.H. Swire. These were two of IX Squadron's most experienced crews.

When the men finally got to bed around 4 am, thoughts of the nightmarish skies over Essen were still playing on their minds. Barely twelve hours later, most of the crew found themselves back in the briefing room preparing for a sortie. They were thankful that at least it was not 'Happy Valley' again.

For some reason, on this operation two other gunners, Sergeants Pelly and Sargent, replaced Alan and Darkie. These changes made the rest of the crew uneasy. They were a team and any disruption was unwelcome. With the exception of the special '1,000 bomber' raids, this was to be the largest raid so far in the war. Kiel, an important naval and submarine base on the Baltic, was the target. En route, they encountered severe icing conditions and arriving over the target they found it obscured by cloud. Despite this, they managed to bomb on the Pathfinder's target indicators.

The next two sorties were both to Duisburg. At the beginning of 'Happy Valley' and well protected by belts of searchlights and flak guns, Duisberg was another of Bomber Command's priority targets. On 8 April, the weather report proved optimistic. Having been told to expect broken cloud over the target, they found that it was totally obscured. Worse still, the German Fighter Control had correctly 'guessed' the target and the night fighters were waiting. The sky seemed full of them, and the gunners watched intently as several shot past. As one turned towards them, they readied their guns to fire if attacked and waited for the fighter to come within range. Tensely, they watched, but to their relief the fighter flew on by.

Disappointed by the results of that raid, Harris ordered another attack on Duisburg the following night. Bill and the crew were briefed again for this operation. It is not hard to imagine the sheer exhaustion they now felt. For over three months, they had lived with constant pressure, fear and uncertainty. The effects were cumulative and fatigue only exacerbated nerves that were already stretched. On top of all that, there was the constant worry that sheer physical tiredness would lead to mistakes or to a fatal lack of alertness. A few seconds' hesitation or inattention could be all that lay between life and death. Grey with fatigue and hollow-eyed, they arrived for the briefing. They would have a second pilot, Sergeant Stout, with them to gain operational experience before taking his own crew on sorties. A fresh-faced new arrival, he looked out of place among these worn veterans of twenty sorties.

The forecast was for thick cloud on the way to the target but broken cloud over Duisburg. Once again, the forecast was wrong and thick cloud blanketed the target, totally obscuring the ground. The Pathfinders found it impossible to mark the target precisely and the target indicators were scattered far and wide. Wilkie, hunched over his bombsight, could not identify the aiming point and finally asked Bill to go around again. Listening over the intercom, the rest of the crew groaned and mentally cursed. No one wanted to linger over any target but particularly not in 'Happy Valley'. With bomb doors open, they were at their most vulnerable and there was always a danger of collision in the swirling mass of aircraft waiting to bomb. Round they went and started the run-in again. The crew listened intently as the usual patter started. The bomb doors were confirmed as open and Wilkie took over, calling directions to Bill, "Left... left... straight...straight..." but instead of "Bombs away," to their horror they heard him telling Bill that he still could not identify the aiming point and to go around yet again. The atmosphere in the aircraft was now electric as once more they turned and circled for another nerve-racking attempt. Everyone who could be spared was watching out for other aircraft and everyone had the same thought: *Get the hell on with it, Wilkie, and let's get out of here.* Again, the bomb doors were opened. "Left… left… straight… straight… hold it…" until at last, "Bombs gone." 'Uncle' was the last aircraft to return that night, landing at 02.40. The squadron had suffered badly. Six aircraft had been dispatched and a note in the squadron ORB reads, 'The Squadron had the misfortune to lose three of these aircraft which failed to return.'[4] It turned out that Wilkie's persistence had paid off: their bomb photo showed the target indicator marker bang in the middle of it. Once again, their accuracy had been spot-on. Sergeant Stout had had a baptism of fire that night, and a lesson on how the job should be done.

IX Squadron had been based at Waddington for eighteen months now. Despite its excellent facilities, there was one vital thing lacking: proper sealed runways for the increasingly heavy Lancasters. In order for new concrete runways to be laid at Waddington, IX Squadron would have to move elsewhere. In 1942, construction had started on a new airfield near the village of Bardney some 7 miles away. It was now complete and ready to become the new home of IX Squadron.

Bardney village lies some 9 miles east of Lincoln beside the River Witham. It has a long and periodically turbulent history. An Anglo-Saxon abbey was built in 675 by King Ethelred of Mercia but was later destroyed by the Vikings. In 1087, a Benedictine abbey was built to replace it. Centuries of monastic use came to an abrupt end in 1538 after six of the Abbey's monks were hanged, drawn and quartered for their part in the 'Lincolnshire Rising', a local uprising against the proposed closure of the Abbey by Henry VIII. Another upheaval happened in 1814 following the passing of an Act of Parliament providing for the widening of the River Witham. This was a mammoth task that required an army of labourers. Some 900 navvies were working on site when one Friday a dispute arose between the navvies and the baker delivering their bread. In no time at all a full-blown riot ensued as the navvies invaded a local pub, broke up the premises and then, having drunk it dry, went on to the next pub. There, the same thing happened and after sacking the pub, they then pelted the baker with his own bread, strung the pub sign up in a tree and set off in search of yet another pub to plunder. However, at the next pub, the quick-thinking landlord had quickly moved his beer barrels outside, managing to preserve his premises if not his beer. Police from nearby Horncastle were summoned but took one look at the scene and retired hastily. It was not until the cavalry arrived with a magistrate who read the Riot Act that order was restored. Today it is a quiet and pretty village.

The new airfield was built on farmland to the northeast of the village beyond Scotgrove Wood. It conformed to the standard bomber airfield pattern of three paved runways, a long main runway northeast/southwest and two shorter runways forming the shape of an A-frame. There were three large hangars and dotted around the perimeter track were dispersals for the bombers. Unlike Waddington, living quarters were separate from the main base. They lay on the other side of the road from the main entrance and were built on farmland to the south between New Park Wood and Birt Hill.

The standard of accommodation was a disappointment after the solid, comfortable buildings of Waddington. Quarters were in cheaply built Nissen huts with thin, unlined walls that offered little protection against the cold. The only heating came from pungent coke stoves in the middle of each hut; those sleeping nearest to them roasted while those away from them froze. Overnight condensation formed on the walls and trickled off the roof, dripping down onto beds and the unfortunates in them.

The move was planned for the 13/14 April, although an advance party had gone ahead to prepare on the 7th. The idea was to move the whole squadron without reducing its operational ability for even a day. All the myriad components that form part of an operational squadron – engineering equipment, huge quantities of spare parts, bombs, catering equipment and stores of every possible kind – had to be packed, loaded, unpacked and sorted. It was a massive operation. Apart from seven crews who were detailed for operations on the 13th, all the other crews flew their Lancasters to the new base that day with the support units following by road. The ORB for the 14th reported with some satisfaction:

> During the day the remainder of the squadron moved to Bardney, and the whole squadron movement was carried out smoothly. On arrival at Bardney all personnel worked vigorously with the result that five crews took off on an operation that night, the target was Stuttgart.[5]

Among those transferred to the new base was a young WAAF Intelligence Officer, Miss Barclay. She was one of only two WAAF officers to be stationed at Bardney at that time – they shared the Officers' Mess with the airmen. She recalls it was there that '…the 9 Squadron personalities began to emerge and become known to Stella [Stella Collier, Administrative Officer] and me. Living with them implanted them in one's memory…'[6] She only mentions a few notable personalities by name. One of those mentioned is Bill Meyer.

Planning for the move had been meticulous, thus ensuring that Bardney could be operational that night. Bill's crew were one of the five dispatched to Stuttgart. As they trundled along the peri-track that night, they found the tarmac on the runways was so fresh that, 'if the aircraft stood on the end of the runway ready to take off, the wheels would start sinking in'.[7]

Once again, a rookie pilot, Sergeant Evans, came with them to be shown the ropes. This was to be a big operation with 462 aircraft. The routing was across northern France at low level. Thick cloud and rain obscured the skies over England, but the weather over the target was expected to be clear with an almost full moon that would make them visible to marauding night fighters. 'Uncle' was airborne at 22.13, climbing into thick cloud with icing conditions. Nearing the target, they saw the red and green target indicators ahead, but these were extinguished by the time they arrived and so they aimed at the fires they could see already burning and dropped their bombs on them. Daylight reconnaissance revealed that despite an element of 'creep-back' there had been substantial damage to the industrial area in the north of the town and the goods station at Unterturkheim.[8] 'Creep-back' occurred as crews in heavily defended areas tended to drop their bombs early on the first fires they saw, wanting to get out of the danger area as quickly as possible. This led to the bombing pattern progressively creeping back from the original aiming point.

Their return routing was ordered to be at low level over France. Bill made sure that it was very low indeed. Darkie wrote in his logbook, 'Zero feet over France'. As they sped across the French countryside, passing over the vineyards of the Champagne region, they watched as the occasional village loomed out of the darkness. Turning after the waypoint at Châlons-en-Champagne, they flew northwest towards Dieppe. In the moonlight, Alan suddenly spotted a heavily laden goods train puffing slowly along. The labouring engine was sending great clouds of smoke into the air as it pulled a long string of wagons through the sleeping countryside. The wagons were bound to be carrying supplies for the Germans and immediately Alan was tempted to have a go at it. He got on the intercom and asked Bill's permission and, on being given the go-ahead, duly blasted off at it, later reporting with glee in his logbook, 'Goods train shot up!!' This enlivened the long flight back. They landed at Bardney at 04.45 to be greeted by their half-frozen ground crew before facing the usual debriefing and at last, falling into bed.

There is no way of knowing if the crew was aware of it, but this was to be their last operation in 'Uncle'. She was 'their' aircraft and had carried them faithfully through nineteen operations and had also made several trips with other crews; she was now in need of an overhaul. 'Uncle' returned to squadron duty early in May and was flown thereafter by various other crews before failing to return from a raid on Gelsenkirchen on 10 July 1943.

The crew now possibly had a couple of days' leave – the next entries in their logbooks are for training exercises on the 19th when they spent an uncomfortable couple of hours being thrown around the skies during a Fighter Affiliation exercise when they were attacked by a squadron of particularly determined Spitfires. At least they had an evening free to spend at the local pub.

Unlike the other services, aircrews, regardless of different rank, would tend to stick together. Their closeness was forged in the fight for survival in the skies. Although off-duty contact between officers and NCOs was officially discouraged, Bill, like many others, disregarded this, attaching more importance to the bonds that bound a crew together. He understood the importance of maintaining morale and took a fatherly interest in his crew's welfare, and so the whole crew would go out together to one of the local pubs. To get away from Bardney, Bill would sometimes suggest they went further afield. This was always popular, as Bill had a stunning 3.5 litre SS 100 Jaguar; with its long, louvered bonnet and flowing lines, it had both looks and speed. Off duty, Bill's sense of fun would be revealed and he would somehow manage to load his whole crew, all seven of them, into his two-seater sports car and whisk them off to a local pub. They piled in and hung on as best they could, the last two clinging for dear life onto the running boards on each side.

Their usual destination was an old coaching inn in the nearby village of Minting. The Sebastopol Inn was very small and its low ceilings were stained a deep brownie yellow by centuries of tobacco smoke. Inside were two tiny rooms with some solid wooden chairs and tables. Fires glowed in the little fireplaces in each room, providing welcome warmth and adding to the smoky atmosphere. Lastly, and most importantly, the beer was cheap. They would squeeze themselves in and talk about the latest news and tell stories about their previous lives while pint after pint disappeared. An alternative and closer option was to go to one of the pubs in Bardney village, perhaps The Nag's Head, The Jolly Sailor or The Black Horse. On these occasions, they would follow Bill on bikes as he led a 'Vic' formation, weaving down the country lanes to and from the local inns. On occasion, it was on someone else's bikes. It was a habit with aircrew to lay their hands on the first bike they found and ride it back to base, where it would be left at the Guardhouse for the irate owner to collect in the morning.

However, on 20 April, it was back to work. This time, the target was Stettin. Despite its turbulent past, Stettin had always been an important trading port as a member of the Hanseatic League and part of the Holy Roman Empire. The city had been linked to Berlin by a canal in 1914. In 1943, it was still an important Baltic port and a major centre of weapons production.

In all, 339 aircraft were ordered for this attack. The force consisted of 194 Lancasters, 134 Halifaxes and eleven Stirlings, with eighty-six Stirlings ordered to attack the Heinkel factory near Rostock while 11 Mosquitos carried out a diversionary raid on Berlin. In addition, eighteen Wellingtons were to lay mines off Brittany ports with three Operational Training Units also taking part. The attack was planned to last from 01.00–01.30 hours.

This operation was unusual in two respects. Firstly, there was a full moon. Bomber Command did not usually operate then, as the bombers were too vulnerable to attack by night fighters. Secondly, the bomber stream was ordered to fly at an extremely low level in order to try and evade the fighters and the heavy flak. The operational orders state that Group 6 were to fly at '500 feet or below' and then, categorically, that Group 5 aircraft were to fly even lower, as 'Low as possible crossing Denmark'.[9] This was despite Bomber Command's disastrous experience a few days earlier in a low-level raid on the Skoda works in Pilsen. The raid left the Skoda Works unscathed as a large asylum 7 miles away was mistaken for the target and bombed instead. Flying at low level with a full moon, the aircraft losses had been 11%; 252 young men had lost their lives in one night.

The target was to be marked for the main force bombers by Pathfinder Stirling and Halifax aircraft equipped with H2S radar, the ground-mapping radar used for blind target identification. It identified large physical features such as rivers and lakes well. Stettin was therefore an ideal target, as it was only 80 kilometres from the Baltic coastline to the north, on the River Oder with Lake Dabie nearby.

Six IX Squadron crews were on the Battle Order, including Sergeant Evans who Bill had taken as his 'Second Dickie' to Stuttgart on the 14th. That night, Bill and the crew were flying in ED 799 WS G-George. It was the ninth operation that 'George' had flown on and her penultimate one as, flown by Sergeant Brown and his crew, she failed to return from a 'Gardening' sortie on 22 April. Bill took off from Bardney at 21.43, followed by Sergeant Evans at 21.49. It was just after last light as they followed the familiar route over Mablethorpe on the Lincolnshire coast before heading out over the North Sea towards Denmark.

Along the east coast of England other bombers were taking off, including Halifax HR 728 of 51 Squadron based at RAF Snaith in Yorkshire. On board was Warrant Officer Eric Brown DFM, who was qualified both as a wireless operator and gunner but was flying as mid-upper gunner that night. Airmen were not supposed to include comments and details in their logs but fortunately some, like Bill, did make brief notes. However, Eric did even better – he kept a diary where he could record events and feelings much more openly. This raid stood out in the memories of all those taking part, but Eric Brown's logbook gives a particularly vivid description of the night's event.

The orders to fly as low as possible were followed to the letter. Over the sea, both Eric and Alan, mid-upper gunners in their respective aircraft, found they could see the crests of the waves breaking in the moonlight; a beautiful sight but one they could not relax and appreciate. From the rear turret, Darkie watched in fascination as below him the downdraught from the propellers drilled parallel trails through the waves. Approaching the Danish coast, the high, undulating ridges of great sand dunes loomed out of the darkness, forcing them to climb abruptly to clear these vast coastal mounds. Eric Brown noted, 'Flew at zero feet across Denmark. Many lights seen shining in the windows of houses. "V" sign flashed by navigator who received a signal in return'.[10] The Danes, overjoyed to see the Allies in action, bravely ignored the blackout restrictions and people rushed out, waving and flashing lights at the passing aircraft. Feeling unable to ignore such a welcome, the navigator of Eric Brown's Halifax had flashed a 'V for Victory' sign with his lamp and was delighted to see it promptly returned from the ground.

While this low-level flying proved very popular with the Danes, it proved tense and nerve-racking for the crews as the bomber stream converged over the village of Bjerregard, some 30 miles north of Esbjerg. A low range of hills ran through the centre of Denmark right through their track. Alan was told to watch out for it and any other obstacle that might be lurking in the dark – there were plenty of them. As they thundered across the countryside, they caught glimpses of farms and villages and the silvery tracings of rivers and lakes glinting in the moonlight. Church spires, high tension cables, trees and the odd hill loomed out of the night, causing hearts to pound and Bill to hastily pull back on the controls. Hedgehopping in the dark in the massive Lancaster was hair-raising and it was with some relief that they started to climb to bombing height when they were over the Baltic.

In addition to coping with the hazards of this aerial steeplechase, there was heavy fire from flak ships and flak batteries to contend with. The RAF Final Raid Report states that, 'Flak defences were very active along the whole route over enemy territory… particularly from coastal area'.[11] Sixty-six aircraft were damaged by flak that night, most of them over Denmark. The report makes clear the dangers of such low-level sorties, noting that 80% of the aircraft whose height at the time of being hit was known were flying at or below 500 feet.

Crews developed an intense hatred for these flak defences and the men manning them, and took every opportunity to attack them. Alan and Darkie got in a few rounds at a couple of flak ships and Eric Brown reported with succinct satisfaction, 'On the way out a ship opened fire on us. A burst from the rear turret silenced the gunner'.[12]

Sergeant Evans, who had flown with Bill on the Stuttgart operation a week earlier, was one of the youngest pilots on the squadron. He was just twenty years old. He and his crew in

Lancaster ED 834 Z-Zola were on only their second operational sortie. It was to prove an eventful trip. Over the Danish coast, a flak battery got them in their sights and a maelstrom of flak raked the whole port side of the aircraft, damaging the fuselage and starting a fire in the cockpit. A bomber pilot was metaphorically in the hot seat every time he flew, but now Sergeant Evans found himself quite literally in that position as a fire blazed away under his seat. As smoke filled the cockpit, members of the crew, hampered by their oxygen/intercom masks, desperately grabbed fire extinguishers and aimed them at the base of the flames, finally managing to put out the fire. The crew, somewhat shaken, then continued towards their target some 85 miles away. They had not got much further before they were hit again, this time in one of the port engines, which burst into flames. The engine was promptly feathered and the fire eventually went out. After two potentially fatal incidents in so short a time, the inexperienced crew felt jittery and tense, which no doubt contributed to what happened next. Such was the damage to the aircraft that a decision was made to jettison the bomb load, which included a huge 4,000lb 'Cookie'. Unfortunately, and the operational report states due to an intercom failure, nobody informed the skipper, who remained unaware that the bombs were about to be dropped and so the aircraft continued at low altitude. The minimum safe altitude for dropping these huge 'Cookies' was nearer 5,000 feet. As a result, when the bombs were dropped, the massive explosion as 4,000 lbs of high explosive detonated seconds after leaving the aircraft nearly blew the Lancaster out of the sky. The Operational Report does not detail this further damage but states, 'The explosion severely damaged the aircraft, but the Captain succeeded in bringing it back'.[13] This laconic statement leaves little doubt that it was something of a miracle that Sergeant Evans managed to get back to base at all. Of a total of 339 aircraft, twenty-one – thirteen Lancasters, seven Halifaxes, and one Stirling – failed to return, representing a loss rate of 6.2% of the force.[14]

Pathfinder marking was very precise on this occasion. Bomber Command Final Raid Report states that the green incendiaries that were the target indicators '…were placed extremely accurately, several being within a few hundred yards of the aiming-point'.[15] The main force then dropped their bombs on these indicators. Many crew reported seeing dense smoke and numerous fires and that the centre of the town was ablaze. There appears to have been little 'creep-back' that night. Bomber Command considered it to be 'the most successful attack beyond the range of Oboe during the Battle of the Ruhr'.[16] Oboe was the blind bombing radar device that combined radar and radio to control the final flight path of an aircraft onto a target.

The success of the raid was confirmed by reconnaissance sorties flown on 21 and 22 April. These showed that the centre of Stettin had been devastated. In the Pommerensdorf district, nearly 100 acres of closely grouped industrial buildings were destroyed, including the whole of an important chemical works, A.G. der Chemischer Produkton-Fabriken Pommerensdorf-Milch. Many factories and utilities, including water and gas works, were damaged, as were the Sachsenberg, Kruger and Stettiner Oderwerke shipbuilding yards. Military installations also suffered, including the pioneer barracks, the police barrack, the Intelligence Division and the Bredewer-Werder naval base. Damage to domestic property was considerable and 40,000 people were reported to have been made homeless by the raid. For a week afterwards, the town was without water, gas or electricity.

For the men that took part in it, though, the most important achievement was to have survived and returned home if not unscathed then at least with one more operation under their belts.

CHAPTER THIRTEEN
EXPERIENCE

By this time, Bill and his crew were one of the most experienced crews on the Squadron, having survived twenty-two sorties. They were also known as one of the most successful crews. Some men, like Alan, counted off the number of sorties in their logbooks. Many did not allow themselves to think further ahead than the next operation. At the beginning of a tour, thirty sorties seemed a hopeless number to contemplate. The odds against survival seemed overwhelming. During their first trips, crews were too busy learning the ropes to think ahead much, but as crews gained experience their confidence slowly grew. Fear was an ever-present companion but men found their own ways to cope with the apprehension they all felt; most developed a certain acceptance of the odds. Don Charlwood, an Australian navigator with 103 Squadron, felt that, 'After a time the most timid of men can become accustomed to the most threatened of lives'.[1]

The Air Ministry recognised the cumulative nature of the stress endured by bomber crews. It was accepted that everyone had their breaking point but, sadly, breakdowns were seen more in the light of a character flaw than a psychological problem. The Ministry attempted to set out guidelines for commanding officers faced with dealing with aircrew who could not, or would not, carry out their duties. These guidelines stressed the importance of ensuring there was no medical disability causing a refusal to fly. However, in addressing the problem of deciding whether a medical condition was to blame, it was noted that, '...there will be a residuum of cases where there is no physical disability... and in fact, nothing wrong except a lack of moral fibre'.[2] This became known as LMF, a term denoting a military crime that lay somewhere between those of cowardice and desertion. The punitive nature of the treatment meted out to those so labelled was designed to serve as a deterrent to others thinking of taking the easy way out. Initial treatment varied depending on individual commanders. In some squadrons, the offender was marched onto the parade ground where, in front of the assembled squadron, the charges and sentence were read out before the badges of rank and flying badges were ripped off his uniform. In others, the man was hastily dispatched from the station and reduced in rank. All men labelled as LMF were reduced to the lowest rank possible, Aircraftman Second Class. Commanders were keen to be rid of them as soon as possible for fear that their behaviour would prove contagious. They were posted away from their squadrons in haste to such places as the Combined Re-Selection Centre at RAF Eastchurch on the Isle of Sheppey in Kent. There they would be evaluated and processed.

However, it proved difficult and sometimes impossible for commanders to distinguish between a man deliberately trying to shirk his duty and one for whom the strain of flying brought on mental or physical incapacity. The stresses to which bomber crews were subjected were enormous. From the moment they saw their names on the Battle Order in the morning, the tension started to build as speculation mounted as to the target. Incessant niggling thoughts of what the night might bring were exacerbated by all-too-vivid memories of horrifying explosions that turned bombers into fireballs. Tiredness took its toll, and mental strain and physical exhaustion compounded each other's effects until there came a point when even the bravest of men felt they could not go on. Combat exhaustion could be, and was, mistaken for cowardice.

One of the most compelling and fundamental elements that overcame the constant fear of dying and prevented men giving up and refusing to fly was that of an even greater fear: that of letting their crewmates down. The mutual trust and reliance on which their lives depended bound each member of a crew to the others. The crew took their lead from their pilot, and Bill had gained their respect and confidence with his quiet self-assurance and calmness in emergencies. Seeing other aircraft blown to pieces and finding faces missing in the mess after sorties was a constant reminder of their own mortality. The first time a friend was lost it hit home hard, but soon they learnt to accept the inevitable 'Failed to Return' beside familiar names on the board. This was not callous; it was a necessity in order to be able to carry on.

And carry on they did. The next few days saw a lull in operations with the days spent in training and testing. Now flying in Lancaster ED 699 L-Love, Bill and his crew were detailed to lead five aircraft in formation flying practice. They also tested L-Love's performance in a Height Climb exercise. L-Love managed a respectable 23,000 feet. This was some 4,000 feet higher than they usually operated at and, as Alan noted, extremely cold at minus 33 degrees. Such low temperatures had unexpected hazards for the gunners. When they came off oxygen and tried to take off their facemasks, they could find that the condensation from their warm breath escaping at the edge of the mask had frozen them to their faces. At their dispersals before take-off, Doctor Wright would pass round jars of ointment to rub on their faces to prevent this.

On 26 April, Duisburg was once again the target. It was another big operation involving Lancasters, Wellingtons, Halifaxes, Stirlings and Mosquitos. A total of 516 aircraft in all. It was a clear night and IX Squadron aircraft were in the forefront of the bomber stream. As they flew at 20,000 feet, the Rhine and the docks were clearly visible as Don aimed for the red target indicators. Bill's operational report comments, 'Too early to see fires on arrival but attack appeared to be opening promisingly'.[3] As always, the flak batteries in 'Happy Valley' sent up wave after wave of shells. On their return, they found L-Love peppered with holes from uncomfortably accurate fire.

Nothing is mentioned in any of the crew's logbooks for the next week so they were probably granted a few days' leave. On 6 May, an operation was planned and Bill and the crew flew an NFT in preparation, only to have the sortie cancelled at the last minute. On 11 May, the crew was on the Battle Order again but after completing another NFT, the sortie was cancelled late in the afternoon. It was not until 12 May that they would fly operationally. Once again, the target was Duisburg.

Duisburg was the largest inland port in Germany thanks to its position on the confluence of the Rhine and Ruhr rivers. As well as an important logistical centre for rail and inland shipping, it was a major industrial centre with rolling mills and steel works and, as such, a prime target. The previous raids had been only partially successful, so Bomber Command was determined to go back once again.

To do the job, the Command dispatched a large force of 572 aircraft. Twelve Lancasters were from IX Squadron, including Bill and his crew in Lancaster L-Love. While cloud shrouded much of England, the weather was expected to be clear over Europe. There was a strong southwest wind blowing that would speed them on their way, but they would be punching into it on their return. The sheer size of the bomber stream and the weather conditions meant that German night fighters were sure to be out in force, and so it proved. The stream suffered a major attack going over the Netherlands and the Junkers 88 night fighters then lay in wait for the returning aircraft, shooting down twenty-five of them between 01.23 and 03.52.[4]

All the crew were very much on the alert and Bill was weaving constantly. As usual, the flak was fierce and accurate. As they tipped to port, Alan heard a sharp crack behind him, and a blast of freezing air rushed into his turret as a piece of shrapnel flew through, missing his head by inches. Brushing off the shards of Perspex that covered him, he looked around and, having assured himself that there was no other damage, informed Bill on the intercom of the unwelcome air conditioning his turret had just acquired. For the rest of the sortie, he endured the howling icy wind blasting straight through his turret.

Approaching Duisburg, yellow track indicators were seen and as they neared the target Bill could clearly see the brilliant red and green target indicators floating down. Mac was able to obtain an accurate GEE fix, enabling them to make a timed run to the target. Despite the fighters, Bill was delighted at the success of the raid, commenting, 'Wizard show. GEE fix on target. Bombed on Red Target Indicator'.

Bomber Command too was satisfied, reporting, 'The Pathfinder marking on this night, however, was near perfect and the Main Force bombing was particularly well concentrated'.[5] Both the old city centre and port area of Duisburg suffered severe damage, with much shipping destroyed in the port.

Having landed at 04.30, Bill was still deep in an exhausted sleep when his batman woke him with the unwelcome news that he was working again that night. Even more unwelcome was the news that their target would be the Skoda Works at Pilsen in Czechoslovakia. This would involve a long, tiring trip and they would be flying over enemy territory for almost all of it. The Skoda Works were a priority target because of the wide range of armaments they produced, including locomotives, machine tools, steam turbines and naval guns. For this sortie, on 13 May, 168 aircraft were dispatched.

The operation involved flying outbound at low level for a considerable distance. Surrounded by high ground, Pilsen lies in a basin where four large rivers converge. The approach was very difficult; Alan recalls it as absolutely nerve-racking. They bombed from the absolute minimum safe height for dropping the 4,000lb 'Cookie' and then had to face the return leg again over enemy territory. It was a long, gruelling seven-and-a-half-hour trip. The Pathfinders were late over the target and the target indicators were very scattered. Other crews expressed doubts as to whether the Pathfinders had actually located the target.[6] It was later found that nearly all the bombs had fallen in open country to the north of the Skoda works.

There followed a nine-day break in Bomber Command operations. The whole squadron spent the time training. There was little time to rest and unwind from the constant strain of operational flying and always the knowledge that soon they would be on operations again. Operations resumed on 23 May with a major raid on Dortmund. A total of 826 aircraft were dispatched, including Bill and his crew, the largest number up to this point in the war with the exception of the 1,000 bomber raids. The weather was clear and the Pathfinder marking was accurate, paving the way for a successful raid that demolished the Hoesch steelworks.

Even when they arrived back over England, it was important to be as watchful as ever. Any feeling of being safe when over home territory was dangerously misleading. Not only did the Luftwaffe bomb RAF airfields, but fighters were also sent to lurk around airfields to attack homecoming aircraft. The Luftwaffe also used some captured British aircraft to infiltrate returning squadrons. The familiar outlines deceived the watching gunners until it was too late, and aircraft had been lost in this way just as they thought they were safely home. As a result, Bill liked the crew to stay in position, keeping a sharp lookout until they were safely on the ground.

On this occasion, Sinc got on the intercom asking for permission to leave his station and use the toilet. He was told firmly, "Not yet." Toilet facilities on the Lancaster consisted of an Elsan chemical toilet. These devices were regarded with such horror that crew went to great lengths to avoid using them. Their situation, right at the back of the aircraft, meant men had to first get there then struggle out of enough clothing before finally balancing on the ice-cold seat. Not a lot of fun at any time but especially not in turbulence. Whenever possible, needs were taken care of by using a pee can. However, this was not one of those occasions and Sinc, increasingly desperate, repeated his request several times before finally being given permission when they were on the downwind leg, preparing to land. No doubt with some relief, he made his way back and was actually seated on the Elsan when they touched down. Lancasters landed with just the main wheels touching, which was usually quite smooth. However, when the tail wheel touched the ground, it would not always be in line and as it centred itself a violent wobble would run through the aircraft. To try and ensure that the wheel would be in line, a deep groove was cut into the tyre tread to help it centre quickly. This was not foolproof. On this occasion, the shimmy effect was considerable and the contents of the Elsan rose up like the Severn Bore, swishing from side to side with Sinclair acting as a rather unsuccessful bung on the top. He emerged covered in nauseating, stinking Elsan fluid and worse besides. Cursing and swearing, he tried his best to clean himself up but to little avail. The rest of the crew, with a marked lack of sympathy, made Sinc sit as far away from them as possible in the crew transport. Going into the briefing, other crews reeled back holding their noses and making pointed remarks on his incontinence. Alan recalls, 'In the interrogation room we had to sit closer and I think it was the quickest debriefing we ever had!'[7]

The next raid was back to the Ruhr again, this time to Düsseldorf, on 25 May. Bill's operational report notes:

> Primary attacked at 1:46:30 from 20,000. Yellow Markers seen on position "2 X" and timed run made from there. Some red T.I.'s seen but had dropped through cloud on arrival so bombed on time and distance run. No bursts seen owing to cloud layer. Very scattered incendiary fires over a very large area.[8]

There were two layers of cloud obscuring the target but once overhead the flak increased, and the air was heavy with the sound of exploding shells and the smell of cordite as chunks of metal thudded into the thin aluminum skin. Mac called out the heading for home and Bill slowly turned onto the new course away from the maelstrom. Tension eased a little as they left the target but not for long. Geordie's sharp eyes spotted a flicker on one of his instruments. The oil pressure wavered and then quickly fell on the port inner engine. Checking the oil temperature gauge confirmed his fears: the temperature on that engine was rising steadily. "Losing oil pressure, temperature rising. Port Inner, Skip," he told Bill.

Bill immediately responded, "Shut it down." Geordie quickly throttled the engine back and feathered its propeller while Bill retrimmed the aircraft to counteract the drag of the dead engine. Flak had torn into the engine, fortunately not setting it alight. The Lancaster could fly perfectly well on three engines but could not maintain their height. On three engines, the aircraft would only maintain around 10,000 feet – it would be downhill all the way back. Immediately, Mac set about recalculating times and remaining fuel. At this lower altitude, they would burn more fuel and their airspeed would be less, factors that would eat into their fuel reserves. Don moved to stand in the astrodome to keep watch. He scanned the skies intently – all were very aware of their increased vulnerability to both flak and fighters.

Losing the port inner presented another set of problems. Other systems powered by this engine included hydraulic pumps that operated the landing gear and flaps. Approaching Lincolnshire, Bill either chose or was directed to land at Woodhall Spa. This may have been because the main runway was longer than Bardney. A more likely explanation is that Bardney did not want their runway blocked by a crashed aircraft should there be further problems and Woodhall Spa was not operating that night. As they flew over Lincolnshire, the shapes of fields and villages slowly became visible. In the distance, through the morning mist, they could see the gooseneck flares guttering and flaring beside the runway. The Lancaster had an emergency system that would lower the undercarriage with compressed air and now Geordie turned on the emergency air cock to engage this. Bill wondered how extensive the damage was and the exact state of the landing gear – there was no way of telling and so he ordered the crew to take up crash positions just in case. Geordie read off the IAS (Indicated Air Speeds) – 130, 120, 115, finally, 110, their target speed, while Bill concentrated on getting the Lancaster down as close to the beginning of the runway as possible. After floating in over the threshold, Bill put her down firmly and immediately told Geordie to throttle back. The Lancaster raced on, most of the runway flashing past before they finally came to a halt. Infinitely slowly, they taxied to a dispersal and stopped before going through a familiar routine: Booster pumps off… Engines off… Ignition off… Finally, silence. For a few seconds, they just relaxed in their seats as relief overcame them. Then each man completed his checks, masks were unplugged, equipment gathered or stowed and, one by one, they left their positions, squeezing along the fuselage to get to the door at the back. Climbing down the ladder, they drew in deep breaths of cool, fresh morning air before quickly going to inspect the damaged engine. Then, bags in hand, they walked stiffly across the tarmac. Here, all was peaceful. The grass glistened in the early-morning dew as the haze slowly lifted. It was a little before 4 am and the first twitters of birds filtered across the airfield, announcing the start of another day.

They were driven back to Bardney in the crew transport. They dozed as, slumped in their seats, exhaustion overcame them, for night after night they had flown through the bitter cold in unpressurised, poorly heated aircraft. The constant vigilance as they faced the multiple dangers of enemy action, collisions, mechanical failures and weather had taken its toll. They had now completed twenty-eight of the thirty missions. The odds against completing a tour were increasing all the time. Knowing they were lucky to have survived so far and tantalizingly close to the magical thirty only added to the pressures they faced. Hope can be a cruel thing, playing on already taut nerves. Bill kept a close eye on all his crew, particularly the youngest ones, Darkie and Alan. After five months, mental and physical exhaustion were showing. Heavy shadows were permanent fixtures under everyone's eyes.

There was no let-up. It was seven thirty before they sank wearily into bed, but once again Bill's batman woke him at lunchtime to tell him he was on the Battle Order for that night. After lunch, the crew drifted into the Briefing Room. A collective groan ran around the briefing room as the target was announced. It was Essen again, at the very heart of the Ruhr Valley. After Berlin, this was the most unpopular target and no one had forgotten their previous experiences there. Late in the afternoon, the sortie was cancelled to everyone's relief. However, it was only a delay. The next day, the 27th, it was Essen again. This was the fourth time Bill and the crew had been there and it seemed to get worse every time.

Unusually, on this raid a second bomb aimer, Sergeant Robinson, came with them to be shown the ropes. Now that it was almost summer, the light evenings meant that take-offs were late in the evening. Tonight it was scheduled at 22.00. The bomber stream converged over Sheringham before routing over Egmond in Holland and continuing to the German border before turning south. The layers of cloud parted occasionally to give Sergeant Robinson in the front of the Lancaster a horrifying view of the cauldron of flak and searchlights over 'Happy Valley'. Once again, skymarking had to be used. Finally, the red and green tracking flares were seen and Don had the release point flares in his bombsight as he dropped the bombs. Sergeant Robinson, without a specific job to concentrate on, could only look out in dismay: how was it possible to stay alive in all this? The flak was particularly heavy again that night. In his logbook, Bill wrote, 'Hot flak over target', while Eric Brown of 51 Squadron who was also flying that night wrote, 'VERY heavy barrage over target. A/C [aircraft] seen to explode in mid-air'. Of the 518 aircraft dispatched that night, twenty-three failed to return. Those who did return thought themselves very fortunate.

Wuppertal was the target on 29 May with 719 aircraft being dispatched. Mac was unwell and unable to fly so he was replaced by Sergeant R. Powell as navigator on this raid on 'Happy Valley'. Bill was seriously worried and uncomfortable about this change. Mac was a meticulous and experienced navigator and Bill had tremendous confidence in him. Now, on this, their second to last sortie, an unknown and untried element was being introduced. The routing that night only added to their worries. The approach to the target was through the 20-mile gap between Düsseldorf and Cologne, both themselves heavily defended. This routing would require extremely accurate navigation. Aware of the dangers, Bomber Command instructed the Pathfinders to drop target indicator markers as aids to navigators to help the bomber stream avoid the most heavily defended areas.

They took off at 22.15 before converging over Southwold and heading out over the North Sea. As they crossed Belgium, German controllers were monitoring the stream and, noting the heading, were sure that such a large force was going to somewhere in the Ruhr Valley. In the darkness over the North Sea, they flew without seeing any of the other aircraft; just the occasional gentle buffeting as they hit the slipstream of a bomber ahead of them reminding them they were not alone. As they approached 'Happy Valley', the usual flares and searchlight beams formed swathes of lethal light arching across the skies. During the 'Battle of the Ruhr', the aim of electronically predicted anti-aircraft guns and searchlights on the ground had become extremely accurate and now they found themselves flying through a seemingly unbroken wall of heavy, accurate flak. Bill, his arms aching, fought to stay on track amidst the constant buffeting. Visibility was good that night and, as they approached, the Pathfinder markers were clearly visible against the red glow of the fires below. They watched as their bombs cascaded down into the inferno beneath.

Wuppertal was situated on the River Wupper, deep in a valley surrounded by steep hills. The raid caused the first example of what became known as a 'firestorm' in the small streets of the old centre of the town. Many of the officials responsible for fire and air raid warnings were out of town relaxing on this Saturday night, and the fire services were unable to control the fires that raged through the old buildings. Bomber Command was delighted with the results, reporting that:

> This attack was aimed at the Barmen half of the long and narrow town of Wuppertal and was the outstanding success of the Battle of the Ruhr. Both Pathfinder marking and Main Force bombing was particularly accurate and a large fire area developed in the narrow streets of the old centre of the town.[9]

The crews were well satisfied too, feeling they had done well despite the daunting opposition they encountered. Bill wrote, 'Excellent Parramatta [Pathfinder technique]. Much flak and searchlights en route'. Eric Brown of 51 Squadron was also delighted, noting:

> Night Fighters up in force. A/c [aircraft] seen to crash in flames all the way from the coast to the target. Air to air tracer seen...Target ablaze as a/c left target. Wuppertal well and truly wapped. Extremely concentrated searchlight belt over the Ruhr. No opposition over the target but the approach and the getaway made up for the quiet time over the target. A first-class raid.[10]

During the first ten days of June, the full moon period curtailed Bomber Command activities. When operations resumed again on 11 June, Bill and the crew were on the Battle Order. This would be Bill's thirtieth operation. If they got through this, they would have made it. Once again, they were in Lancaster ED 699 L-Love. Alan was ill and in his place as mid-upper gunner was Sergeant J. Elliott. In addition to the usual pre-operation nerves there was the fear that despite having come so tantalisingly close to surviving a tour, they might be lost on this, their last operation. It had happened to many crews. For six months now they had lived with the constant knowledge that every operation could well be their last – a mental accommodation had been made that accepted this. Thinking about the chances of surviving was intolerable and such thoughts were quickly dismissed – now insidiously these thoughts crept back, exacerbating the ever-present fear they had learned to live with.

The day was overcast; thick grey clouds slunk across the sky, threatening rain later. The air was heavy and oppressive. Departure would be late in the evening, leaving the crew with long hours to fill. The hours and minutes ticked slowly by till it was time for the briefing. Other crews stopped them to say good luck and ask how they had managed it, both envious of and awed by their achievement. These good wishes made them uncomfortable

– they seemed to tempt fate. They tried to shrug them off with answers that ran along similar superstitious lines: "Thanks, but you never know… "

By the afternoon, rain was falling; thunder rumbled ominously while distant lightning flashed. The electric tension in the air matched their mood perfectly. They entered the briefing room for the last time. Would it be an easy target or the heartland of Germany? "The target for tonight is… Düsseldorf." No easy final trip then; it was back yet again to 'Happy Valley'.

Bomber Command ordered 783 aircraft to take part in this operation. Take-off in the darkness at 23.40 meant a return in the early-morning light; this would increase their vulnerability to fighter attacks.

In the evening, the familiar routine took over: the pre-operation meal, then time to change. Identities were discarded as they emptied their pockets and got into their flying gear before finally piling on Mae Wests and parachute harnesses. During the evening, the weather worsened, the clouds blackened and sheets of driving rain swept across the apron. On the bus to their dispersal, no one had much to say. Each sat filled with their own thoughts. One way or another, this would be the last time they went through these rituals together. Climbing down from the bus, a final volley of 'Good lucks' rang in their ears. Hunched and wet, Geordie and Bill trudged through the downpour to do the final checks while the rest of the crew dashed for shelter under the wing to smoke their final cigarettes.

As Bill strapped himself in, the rain beat down on the glass canopy of the cockpit, distorting the world outside. The lights were a wet blur as L-Love thundered down the runway, clambering slowly up into the cloud above. As they crossed the North Sea and flew towards the Belgian coast, the moon shone, touching the clouds with silvery light. It was beautiful but unwelcome, leaving them uncomfortably exposed. As they reached the turning point on the German border, Mac gave Bill a new heading and they turned north. The clouds were thinning now and in the distance ahead shone the brilliantly lit-up skies of 'Happy Valley'.

The cloud thinned and dispersed and now they could see Düsseldorf below, outlined in a mass of flames. In the centre, a great column of black smoke rose out of the inferno, towering into the sky almost to their height of 19,000 feet. They started the run-in. Don's voice came over the intercom: "Right... Right... Hold it... Steady... Steady..." a long pause "...Bombs gone." Bomb doors closed, they turned to pick their way through the barrage of flak and searchlights. Approaching the Dutch coast, Darkie, peering out of the rear turret, could still see the glow of the fires in the distance. Now they were out over the sea, time to lose height and come off oxygen. Tiredness vanished as relief and exhilaration flooded through them. As the English coast loomed out of the early-morning haze, they chattered excitedly over the intercom. Then, in the soft half-light of the early dawn, Lincoln Cathedral came in sight, rising above the town, welcoming them home as it had on so many other mornings, a reassuring symbol of permanence and endurance.

Calling Control, Bill heard for the last time those welcome words, "L-Love. Pancake. Pancake." This was their permission to land. Bill brought L-Love downwind and settled onto the glide path while over the intercom came wild whoops of joy as they touched down. Against all the odds, they had made it.

One by one, the mighty Merlins were shut down and the checks completed. Bill sat, still savouring the moment as the tension drained slowly from his body. Relief flooded through him; he had felt responsible for the six young men under him and now he had brought them safely home. Twisting out of his seat, he patted L-Love's control yoke and idly wondered who would be flying her tomorrow. Excited chatter filled the aircraft as the crew gathered their gear up for the last time. Their ground crew were waiting, their tired faces wreathed in smiles, eager to shake their hands and congratulate them. With a final glance at L-Love, they were whisked away in the crew truck and the realisation started to sink in: tomorrow, they would not be gearing themselves up for another night in the skies over Germany. It was over for now. They arrived in the debriefing room, tired but exhilarated, to more congratulations from staff and other crews before a final post-operational breakfast and bed.

The next day, the squadron were on ops. again. The Battle Order was posted and briefings held and all the myriad preparations made; only now the crew were mere observers of this familiar routine that had been their lives for six months. Although not all of the crew had completed the statutory thirty sorties that Bill had, their commanding officer considered their outstanding record entitled them all to finish operations together. The next day, they would leave Bardney. Their completion of a tour of duty entitled them to two weeks' leave, but first came a riotous evening of celebration. Round after round of pints disappeared as raucous voices sung traditional songs and Mac thumped happily away on the piano.

The next morning, there were some very heavy heads as they said their final goodbyes. As he got into his car to drive away, Bill was filled with mixed emotions. There was intense relief that his hand-picked crew had made it through and pride in their achievements but also sadness to be leaving a great squadron and the men with whom such a close bond had developed. For six months, his whole existence had been the crew and the squadron. Now the thought of normal life, asleep in your bed every night, seemed slightly unreal.

In June, Bill was recommended for a DFC, the Distinguished Flying Cross. The recommendation from his Commanding Officer was duly endorsed by Air Vice Marshal R.A. Cochrane, the Commanding Officer of No. 5 Group. It states:

> This officer has carried out 30 sorties against enemy targets, involving 175 hours flying. He has at all times displayed the greatest determination to carry out his tasks to the best of his ability. His courage and leadership have made his crew extremely successful, and his tenacity has produced good results in the number of night photographs he has obtained of his targets. He is strongly recommended for the award of the Distinguished Flying Cross.[11]

The recommendation went up the chain of command and in due course Bill heard that the award had been approved. It was announced in the *London Gazette* on Friday, 13 August 1943. Clearly, Bill's leadership qualities and character had welded together a crew whose performance had been outstanding. The younger members of the crew had come to rely on this 'old man' of thirty-three whose quiet manner masked a fierce determination to both do the job well and to ensure his crew had the best chance of surviving. Alan recalls that from the minute he joined the crew, he had an absolute certainty that Bill would get him through his tour. He also remembers that he had no such comfortable feeling with the next crew he joined.

It is clear that Mac had admired Bill enormously. He described him in such terms to his father that Mr McCorkindale senior was moved to write to Bill to thank him for looking after his son and getting him through the tour and to congratulate him on the award of his DFC. The gracious letter, included below, that Bill wrote in reply, speaks volumes of the kind of man Bill was.[12]

24th August 1943

Dear Mr McCorkindale,

I appreciate the sentiments expressed in your letter very much indeed. At the time when I received my decoration I knew that your son had been recommended for the D.F.M. and I was delighted when I heard a few days later that it had actually come through.

There is a tendency to attach too much importance to the pilot, when each individual member of a crew is just as important in his own way. This applies in particular to the navigator, who is the kingpin of the whole outfit. And that is where we were so lucky – I was at all times able to place absolute reliance on Neil's work and well remember how uncomfortable I felt on the one occasion when, owing to illness, I had to take another navigator. He kept on working away calmly whatever the emergency, which is the main reason why we had such a trouble-free tour. Never was a medal better earned.

It is I, therefore, who should be and am grateful to you for contributing in so vital a way to the success of our efforts. Were it not for the sterling work put in by Mac (as we all call him) I doubt very much whether I would be here today.

With very best wishes, I am

Yours sincerely

W.A. Meyer

On completion of their tour with IX Squadron, Mac, Sinc and Darkie received the DFM, the Distinguished Flying Medal. The DFM was the equivalent of a DFC but was awarded to non-commissioned officers. While it was common for a pilot officer who managed to complete a tour to be awarded the DFC, it was quite rare for non-commissioned officers to be rewarded with DFMs – it meant their performance had been really exceptional. DFCs and DFMs were only granted, rather unfairly, to surviving crew members with the proviso that if the recommendation had already been made, it was allowed to go ahead if they were subsequently killed.

CHAPTER FOURTEEN
TRAINING OTHERS

For his precious two weeks of leave, Bill went home to London. His mother had moved back to London now and was living in a flat in Pont Street. Like all mothers, she worried constantly about her son's safety. Bill, in turn, was concerned about her. Not only did she have no family in England to support her, but her heavily accented English sometimes caused difficulties at a time when anti-German sentiment was rising.

No bombs had fallen on London recently, and the light summer evenings lent an illusion of normality before night fell and the blackout resumed. Although traffic was lighter, the pavements around Piccadilly were filled with American servicemen on leave from their bases in East Anglia and keen to see what London had to offer. At the Haymarket Theatre, Noel Coward's comedy *Present Laughter* alternated with his more serious *This Happy Breed*. Newsreels played in cinemas and were popular as a means of keeping up to date with events at home and for news of the war. Recently, the news had been more encouraging. In February, after terrible losses were suffered on both sides, the Battle of Stalingrad had finally ended with the surrender of the German 6th Army under General Paulus and in May, German and Italian forces had surrendered to the Allies in North Africa.

By now, the transformation that London had undergone since the start of the war felt quite familiar to Bill. There were sandbagged buildings and protective hoardings everywhere. Posters on the hoardings focused on encouraging the population with slogans such as 'Dig for Victory' while others warned, 'Careless Talk Costs Lives'. The rubble-filled gaps and damaged buildings in many streets remained, with facades fallen away to reveal the remnants of people's lives. Staircases, bedrooms, living rooms and personal belongings all lay pitifully exposed to view.

The two weeks passed quickly and all too soon it was time for Bill to leave for his next posting. On completion of a tour of duty, airmen were usually sent for six months to OTUs to act as instructors for trainee crews. They were known as 'screen' instructors. The term 'screen' was used to identify the person so-called as having experienced active service; in practice, someone who had survived one tour of duty. They were not qualified instructors and their job as 'screen' was to try and pass on their skills, practical knowledge and tips to rookie aircrews. Bill and his crew were posted individually to No. 82 OTU at RAF Ossington.

This leave was just long enough for Bill to begin to become reacquainted with some of the comforts of civilian life, but visiting some of the old familiar haunts brought a strange feeling of unreality. There was a feeling of detachment, of visiting a life that belonged to someone else. On the 27 June, Bill drove up to Derbyshire and reported at RAF Church Broughton. There he was to spend a week at 93 Group Instructor's School.

Church Broughton was a quiet village some 10 miles southwest of Derby. The airfield there was completed in October 1942 to the standard RAF pattern, with three concrete runways and the usual scattering of Nissen huts. It was part of 93 Operational Training Group and a satellite of RAF Lichfield. There, the officers escaped the misery of living in Nissen huts. Instead, they were billeted in some splendour at nearby Foston Hall, a grand Victorian pile set in beautiful gardens. It is used nowadays by Her Majesty's Government as a women's prison. Bill found he would be flying a Wellington bomber at Ossington – this was the aircraft he would be instructing on at the OTU. Instructors there gave him a few ideas on what to concentrate on with rookie pilots. He was given just six hours of flying to familiarise himself with the Wellington which he was then expected to instruct others on.

The Wellington – affectionately known as the 'Wimpey' after a character, J. Wellington Wimpey, in the Popeye cartoons of the period – was a twin-engine bomber that had been the frontline bomber before being replaced by the four-engine Lancaster. Designed by Dr Barnes Wallis, who invented the bouncing bombs used by the Dambusters, the Wimpey was renowned for the amount of punishment it could take. This was due to the geodetic latticework construction that allowed it to fly on even when large holes were blown in it. Its disadvantages were its slow speed, a low operational ceiling and the limited bomb load it could carry.

At the end of the week, Bill made his way across the country to RAF Ossington in Nottinghamshire. The lack of signposts meant constant stops to map-read until, nearing the airfield, the sight and sound of aircraft taking off and landing guided him back to a familiar world.

RAF Ossington was situated to the west of the village of Ossington. The airfield had been built in 1941 in the grounds of Ossington Hall, a stately home that dated from Tudor times. The Hall itself was used for accommodation and, as the base expanded, further accommodation was built outside the village. The tempo of life at the OTU was very different from an operational squadron. Gone was the tension of waiting to see whether you were on operations that night and what the target was. It was possible to make plans with some certainty of being able to carry them out. However, life on an OTU had its own dangers.

At No 82 OTU, training was carried out on Wellingtons, Martinets and Tomahawks but Bill would only fly Wellingtons. After a couple of brief familiarisation flights, he started acting as 'screen' on 11 July, spending two days instilling the finer points of circuits and landings into Sergeant Arrowsmith. On arrival at the OTU, the mass of recently qualified aircrew would have just formed up into crews. They had not had much time to practise their individual skills, let alone get to know each other and learn to work together. They were now undergoing the same process that Bill and his crew had gone through, of welding themselves into a crew. Meanwhile, the 'screens' tried to pass on their skills and experience.

Alan Hart remembered explaining to air gunners that if you had to come out of the rear turret in a hurry, you opened the doors behind you, grabbed and clipped on your parachute then rotated your turret and fell out backwards; but that the first and most vital thing was to remove your safety strap so that you were not tied to the aircraft. On another occasion, Alan was asked where the Very pistol went. This vital piece of equipment fired off the 'Colours of the Day', a visual code to confirm your identity and prevent your own side shooting at you. Little things such as the best way to get out through the escape hatches and how best to stow your parachute could make the difference between life and death. From now on, Bill would fly with different crews almost every day. It was strange and unsettling after the trusted bonds formed flying with his crew and, in its own way, quite nerve-racking.

The other members of Bill's crew arrived during the first two weeks of August. While the rest of the crew could see each other in the Sergeants' Mess, Bill, in the Officers' Mess, would only see them occasionally. On 20 August, they had something of a reunion as Bill, Darkie and Mac's logbooks record that they flew together with Bill in command in Wellington 'K' on a cross-country flight: Ossington – St Bees – Stranraer – St Abbs – York – Ossington. Bill's logbook also records flights with 'crew' on 1 and 14 August. On 5 August, Alan Hart acted as rear gunner on an air test with Bill, but it was Darkie who made the most flights with Bill. Darkie clearly felt enormous respect, admiration and liking for Bill who, in turn, thought a great deal of this young man who had shown such determination and skill. On five occasions, Darkie appears to have flown with Bill, and it is Bill who signed off the monthly total in his logbook for August. There may have been other occasions when some of the crew flew together, but these flights were probably the last that Bill flew with members of his IX Squadron crew.

After their six months at the OTU, the crew were all posted to different squadrons. Mac, Neil McCorkindale, flew with several Pathfinder squadrons. He was fortunate in that these squadrons flew the De Havilland Mosquito. The Mosquito was a two-crew fighter-bomber. Made of wood for lightness, it was designed to sacrifice armaments for speed. It was extremely successful and the loss rate was 1/10 of that of Lancasters. After the war, Mac returned to Scotland to become County Chief Librarian in Aberdeen.

Alan Hart was fortunate to survive his next tour of duty. Alan admits he was a somewhat lippy youngster and had got on the wrong side of his Commanding Officer. As a result, he was posted to 101 Squadron, a Special Duties squadron flying what was known as the 'Airborne Cigar' or 'ABC' for short; this was Radio Counter Measures. They flew with an additional German-speaking crew member whose task it was to jam enemy flight controllers' broadcasts and also occasionally to transmit misinformation to mislead and confuse German fighters. However, the enemy could pinpoint the equipment used to do this and 101 Squadron had the highest casualty rate of any squadron. Despite his CO's best efforts, Alan survived and lived a long and happy life in Loughborough where he became a quality manager in an aeronautical engineering factory. He died in 2014.

Geordie (Wilson Hunter) and Wilkie (Donald Willbee) also survived their second tours and came safely home after the war, but it has proved impossible to trace either them or their descendants.

Sinc (Stafford Sinclair) and Darkie (Thomas Johnson) did not survive the war. Sinc was promoted to Flying Officer in the autumn of 1943 and, having completed a conversion course onto the B17 Flying Fortress, he joined 214 Squadron, another Special Duties Squadron tasked with jamming enemy radar and providing a radar screen for other Bomber Command aircraft ahead of the bombing stream. This meant that they were out on their own without the protection of the bomber stream. He came heartbreakingly close to getting through his tour, but his plane was seen to go down in flames over the River Elbe on 22 March 1945 during a raid on Hamburg. It was one of the last raids of the war. His name is commemorated on the Runnymede Memorial.

Darkie survived another tour of duty and his outstanding abilities earned him promotion to Warrant Officer. He was then sent to instruct at No. 10 Air Gunnery School based at RAF Walney Island, near Barrow-in-Furness. On 2 January 1945, his aircraft, Anson LT 741, failed to return from a training flight. Despite a series of air and sea searches during the following days, the aircraft was not located until eight days later when it was found on Blackcombe Screes in Cumbria. The aircraft had crashed near the top on a steep and rocky face and disintegrated. Having survived the terrible dangers of sorties over Germany, it seems especially sad that a training accident should claim Darkie's life so shortly before the war ended. His grave is in Liverpool's Allerton Cemetery.

Being posted to an OTU was intended to give airmen a 'rest' from the danger and stress of operational flying. In practice, it did not turn out quite like that. Alan stated that, 'It sometimes was much more dangerous flying with untrained aircrew... I mean not trained in working together...'[1] A glance at the Operations Record Book confirms this. In the returns for the month of September 1943, under a column headed 'Aircraft Wasted', are listed nine aircraft. Three had been discovered as unusable on inspection; this alone says much about the state of the aircraft used for training. Trainee crews managed to write off another six. The Aircraft Serviceability Returns are also startling – on average, almost half the aircraft of all types were unserviceable each day. This was partly due to the condition of the aircraft in the first place, beaten-up old veterans no longer fit for operational flying, but undoubtedly the trainee crews also managed to provide plenty of work for the fitters and mechanics.

Bill was to find out first-hand just how dangerous it could be. On 23 September, he was flying as 'screen' with Flight Sergeant Watkins and his crew in Wellington Mk X HE 265-Y of 'B' Flight. The Wellington had one pilot but, unlike the Lancaster, there was no Flight Engineer and thus no flight instruments on the right side of the aircraft. The pilot sat on a raised seat on the left-hand side while Bill, as 'screen', would have stood beside him at a lower level on the right. A Wellington usually had a crew of five but on this occasion there were four on board. They took off and were flying northeast and nearing Lincoln when suddenly the oil pressure dropped sharply in the port engine and it had to be quickly feathered. The aircraft was at 1,500 feet. A quick look at the map revealed the nearest airfield was RAF Skellingthorpe, close to Lincoln, and a decision was made to land there. There was now no hydraulic power to lower the undercarriage as power for that was drawn off the port engine. With that engine feathered, the undercarriage could only be lowered by vigorous hand pumping. This task fell to Bill while the pilot concentrated on flying the Wellington.

An engine failure in a twin-engine piston aircraft makes handling much more difficult for both take-off and landing, but especially on and just after take-off. The aircraft will lose not half but nearer 80% of its climb capability. There are also control problems with asymmetric thrust, causing the aircraft to yaw and roll in the direction of the dead engine. This has to be corrected by use of the rudder which in itself depends for its effect on airflow across the surface. Due to the way the propellers (at this time not counter-rotating) produced thrust, losing the port engine was more dangerous and it was essential to maintain minimum control speed with the critical engine inoperative. Aircraft normally land into wind, the wind flow over the wings giving greater airspeed and making stalling less likely. Taking off or landing downwind, with the wind behind you, significantly lengthens the take-off and landing distance.

With the wheels down, they would have had trouble maintaining height. This was probably why the Wellington now attempted a downwind landing at Skellingbourne, initiating a sequence of events that led to disaster. As they approached the runway, Flying Control at Skellingthorpe fired off a red flare at them, indicating that they were forbidden to land. Although already low over the threshold, on seeing this, the pilot attempted to overshoot. Without the ability to raise the undercarriage quickly, with its one engine screaming, Wellington Y-Yoke never had a chance. In an effort to clear the trees at the end of the runway, minimum control speed was lost and the aircraft stalled at treetop height and came crashing down into the woods.

As Y-Yoke plunged through the trees, there was a terrible sound of rending metal as panels bent and tore away and the wings broke, rupturing the fuel tanks and allowing fuel to pour over the fuselage. At the same time, the intricate pipework carrying hydraulic fluids and oils throughout the aircraft ruptured, sending further quantities of highly inflammable liquid flowing through the airframe. As is almost inevitable in a crash, a spark ignited these fluids and in seconds the aircraft was ablaze. For an instant, the shock of the impact stunned the crew. Then came the realisation that the aircraft might explode at any moment. Coughing and gasping, they struggled out of their harnesses and fought their way towards the exit. Speed was vital; curls of flame were already edging along the fuselage, licking up towards the door and filling the aircraft with smoke and fumes. They reached the door only to find it had jammed. Terrified of being trapped in an inferno, they pushed and kicked furiously at it, finally managing to force it open. Flames were now leaping up at them through the doorway. Realising that their only chance was to jump through the flames before the aircraft exploded, they hoped for the best and jumped. Everyone managed to get out but one crewmember's injuries were serious and Bill suffered burns. The aircraft was completely burnt out.

Even when new, and with optimum performance, the Wellington was known to be a handful on one engine and Y-Yoke was an old aircraft deemed unfit for active service. With the benefit of hindsight, it is clear that the red flare should have been ignored and the landing completed. A pilot with limited experience would have been unlikely to have the self-confidence to ignore his training and disobey the flare. Bill certainly should have realised this; however, it would have been impossible for him to take over the handling of the aircraft. Nevertheless, Bill, as the senior officer, was responsible for the aircraft. The record states that:

> Captain F/L Meyer screened with a 6 course crew attempted a downwind landing with port engine failed at Skellingthorpe Airfield. Given RED by F.C.O., tried to go round and stalled into a wood. Crew of 4 injured. Aircraft, Cat. E burned out.[2]

Every accident and aircraft loss was recorded on an 'Accident Card'. There were different types for operational squadrons and OTUs. They were an early type of punch card with headings all round the edge of the card that listed the various causes and degrees of severity of an accident, the number and type of casualties, the weather, various possible defects, the stage of the flight when it occurred and any errors that had been made. The relevant section would then be punched out. In the middle of the card on one side the names of the crew and details of the aircraft, its engines and its home base. The reverse contained a brief résumé of the accident and the conclusion of the inquiry that followed it.

It was noted that the central main bearing had failed in the port engine and that the pilot had made an error of judgement in not disregarding the red flare. It also drew attention to a regulation stating that the pilot should have fired off a Very flare to indicate the emergency so that Flying Control on the ground would have understood the situation. In this case, there certainly was not time for all that. The incident seems to have been accepted as just another unfortunate training accident. There are innumerable incidences in OTU records of crews being killed either practising one-engine overshoots or after engine failures.

The record states that Bill was 'Slightly Injured'. These injuries were burns to the hands and face and were sufficiently serious for him to be treated at the RAF hospital at Rauceby. Originally built as a mental institution, Rauceby was taken over by the RAF in 1940 to serve as a specialist Crash and Burns Unit for all the

RAF bases in Lincolnshire. This unit undertook pioneering work in plastic surgery. Sir Archibald MacIndoe, the famous surgeon who specialised in reconstructive surgery, worked there. He had founded the 'Guinea Pig Club' at Queen Victoria Hospital in East Grinstead to help the rehabilitation of badly burned aircrew. Bill's burns must have taken some time to heal for it was two months before, on the 24 November, he was pronounced fit.

It was now over five months since Bill had left IX Squadron. It was not considered worthwhile sending him back to the OTU and he was given a week's leave. Bill had taken the decision to volunteer for the Pathfinders, the elite group that led operations, when he went back to operational flying. With his excellent record, he was immediately accepted and was now sent to RAF Upwood to complete a course run to train Pathfinders in the specialist navigational and targeting skills that they needed. If he passed this course, he would be joining an elite Pathfinder unit, 97 (Straits Settlements) Squadron.

CHAPTER FIFTEEN
THE PATHFINDERS

Finding and bombing targets proved much more difficult than Bomber Command had anticipated. In 1941, it was found that less than one third of crews were bombing within 5 miles of their targets. All too often, bombers were getting lost at night, with even such conspicuous targets as Berlin or Essen sometimes being largely missed. The Air Ministry decided that an elite force should be created to lead bombing raids and pinpoint targets more accurately. Sir Arthur Harris, Commander-in-Chief of Bomber Command, was strongly against the idea and fought tooth and nail to prevent it. Harris believed that the creation of an elite force, consisting of the best crews, would lead to jealousy and bad feeling in the Command. On being given a direct order to create such a force, Harris complied but insisted on installing his own choice of commander for this new force and, ignoring the demands of seniority, he chose as commander a relatively junior officer, an Australian in the RAF, Group Captain D.C.T. Bennett.

Donald Bennett was born in Towoomba in Queensland, Australia. He had an unlikely start to his RAF career, having left school to become a jackaroo (drover) on his father's cattle ranch. His initial application to join the RAAF (Royal Australian Air Force) in Brisbane was rejected on health grounds. Undeterred, with characteristic single-mindedness, he simply took himself off to Melbourne and applied again. There he succeeded in joining the RAAF and a year later transferred to the RAF. He became an instructor on flying boats before resigning due to the poor prospects of promotion in peacetime.

After a stint in civilian flying, Bennett rejoined the RAF in 1941, becoming CO of both Nos. 77 and 10 Bomber Squadrons in succession. Unlike some squadron commanders, Bennett flew with his men as often as possible – he wanted to know the problems they faced and how they performed. While CO of 10 Squadron, he was shot down over Norway during an attack on the German battleship *Tirpitz*. Landing in deep snow, he evaded German soldiers and police and set off on an epic journey through the snow-covered mountains to neutral Sweden. He finally reached England, where he was awarded the DSO for his exploits. Shortly after this, in July 1942, he was given command of the new Pathfinder Force.

Bennett was not just an exceptional pilot; he also had an unparalleled knowledge of all aspects of flying. He had qualified as a First Class Navigator, a ground engineer and as a wireless operator. No one could have had better qualifications for the job. Bennett brought to the Pathfinders his outstanding abilities, ideas that had been shaped by personal experience as a squadron commander and his familiarity with bomber operations. His single-minded determination to forge the Pathfinders into an outstanding force could make him appear harsh and severe. Arthur Harris, himself noted for his fiery temper wrote, 'He could not suffer fools gladly, and by his own high standards there were many fools'.[1]

Pathfinder Force became operational in August 1942 and originally consisted of five squadrons, one from each operational bomber group, using a variety of aircraft. Bennett was determined that the Pathfinder Force should have the best men, that they should be well trained and that they should have the most advanced equipment. He lost no time in putting his ideas into practice, treading on as many official toes as he needed to in the process.

The Pathfinders' task was twofold: firstly to lead the bombers of main force to their targets and secondly to identify and mark them using a variety of coloured flares that floated down over the target. Harris described their role to Winston Churchill with stark realism: "They will always be in the forefront of the battle. The full fury of untouched defences will always confront them. Tied to their 'aids', they will have to restrict evasive action to a minimum. We shall ask much indeed of these young men."[2]

And indeed much was asked of them. While an ordinary tour of duty consisted of thirty operations, for the Pathfinders it consisted of a minimum of forty-five operations. Not only was their tour of duty fifty percent longer but also these crews were in far greater danger. A directive to the Pathfinders reads, 'Evasive action must be kept within very small limits'.[3] This was in order to use H2S, the primitive radar aid, to bomb accurately. The pilot, who would normally weave the aircraft from side to side to enable the gunners to peer beneath to spot fighters, would have to maintain straight and level flight for at least six minutes. Ample opportunity for a fighter to creep up underneath from behind and take aim at the unsuspecting bomber, as the Germans quickly learnt. Despite the dangers, there was no lack of volunteers. Many young men wanted nothing more than to wear the coveted Pathfinder badge, a small golden eagle, but only the very best were accepted. To prevent identification in case of capture, the golden eagle was never worn on operations but remained a secret badge of honour.

By January 1943, the importance of the role of the Pathfinders had become clear and the force evolved into No. 8 (Pathfinder Force) Group with the motto, 'We Guide to Strike'. While the force initially included an unwieldy collection of Wellingtons, Stirlings, Halifaxes and Lancasters, by 1943 it had standardised and now only flew Mosquitoes and Lancasters. Oboe and H2S, as previously described, were the two main navigation aids used by the force to find and identify the target. Both aids had the same drawback. A signal was transmitted and this enabled German fighters to home in on the transmissions. This was less of a problem for the fast Mosquitoes but a very real one for the slower Lancasters.

Every morning, Harris would meet his staff officers and decide on the target for that night, and then a Mosquito from the Meteorological Flight would fly across Germany to assess the weather. These aircraft were unarmed and thus very light – they relied on the extra speed this gave them to keep out of trouble. Weather, intelligence and squadron operational availability were assessed before the target was chosen and the route to target and back decided. This was usually a roundabout route designed to prevent the Germans guessing what the target was until the last possible moment. Often, some squadrons were used as decoys and sent to other targets to divert attention from the real target. Once the size of the force and the bomb load had been determined, Pathfinder tactics were then decided on and detailed plans worked out and transmitted to the stations.

Even with the help of the new aids, navigation was still difficult and inaccurate. Wind and bad weather played havoc with efforts to stay on track. Often, the aids themselves went wrong and transmissions were broken. There were enemy fighters lying in wait for them, directed by controllers who tried to second-guess both routes and targets. Flak ships lined the coastlines of occupied Europe, and inland, the ever-probing searchlights and flak batteries waited.

Planning ensured that a constant stream of bombers flowed across the target in a concentrated mass in as short a time as possible. The advantages of this strategy were that German defences would be saturated while exposure of the crews to the dangers of being directly over the target area would be limited. The inundation of bombs from the dense stream would cause the greatest disruption and destruction as it would both cause panic in the population and overwhelm efforts at fire-fighting. Take-off times from different airfields had to be carefully planned and coordinated so that the bombers, flying the same route, would arrive over the target in a constant stream. From the late afternoon onwards, on most days, the bomber stream could be seen winding out across the English coast with the Pathfinders at its head.

The Pathfinders had various methods of marking targets, the choice depending on the weather and the type of target. The names of the various methods were unusual and must have puzzled many airmen. Bennett named them after various towns in his home country and so aircrew found themselves using techniques called a 'Parramatta', a 'Wanganui' or a 'Newhaven'.

A large target called for a 'Parramatta'. In this instance, the original primary target indicators were continually replaced by secondary markers as they burnt out. If the target was small, the 'Newhaven' method was used, with the target first being illuminated by dropping flares onto it before the aiming point was identified and the target indicators dropped. Finally, in cloud and bad visibility, the 'Wanganui' was the answer. Having identified the target with Oboe or H2S, the Pathfinders dropped target indicator flares suspended from parachutes, and these provided airborne aiming points for the crews. The prefix 'Musical' was added if the Pathfinders were using Oboe. The colours that these flares burnt varied to prevent the Germans lighting decoy fires on the ground. With exotic names such as 'Pink Pansies', 'Red Spots' and 'Smoke Puffs', they came floating down, their red, yellow or green lights sparkling in the night sky. With bitter irony, the Germans knew them as 'Christbaum', Christmas trees.

Aircrew joined the Pathfinders in several ways. Most were highly regarded, experienced individuals and crews, but there were also crews who had shown particular ability in training and who came directly from their OTUs with no operational experience. Sometimes Group Captain Hamish Mahaddie, the group's Training Inspector, recruited crews on his visits to squadrons. Due to his success in stealing away the best crews, he became known as Donald Bennett's 'Horse Thief'.

The final step before joining an operational Pathfinder squadron was a ten-to-fourteen-day course that concentrated on advanced navigation and target marking techniques. Usually, only three or four crews attended at one time, and a highlight of the course was the chance to meet their commander in person as Bennett made a point of coming to address each new intake.

Tall, thin, intense and focused, Bennett seized the opportunity to instil in his men the high standards he expected of them. He left them in no doubt of the supreme importance of their role and the enormous responsibility they would carry. His words inspired but warned as well; only excellence would do.

The course Bill attended took place at the PFF NTU (Pathfinder Navigation Training Unit). This unit had moved from its original base at Gransden Lodge in June 1943 and was now at RAF Upwood, north of Huntingdon and near the Pathfinder Headquarters at RAF Wyton.

Bill arrived at RAF Upwood on 1 December 1943 and training started immediately. The instructors were experienced crew who had already completed tours as Pathfinders. The course concentrated on the use of the latest aids and polishing their flying and navigation skills. These were put to the test on practice exercises that involved approaching a large city, such as Birmingham, and then doing a dummy bombing run using H2S. To make it as realistic as possible, the exercise would be flown to a strict timetable, just as a real raid would be, and target photos would be taken on the bombing run. The crews' performance would be assessed and if a crew was found off-schedule or inaccurate on several occasions, the crew would be sent back to a main force squadron. Probably because of the extra risks they would run, all Pathfinder aircrew were also expected to be able to undertake the duties of another member of the crew in addition to their own.

Bill was delighted to learn he had passed his course and, on 9 December, he packed up his kit, loaded it into the car and drove south to report for duty at RAF Bourn in Cambridgeshire, where 97 Squadron was based.

CHAPTER SIXTEEN
97 SQUADRON

Bill was now joining another of the RAF's elite squadrons; 97 Squadron had been formed as a training squadron on 1 December 1917 and first saw action in World War I over France in 1918. Following a brief deployment in India, where it provided an experimental mail service, the squadron was stood down. Although there were brief periods in the late 1930s when it was resurrected, it was not until 1941 that it was reformed as an operational squadron. This was made possible by a generous donation given by the Malay Straits Settlements (territory now Malaysia and Singapore) to the British Government to be used for the purchase of some Avro Manchester aircraft. In recognition of this gift, the squadron was reformed as No. 97 (Straits Settlements) Squadron in February 1941. It was to be based at RAF Waddington as a heavy bomber squadron and part of No. 5 Group. The Squadron motto was 'Achieve Your Aim', an apt motto for a Pathfinder squadron. In 1942, the squadron converted to Lancasters and in April 1943, it moved to Bourn, in Cambridgeshire, when it became part of No. 8 Group, the Pathfinders.

RAF Bourn was constructed in 1941/42 as a satellite to nearby RAF Oakington. The little village of Bourn that gave the station its name is mentioned in the Domesday Book, and its settlement can be traced back to Roman times. Over the centuries, Bourn's population rose and fell in parallel with various economic or physical disasters. Today, the village has grown but the heart of it remains remarkably unchanged, with the same timber-framed thatched cottages edging the roads.

The airfield was built on high flat land to the north of the village. Some 4,000 acres of farmland between Highfield Farm in the east, Bourn Grange in the south and Great Common Farm in the west had been taken over, together with a local school, Childerley Gate. The A45 St Neots–Cambridge road formed the northern boundary. The three runways formed an extended 'A' when seen from the air. Most of the personnel quarters, including the sick bay, were situated to the west of the field, straddling the local road known as the Broadway. These quarters, and almost all the other buildings, were either prefab or Nissen huts that sprang up in hasty clumps as they were needed. As at Bardney, in the winter, smoke from the coke fires in the huts belched forth, hanging heavily in the cold, damp air and catching in throats. Cinders from these stoves were used to form the paths between the huts, adding their own tang to the damp air. Like many wartime airfields there was a rough-and-ready, improvised feel to the place.

It was a miserable day as Bill drove the short distance from Upton to RAF Bourn with wipers beating full-on against the driving rain. A cold, white mist hung over the airfield. As he drove through the main gate, the solid grey mass that was the Control Tower could be seen standing out against a cluster of Nissen huts. Looking around, Bill glimpsed the distant shapes of tarpaulin-clad Lancasters rising out of the mist. A few men could be seen scurrying between the huts but the field was unusually quiet; flying had been cancelled for the past few days due to bad weather. For once, the ground crews had plenty of time to finish all the work that was needed on the aircraft.

When Bill joined 97 Squadron, it was initially as a Flight Officer; whether this was because of the accident or because all RAF reserve ranks were temporary remains unclear. By the end of February, he was listed as a Flight Lieutenant again.

On reporting for duty, Bill was told that he was in 'A' Flight and to go and report to his Flight Commander, Squadron Leader Charles MacKenzie Dunnicliffe. Dunnicliffe was an outstanding officer who was about to take temporary command of the squadron. He welcomed Bill and told him he would be flying with a highly regarded crew who had completed thirty operations but whose pilot had decided not to continue. It was possible to opt to get all operational flying over in one go and complete the forty-five operations required for this. The alternative was six months' 'resting', acting as an instructor at an OTU before returning to complete the tour. After much debate, it became clear that all but one of the crew were keen to continue for the forty-five operations. The exception was the skipper, Stephen Dawson.

Bill was eager to meet his new crew, two of whom were officers. The squadron had been stood down so he knew exactly where to find them; propping up the bar in the Officers' Mess. It was dark now as, dodging the puddles, he made his way to the mess. Entering, he found himself in a room filled with thick tobacco smoke and rowdy laughter. Edging his way through the crowd, he reached the bar and, after a few enquiries, found Reginald Pike and Bernard Starie, his air bomber and navigator respectively, and introduced himself. Bernard, a married man, had been the 'old man' of the crew at thirty-one. Reg, like the rest of the crew, was a lot younger. Reg was quiet at first, slightly in awe of this older man, but Bill quickly put him at ease and he was soon his usual talkative self. Pint followed pint as they talked till late into the evening, sizing each other up and relating their experiences.

The next morning, Bill found himself with the rest of the aircrew from RAF Bourn, boarding coaches for an educational visit. While a day or two could easily be filled with lectures and training, now, after a week when cold, misty weather prevented any flying, the CO was running out of ideas. This is probably why a visit to the RAF Engineering shops at Henlow was arranged on 10 December. RAF Henlow was one of the biggest maintenance bases in the country, specialising in repairing, modifying and assembling aircraft. It was an opportunity for an interesting exchange of views. The mechanics, who had to repair the damaged aircraft, seized the opportunity to bend the ears of the crews who provided them with so much work.

The next few days were spent in ground training. Bill sat through training films he had seen many times before and heard the same old lectures once again. Sometime during this period he met the rest of his crew, but it would be over a week before he was able to fly with them. This was mostly due to the terrible weather that December, weather that was to have tragic consequences for the squadron and provide a salutary reminder of the harsh realities of operational flying.

When Bill arrived at IX Squadron, he had brought with him his own crew, carefully chosen, who had had time to get to know each other well during training. This was different; he now had no choice in the matter. He had been allocated a crew whose pilot had decided to take a break before completing his tour, much to the disappointment of his crew. The crew were:

> Flight Lieutenant Bernard Starie DFC, Navigator
> Flight Sergeant Thomas Shaw DFM, Flight Engineer
> Pilot Officer Reginald Pike DFM, Air Bomber
> Pilot Officer James McLeish DFC, Wireless Operator
> Pilot Officer Archibald Barrowman DFC, Mid-Upper Gunner
> Flight Sergeant Albert Roberts DFM, Rear Gunner

Reginald Pike, the air bomber, was a good-looking, popular young man, full of fun and cockney good humour. He came from a large family in East London. Reg had wanted to join the RAF and become a pilot, and his family were tremendously proud when he volunteered in 1941. Having gone through the usual rigmarole of interviews and medicals, he was accepted for training as 'Pilot/Observer'. After completing his initial training in England, he was advised that he was being sent to Canada to complete his flying training. However, this was not to be. In a letter to his father in June 1942, Reg swallowed his disappointment and wrote, 'Mum has probably told you that I was washed out as a pilot, and I've re-mustered as Air Bomber and so shall probably be home before Christmas'.[1]

Wasting no time on regrets, Reg immediately got to grips with his new role. July found him at No. 4 Bombing and Gunnery School, in Fingal, Ontario, where he passed out with excellent marks. Next stop was the Air Observer School, No. 8 at Ancienne Lorette in Quebec, an airfield that has now become the Jean-Lesage International Airport. Here, under civilian instructors, he spent a month learning the finer points of pinpointing targets and estimating distances. This course finished in mid-October 1942 and Reg then faced the Atlantic crossing again before arriving back in England in late November. In January 1943, he was sent to No. 14 OTU at RAF Cottesmore in Rutland where he spent the first month brushing up his skills and getting used to the Wellington bomber. In February, he and the rest of the crew started flying together. As Reg had already had some flying training, it was decided that he should be the one to take over flying the aircraft in an emergency, and the pilot, Steve Dawson, made a point of giving him a couple of hours at the controls. The crew had completed thirty operations and Reg Pike received a commission and was also awarded a DFM (Distinguished Flying Medal). It was announced in the *London Gazette* on 25 November 1943. The citation reads:

> The success of this crew and the valuable contribution they have made to the squadron's operational effort is largely due to Flight Sergeant Pike's accurate bombing. At all times, he has displayed commendable resolution and keenness.

The wireless operator, James Campbell McLeish, was born in Dennistoun, Glasgow on 5 January 1920. His father, James McLeish senior, was a master plumber working for Beardmore's in Glasgow. James and his wife, Lillias, had five children. Sadly, one died in infancy. James junior was the youngest one of the family and as such, was thoroughly spoilt by his two older sisters and his brother. A clever boy, he attended Whitehill Secondary School in Dennistoun, Glasgow where he was on the Roll of Honour. After school, he started work as a telegraph boy before working for the Post Office on the night mail. He was known as a very nice young man 'with a bit of a daring attitude'.[2] No doubt this is why he volunteered for the RAF. One family photo shows James posing on his motorbike with a pretty girl behind him while another shows him smiling broadly as he stands under a Lancaster at Bourn. James McLeish proved to be an outstanding Wireless Operator during his first thirty operations. He was not only commissioned as Pilot Officer on 28 December 1943, but he was also awarded the DFC.

Archie Barrowman, the mid-upper gunner, was a Canadian. Although born in Scotland, his parents had moved to Canada when he was still a baby. They settled in the little town of Tisdale in Saskatchewan where his father became the janitor at the local school. Tisdale was a small, rural community in an area where agriculture was dominant. In these peaceful surroundings Archie grew up and went to school. After leaving school he went to work in the local dairy. In January 1942, the war was not going well and Archie must have heard first-hand through family members in Scotland of the deprivations and bombings that Britain was suffering. Early that January, Archie travelled to Saskatoon, the largest city in Saskatchewan, and there, on 8 January 1942, he volunteered to join the Royal Canadian Air Force.

Canada had joined the British Commonwealth Air Training Plan, and training schools had been set up all over Canada. Having passed the initial assessments, Archie was now sent to one of them, No. 7 Initial Training School, in Saskatoon. Here, he found himself back at school in a very literal sense as the training school was based in the premises of two schools, the Normal School and Bedford Road Collegiate. Having passed that course at the beginning of August, Archie was sent on to No. 3 Bombing and Gunnery School in MacDonald, Manitoba. There he completed a three-month gunnery course before graduating on 23 October 1942. He was then given embarkation leave before facing the Atlantic crossing. Archie's exceptional performance in the mid-upper turret earned him a commission and a DFC. His citation reads:

> He is an Air Gunner in a crew which has on several occasions been engaged by the enemy defences and sustained damage from flak. Also they have been attacked by enemy night fighters. Despite this they have dauntlessly pressed home their attacks with great effect. By his skill as an Air Gunner and eagerness to operate against the enemy he has proved himself a most valuable member of the squadron and his crew.[3]

Unfortunately, it has proved much more difficult to find details about, or trace relatives of, the rest of this crew. Bernard Starie came from Surrey and was married but only distant relatives are alive today. It is clear that he was a first-class navigator and served with distinction. He was promoted to Flight Lieutenant and awarded the DFC on completion of thirty sorties. Albert Roberts came from Whiston, near Sheffield in South Yorkshire, but it has proved impossible to trace his family or that of Thomas Shaw. They too had performed exceptionally and were both awarded DFMs on completion of thirty sorties. Thomas Shaw's DFM is now in the Imperial War Museum's collection.

In the winter of 1943, this crew, under the command of Stephen Dawson, had done well in their training at RAF Cottesmore and were keen to go to a Pathfinder squadron. They arrived at 97 Squadron at Bourn towards the end of May. For a young 'sprog' crew, untested in combat, this was quite an eye-opener. As new boys, on probation at that, the other crews largely ignored them. They were left to find their feet and absorb all they could of operational life. The first two weeks were mostly spent attending lectures and doing various flying tests, to see if they were up to the high standard required. Only after passing these preliminary tests were they sent on to the Pathfinder Training Unit, then based at RAF Gransden Lodge, for a week's final training.

Having passed their course at Gransden Lodge, the crew returned to 97 Squadron at Bourn. On 21 June, their first operation together was to Krefeld. At the end of July 1943, Bomber Command made a series of raids on Hamburg, which the crew took part in. This was 'Operation Gomorrah', also known as the Battle of Hamburg. During the first raid on 24 July, Reg Pike noted in his logbook that they carried 'Window' for the first time. 'Window' was a brilliantly simple device designed to confuse German radar. It consisted of bundles of foil that were pushed out of the flare tube and, as they scattered, presented myriad confusing targets on the radar screens below, hindering identification of the bombers. In due course, countermeasures were found, but initially it was highly successful.

On 27 July, the crew returned to Hamburg. Hamburg, situated on the coast, was a perfect target for H2S radar, and the bombing was once again concentrated and accurate. The weather had been unusually hot and dry and the city was still smouldering from the last attack – fresh fires started easily due to the density of the buildings and narrow streets. This combination led to fires joining together, and a tremendous firestorm was born. The inferno raged through streets and courtyards, destroying the centre of the city. Some 40,000 people died, mostly from carbon monoxide poisoning as the fires consumed all available oxygen.

On 22 November, Steve Dawson, now a Flight Lieutenant, flew with his crew for the last time. The target was a tough one – Berlin – but they returned unscathed from this their thirtieth operation. It must have been an agonising decision for Steve to leave his crew after all they had gone through together. However, he was a married man with a young child. They understood that he felt the chance of spending six months in comparative safety with more opportunity to see his family was not to be turned down. The rest of the crew decided that they still wanted to carry on and waited, with some apprehension, to meet their next skipper.

Reg was now Pilot Officer Pike. A smart new uniform had to be acquired before he moved into the more comfortable surroundings of the Officers' Mess. His delighted family insisted on a formal photograph of him in his new uniform with his Pathfinder Wings. A photo had been taken when he qualified as an air bomber; it shows a relaxed, slightly round-faced young man, his side cap clinging on at an impossible angle. In the photo of him as an officer, his new cap is still at a slightly jaunty angle but the eyes have changed; they reflect all that he has been through. Now a man's face stares out in place of that of a boy.

It was now six months since Bill had last flown operationally and Bomber Command's strategic aims had evolved. On 10 June 1943, the Pointblank Directive had been issued, elaborating on the strategic aims of the Casablanca Directive. Pointblank's aim was to focus American and British efforts on destroying the Luftwaffe. This would enable bombers to attack specific targets unhindered by fighters. To do this meant concentrating attacks on factories that made any kind of component for the Luftwaffe rather than all economic or military targets. However, Harris was determined to still pursue the broader objectives laid down in the Casablanca Directive, and the final wording of Pointblank was loose enough to allow him to continue to pursue his own agenda.

In November 1943, Harris wrote to Churchill advocating a bombing campaign against Berlin: 'It will cost us 400-500 aircraft. It will cost Germany the war'.[4] He was preaching to the converted. Martin Middlebrook points out that correspondence between Churchill and the War Office reveals that Churchill had been pushing for attacks on Berlin for some time.[5] Berlin was the cultural, political and economic centre of Germany. As the very heart of the Third Reich, it presented a tempting target. Realising he did not have adequate resources, Arthur Harris had delayed an all-out attack on it in 1942. In 1943, it was a different matter. Encouraged by the successes of Bomber Command in raids such as those on Hamburg, and now with more planes and better navigation equipment, he was ready to turn his attention to Berlin. Harris firmly believed that bombing Berlin would destroy civilian morale and hasten the end of the war.

However, Berlin was an altogether different proposition. Infinitely larger and better defended, the buildings were mainly solid brick and stone, unlike the wood constructions that burnt so well in Hamburg. There was also the much greater distance – Berlin was some 650 miles away and that meant each operation took an average of an exhausting seven and a half hours. Since the end of March 1943, there had only been two raids on Berlin, both in August. On 18 November 1943, Bomber Harris launched in earnest what become known as the Battle of Berlin. It was the second raid, out of a total of sixteen, on the 22 November that was the most successful. Despite cloudy conditions over the target, a vast area was set ablaze that stretched from the central districts westwards across the mainly residential areas of Tiergarten and Charlottenburg and as far as the suburb of Spandau.

Berlin was attacked again on 2 December but it was not a successful raid and the losses were heavy. Ed Murrow, the famous American broadcaster, accompanied a crew on this raid. Reporting on his experiences, he titled the broadcast 'Orchestrated Hell'. It was an apt description of the conditions that bomber crews endured night after night.

During the spring of 1943, with IX Squadron, Bill had flown through the Battle of the Ruhr. Now he returned to operational flying just as the main part of the Battle of Berlin got underway.

CHAPTER SEVENTEEN
LIFE AND DEATH

After twelve days when bad weather prevented all operational flying, Harris was keen to resume the battle and on the night of 16 December the chosen target was Berlin. Twenty-one aircraft from 97 Squadron were briefed for the operation. The forecast was that fog would keep the German night fighters grounded but, ominously, that fog might close in on Bomber Command's own airfields just around the time the aircraft were due to return. That morning at Bourn the weather was still cold and misty and it did not look promising. At the briefing the Met Officer stated that he was sure that the raid would be cancelled due to this risk of fog.[1] It was not.

The route planned was for a direct flight to Berlin and then for a long return going north over the Baltic before turning for home over Denmark. However, it turned out that not all the German fighters were grounded, and the bomber stream was attacked as it crossed the Dutch coast. The sortie went according to plan; there was the usual flak but the thick cloud covering Berlin prevented the searchlights picking out and coning their targets. After dropping their bombs, the Lancasters then turned north on their long routing home, unhindered by the German fighters, who were unable to follow them.

Over England, the meteorologists' predictions were proving accurate. Almost the whole country, with the exception of Scotland

and the west of England, was now covered in low cloud and fog. Everywhere aircraft were arriving overhead their fields, their crews exhausted, some damaged, others short of fuel, only to find that they had to wait, stacked in circuits 500 feet apart before they had a chance to try and land. This was the predicament that faced the returning crews at Bourn. There, the fog swirled thickly above the field, blanketing the flare path and landing lights and enveloping those trying to land. One of the first to return was Charles Owen. Despite most of his navigation aids having packed up on the flight back, his navigator managed to find the way back to Bourn:

> Homed onto base on SBA beam, breaking cloud at 250 feet to find fog, rain and visibility about 300 yards and deteriorating. R/T then packed up, so after circling for ten minutes at 200 feet, landed without permission in appalling conditions.[2]

With no R/T (radio telephone) and no navigation aids, Owen knew their only chance was to attempt a landing there and then. The weather was deteriorating, the thickening fog closing in as he brought the Lancaster ever lower, fighting to catch a glimpse of the flare path through the blackness beneath. With the help of the flight engineer, he managed to pick out a flicker from the flare path and, realising they were much too high, started to sideslip to bring them onto the runway. Sideslipping is a means of losing height fast – the aircraft is banked with opposite rudder applied to stop the aircraft turning. The sideslip must be halted in time to round out and land. Despite Owen's skill, they still landed halfway down the runway. They were lucky to arrive back early before a stack of aircraft had built up overhead the field.

Many of those now circling above would not be so fortunate. Aircraft still arriving were being told to circle at ever-higher altitudes as the numbers waiting to land grew. Some attempted to land using Standard Beam Approach (SBA). At 20.00 that night, a fault had been reported on the SBA, although it is unclear what this was.[3] Those who chose to try to use it faced making a very precise approach while descending ever lower through the fog. Using this system required skill and practice and not all the squadron had been well trained in its use. On their descent using SBA, pilots reached a decision height where, if they could still not see the runway or were not happy with the approach, they would have to overshoot and go around again, a process that used up precious minutes and precious fuel. Sometimes it took three nail-biting attempts before they managed to land. Above, in the circling aircraft, the tension mounted as the flight engineers made crucial calculations as to how much fuel they had left. The answers were alarming; they were faced with a situation that was critical. Some crews, realising they would run out of fuel before they got a chance to try to land, decided they would have to try their luck elsewhere.

At RAF Graveley, 6 miles to the northwest, a new top-secret system to assist aircraft land in foggy conditions had recently been installed; it was one of only three stations where the system was operational at that time. It was known as FIDO, standing for Fog Investigation and Dispersal Operation. Despite its sophisticated title, the principles behind FIDO were very simple; it involved laying a pair of pipes pierced with holes along each side of the runway, extending out into the approach area. Petrol would then be pumped along pipes that were designed to vaporise the fuel as it emerged from the holes. To start it, one of the ground crew had the unenviable task of lighting it and running for his life as a brilliant orange flame raced along the pipework. Clouds of oily black smoke billowed up into the sky at first, before the system warmed up and burnt cleanly. The intense heat then burnt off the fog and provided a flare path along the runway. The system could use a staggering 100,000 gallons (454,600 litres) of precious petrol an hour and was only to be used in emergencies.

There had been concerns that the glare and turbulence created by the flames would make using FIDO impractical. The Pathfinder's leader, Donald Bennett, flew into Graveley in February 1943, and first tested the system. Approaching the flame-ringed flare path, he found himself reminded of 'seeing lions jump through a hoop of flame at the circus', but despite the glare and considerable buffeting from the updraft, he found it perfectly manageable.[4] Others were not so relaxed, finding that descending towards a threshold that was a blazing inferno was more than a little disconcerting. Alan Hart found it 'Quite awe-inspiring when you flew down the middle of these two pipelines that were burning merrily away'.[5]

On the night of the 16th, RAF Graveley had been stood down from operations but it was nearby and it was equipped with FIDO. The conditions were as bad as at Bourn but, surprisingly, FIDO was not lit up until just before 1 am, after some planes had already been diverted and had just managed to land there. Three of 97 Squadron's aircraft that tried to locate the field and land were not so lucky. Two crashed in nearby fields. The other came heartbreakingly close to making it. This was the crew of Squadron Leader Deverill, one of the squadron's most experienced and decorated pilots. They had identified the runway and were on the approach when at the last minute they ran out of fuel, the engines cut out and the Lancaster crashed onto the bomb dump. Only quick action by ground crews prevented the crashed plane setting fire to the dump and an even greater loss of life.

By now the situation at Bourn had worsened. A Lancaster, trying to land, had crashed and burned on the edge of the field. Time was running out for the aircraft circling above. On the ground, Flying Control could not tell if the wreckage from this crash was obstructing the runway and had no choice but to tell the aircraft above to continue to orbit. Two other Lancasters did land some eight minutes later but a third crew, desperately seeking somewhere to land, crashed nearby. The crew had been on their very first operation. Their story, and that of many of the other 97 Squadron crews, is told in full by Jennie Gray in her moving book, *Fire by Night*.

Meanwhile, two more crews had realised they would not get a chance to land before running out of fuel. They had to make a difficult decision, whether to abandon their aircraft and parachute to safety. It was not an easy option, given the value of the aircraft and its equipment. Baling out at night was a risky business at any time and with the blackout in force, shadows and vague shapes on the ground were all that were visible. This night, it was even worse. With the cloud and fog obliterating everything, there was no chance of seeing where you would come down; you had to jump blind. Unsurprisingly, men were very reluctant to exchange the solidity of an aircraft and rely on a piece of flimsy silk to get back to earth. One Lancaster crew tried first to divert to Graveley but, despite once catching a glimpse of the roaring FIDO burn off, were unable to locate the field. Having been left with no choice, the pilot then engaged the autopilot, aimed the aircraft towards the North Sea and, after ensuring that his crew had left the aircraft, jumped after them. The other crew also bailed out. Both the crews landed safely, while their aircraft flew on before crashing when the fuel ran out.

With one aircraft shot down over Berlin, 97 Squadron lost eight of the twenty-one aircraft that took off that night, and thirty-five young men lost their lives. The ORB states bleakly that '…the squadron had a disastrous night'.[6] When the terrible news reached Pathfinder HQ, it brought the head of the Pathfinders himself, Donald Bennett, hot foot to Bourn to assess the situation. Wasting no time, he arrived around 2 am just as the survivors of one of the crashes were being taken to hospital.

Bomber Command lost thirty-one aircraft in all due to the fog as, over and around bomber stations throughout the country, aircraft crashed or were abandoned as crews bailed out. That night the losses due to the weather were the heaviest of the whole war. That dreadful night came to be called 'Black Thursday'. 97 Squadron suffered the heaviest losses of all.

As dawn broke on the 17th, the enormity of the squadron's losses hit home. Airmen were used to seeing the gaps at mess tables and sudden empty beds, but this was loss on an unprecedented scale. Airmen and ground crew alike were gripped by disbelief, stunned by the extent of their losses as they made their way through the fog that persisted, swirling thickly around the huts. For Bill, it was a harsh reminder of what operational flying entailed.

That morning, their commanding officer, Squadron Leader Dunnicliffe, addressed his men. Dunnicliffe had only just assumed temporary command of the squadron. He had taken over from Group Captain Fresson on 15 December, just in time to be confronted by the loss of a quarter of his squadron. After going through what had happened the previous night, he sought to reassure his men, promising them that both crews and aircraft would be replaced as soon as possible. Dunnicliffe now had the unenviable task of writing twenty-eight letters of condolence to the families of twenty-eight airmen and a further eight to families to inform their relatives that they had 'Failed to Return'. It turned out later that they had died that night over Berlin.

For the next two days, the ORB records are stark and brief, simply stating, 'No flying'. Usually on non-flying days, training of some kind was carried out, but it was not until the 19th that this was resumed. Bill and his new crew then had their first opportunity to fly together doing an hour's local flying. For Bill, this was a chance to familiarise himself again with the Lancaster.

Climbing aboard, he was immediately overwhelmed by the evocative smell of an operational Lancaster. That rich blend of sweat, oil and fuel brought memories flooding back of the tension-filled nights over Germany in the cold and dark. Now he had to face it all again; and with a strange crew, it would not be easy. Working his way forward, he glanced around at the familiar layout; the wireless operator's station, the navigator's cubicle with the curtain drawn back – everything was just the same. He stepped up over the main spar, barking his shins in the process as he had so many times in the past. Then, stowing his parachute, he settled himself into the pilot's seat and buckled up the harness. It was as if he had never been away.

Probably due to the difficulties pilots had encountered using SBA on the 16th, they also had an hour and a half's practice using SBA that night. The squadron could not afford such losses again. Neither could Bomber Command. On 23 December, an order went out to all Pathfinders stating they must complete 'At least two SBA practice approaches per week'.[7]

The following day, for the first time in six months, Bill saw his name up on the Battle Order for operations that night. It was a strange feeling; the old familiar tension ran through him. More than that, there were new concerns. There had not been enough time to get to know his new crew well or for them to get used to working as a team. They had only flown together for two and a half hours. Even worse, his Flight Engineer, Tom Shaw, was unable to fly that night and was replaced by Flight Sergeant Davis. The crew were worried too; they liked what they had seen of their new skipper, but how would he be on ops?

There was the usual guessing game as to what the target would be. In the cigarette-laden air of the briefing room, crews sat huddled together chatting. Finally, the squadron and base commanders strode in and silence fell as the doors closed behind them. Then came the time-honoured words: 'The target for tonight...' It was Frankfurt. Although commanding officers were not encouraged to fly on operations, Squadron Leader Dunnicliffe insisted on flying that night. After the devastation of three nights ago, his going on operations that night was an act of solidarity and encouragement for the crews.

A sigh of relief went around the room when the target was announced; at least it was not back to Berlin or 'Happy Valley' yet again. Only one person did not share their relief. Bill's heart had skipped a beat when he had heard the target; this was one he had hoped never to be sent to. Some of his family lived in Frankfurt. While contact had been impossible since the start of the war, Bill had happy memories of holidays spent with his aunt, uncle and cousins in the pre-war years. He had stayed with them at their house in the centre of the city, near the main railway station. He listened intently as details of the sortie were revealed. With a heavy heart, he heard they would be bombing the centre and, in particular, the main railway station. It came as no surprise; transport hubs were always prime targets. The demands of war could be cruel, and acts that were unconscionable in peacetime became necessities of war, but that did not make them any easier. He would, as always, do his best, but it is not difficult to imagine the distressing thoughts running through his mind.

Trying to put such thoughts aside, Bill went to join his crew for their traditional meal. He wanted to talk to them, to gauge their mood before this their first operation together and try and reassure them. He quickly ran through how he liked things done, his calm assurance giving them confidence. Afterwards, they faced the lengthy process of struggling into heavy flying gear, each contemplating what had to be faced in the dark hours ahead. Waiting for the crew bus in the chilly night air, Bill and his new crew wondered how things would work out. While there was mutual respect for each other's experience, they were all aware that they were not yet that seamless entity, a crew.

Within Pathfinder Squadrons there were various roles of ascending difficulty. The most experienced and accurate crews were 'Blind Markers', who would locate the target using H2S and then mark it with target indicators. 'Blind Backers-Up' performed the same task but flew in the bomber stream, re-marking the target at set intervals. 'Visual Markers' would locate and mark the target visually. Finally, there were 'Supporters', who were usually new crews fresh from training. They carried a normal bomb load rather than markers, and it was their task to arrive on target precisely on time and bomb accurately as an additional marker for the main force. For this, Bill's first flight with the squadron, they were allocated a role as a 'Supporter'.

They had been given Lancaster JB-361 B-Beer (in the phonetic alphabet of the period), which was the aircraft the crew had previously always used and which Bill would continue to use. Crews got used to flying in 'their' aircraft – its individual feel, handling and peculiarities became familiar and reassuring. Familiarity and ritual were important to airmen. Men carried good luck charms or mascots of every variety from coins, small toys or items of clothing, and to go on an operation without your charm was deeply worrying. Some had a particular ritual they had to go through such as putting clothes on in a certain order. Often, the aircraft themselves were bedecked with lucky mascots.

Don Charlwood describes how, on having to use another crew's aircraft one night, they were instructed at great length as to the steps to take to prevent disaster. First of all, 'Yohodi, a fearsome being with a red and blue complexion', who was painted on the fuselage near the rear turret, had to be kept happy in order to keep the guns from freezing up. This involved rubbing his belly three times. Then Don was to 'Rub the horseshoe over the navigator's table'.[8] This was to prevent getting lost. Unfortunately, Don misunderstood and taking the statement literally went to the trouble of untangling the said horseshoe from the mass of wire that held it over the table and literally rubbed it over the table rather than simply rubbing the horseshoe. However, the precautions worked and they got back safely, although the aircraft's usual crew were horrified when they heard that their lucky horseshoe had been taken down. In the Lancaster that Don usually flew, the lucky charm was a 'grimy toy rabbit, which we called Nunc Nunc, whose rear end was solemnly kissed after each operation'.[9]

It was now mid-winter, one day away from the shortest day of the year. Thoughts of Black Thursday were still on everyone's minds. In the chilly dark, the crew clambered onto the bus. There was half-hearted chatter as they were driven round the peri-track to their dispersal. There, a great shadowy shape loomed out of the darkness. Their Lancaster waited. Slowly, Bill climbed out and walked over to her, his breath white smoke in the frosty air. Together with the flight engineer, he circled JB-361 doing the final checks. Then, rubbing his hands for warmth, he joined the rest of the crew as they smoked their last cigarettes. The crew were restless; all were keyed up and there was a sense of relief as they came to mount the rickety ladder at the back of the Lancaster.

Each found their place, stowed their parachutes and checked their equipment. Bill gave a thumbs-up sign to the ground crew on the battery cart. There were puffs of smoke tinged with flame as one by one the great Merlin engines crackled into life filling the air with noise and vibration. Flt Sgt Davis, the flight engineer, checked the oil pressure and magneto drops then Bill's soft voice came over the intercom, checking round the crew positions to see that all were ready. Finally, they moved slowly out onto the peri-track, joining the line of other Lancasters zigzagging their way to the end of the runway. They waited, watching as, one by one, the Lancasters lifted heavily into the darkness. At last it was their turn. The green Aldis light flashed out at them and they turned onto the runway threshold. The vibration and noise were deafening as, engines at full power, they thundered down the runway before lifting heavily off the ground and clawing their way into the dark night sky. Lancaster JB-361 was one of the last to take off that night, getting airborne at 17.35.

Six hundred and fifty aircraft were taking part in this operation. They found the Luftwaffe waiting for them. German controllers had plotted the direction of the bomber stream and correctly deduced that the target was Frankfurt. En route, they found flares lighting up the sky; the Germans were using them to help them spot their prey. Over Frankfurt, more searchlights lit up the cloud base, shining through the thinner cloud and illuminating the silhouettes of the bombers for the waiting night fighters.

Having deduced where the bombers were heading, the Germans had plenty of time to alert their defences and light a decoy fire 5 miles southeast of the city. Such decoys were used frequently by the Germans to protect cities or vital installations. They were often successful as there was a tendency for bombers to attack fires thinking they were the targets burning. However, although some aircraft bombed the decoy because it was laid to the south of the city and the stream approached from the north, when the usual creep-back occurred, some of their bombs landed accurately on the centre of Frankfurt. Allowing no hint of the anguish he had felt, Bill wrote tersely in his logbook that it was an 'Easy Supporter trip'. Forty-one aircraft were lost that night but 97 Squadron were fortunate. In the ORB for the night, the Duty Officer wrote, no doubt with a deep sense of relief, that, 'All the above aircraft and crews returned safely to base'.[10]

In fact, the raid did more damage than Bomber Command realised at the time. The main railway station and the area around were almost completely destroyed. It is sad that Bill was not to know that in Niedenau, the street where the Meyer family lived, although only four of the whole street of beautiful old houses remained standing after that night, one of the four was Bill's family's house. It had survived and is still standing today. It has become a boutique hotel.

The shock of the events of the 16th were still very much on everyone's minds when on 22 December the burial took place of eight of 97 Squadron's dead at Cambridge City Cemetery. The Station and Squadron Commanding Officers attended, as did a number of officers and NCOs. The bodies of twenty other aircrew from the squadron who died that night were conveyed to their home towns for burial. A member of the squadron accompanied each coffin.

The next couple of days saw Bill and the crew practising bombing runs on Northampton using H2S and doing a brief flying test on JB-361. They were getting used to each other. When the original members of this crew had come together and crewed up they had all been together in the Sergeants' Mess and, training together from the start, there was inevitably a somewhat relaxed attitude to their operating procedure. The uncertainty as to whom they would be flying with had worried them all considerably, and so it was with some relief that Reg wrote to his family that their new pilot was not only a 'good un' but that under him things had tightened up a bit, which he felt was all to the crew's benefit. Meticulous attention to detail and discipline in the air might just improve the odds a bit, and every bit helped.

They were working again on the 23$^{rd.}$ as Bill Coates, on only his third operation, remarked in his diary: 'Just to foster the Christmas spirit in the Big City… Command decided to make us work for our Christmas'.[11] The target was once again Berlin. To prevent the Germans detecting the target early on as they did on the Frankfurt raid, Bomber Command planned much larger course changes for the routing. This had disadvantages; the trip would be far longer and more tiring for the crews and more difficult for the navigators. Also, because of the increased fuel that would be needed, the bomb load would have to be lighter.

The Command also introduced a new procedure. Some crews, usually experienced Pathfinders, were designated to be 'Wind Finders'. This entailed their navigators calculating the winds they were experiencing and radioing them back to Group radio stations. An average wind was calculated from the figures returned. That was then broadcast to the bomber stream every half hour with the idea that everyone would use the same wind and arrive over the target in a more concentrated stream that would offer greater protection from fighters and flak.

Bill and the crew were on the Battle Order again for this raid. He had slipped into the pattern of operational life as though he had never been away. The morning passed slowly. There was no need to do an NFT, a flying test, as they had completed one the previous day in JB-361. At the briefing, they were given a take-off time for late afternoon, but this was later changed as the weather was forecast to deteriorate overnight. The raid was delayed for seven hours. Such delays were nerve-racking and stressful; it was worse still when raids were scrubbed at the very last minute. All the performance of briefing, gathering papers and equipment, getting into flying gear and the mental preparation was wasted and would have to be gone through again for another operation to be ticked off. On this occasion, the seven-hour delay was to allow the bombers to return at first light, giving them a better chance of landing if the weather had worsened. Black Thursday was still on everyone's minds.

It was not until after midnight that the squadron started taking off. A strong and penetrating wind blew across the airfield, whistling around the aircraft. While the inspection was carried out, the rest of the crew stood hunched up, backs to the wind, smoking their last cigarettes. By the time they had finished, the cold had chilled them to the bone and they hastened to climb on board.

Seventeen of the squadron's Lancasters were operating, and it took nearly forty minutes before they were all airborne. Bill was acting as an under training Blind Marker that night. The German controllers did not immediately identify the target and cloud cover and icing made conditions difficult for German fighters, but over Berlin the flak was as relentless as ever. It was a long trip back, punching into strong headwinds as they crossed northern Germany and Holland. Once well out over the North Sea, the tension eased a little. After the long hours spent at 20,000 feet in sub-zero temperatures, they were able to descend over the sea and come off oxygen. The flasks of coffee were passed around; a welcome taste of warmth and a chance to get the rubbery taste of the oxygen mask out of their mouths. A grey misty dawn was breaking as they landed back at 07.20 am. At their dispersal, the engines were silenced; cold, fresh morning air drifted in through the now open door. Slowly, they gathered their gear and stumbled out. It was Christmas Eve. This operation had involved some twenty-four hours of waiting or working. In his logbook, Bill wrote, 'Tiring but easy trip'. A considerable understatement considering the hours of preparation and delay, the eyeball-searing searchlights and fiery streams of flak seeking them out over Berlin and, finally, fighting the exhaustion that set in on the return journey.

For Bomber Command, it was not a successful raid. Equipment often failed and reports show that thirteen of the twenty-three Primary Blind Markers who were meant to use H2S to mark the target were unable to do so as their sets were not working or were unreliable. The final plot photos revealed that nothing had been dropped in the target area; seventy were plotted outside the area and seventy-five remained unplotted as they were even further away.[12]

The weather now worsened; there was to be no flying, operational or otherwise, for the next couple of days. Some ground training took place on the 24th but now men's minds were focused on making the most of Christmas. A determined effort had been made to introduce some Christmas spirit. The Officers' Mess had been transformed; holly and ivy were strung up for decoration and in the evening the celebrations started. Christmas and other celebrations in the mess were usually riotous, boozy affairs. Sing-songs, practical jokes, all sorts of wild and boisterous games went on and almost anything could happen and did. Nothing was too extreme. It was not unknown for fire extinguishers to be set off, flares too. Men 'walked' on the ceiling, pianos were known to catch fire or roll downstairs… anything to release the intolerable tension under which they lived. Pushing themselves to extremes on operations, aircrew took their recreation to similar lengths. This was tolerated by those in authority who recognised the need to let off steam despite that fact that it often got somewhat out of hand. This year, though, at the back of everyone's minds were the squadron's recent terrible losses.

At breakfast on Christmas morning there were some sore heads around. Many attended church, after which it was time for the officers, including Bill, Reg and Bernard, to go down to serve the other ranks their Christmas lunch. Their own Christmas meal would be served in the evening.

Christmas passed by quickly and the next few days were spent in more training. Bill and his new crew were getting used to working together. The crew were keen to have a ride in Bill's Jaguar so they all piled in for a trip to a local pub one evening. On the 29th, it was back to work. After doing an air test in the late morning, they waited to see what the target would be.

It was Berlin. Once again, Bill was an under training Blind Marker carrying no flares but a 4,000lb 'Cookie' and five 1,000lb general purpose bombs. It was to be a maximum effort with 712 aircraft dispatched. Bomber Command tried a new tactic. As Martin Middlebrook explains:

> An ingenious feature of the tactical plan was a 'double spoof' by Mosquitoes. There would first be a diversionary raid on Magdeburg, which was intended to look like a diversion but this would be followed by a second Mosquito raid on Leipzig which, it was hoped, would look like the opening of the main raid and draw off the German fighters leaving the bombers unmolested as they flew on to Berlin.[13]

The ruse worked and the German controllers sent their fighters to Magdeburg and by the time they switched to Berlin the raid was nearly over. However, the flak was another matter. Berlin was defended by three massive flak towers built in a triangular pattern that formed a defensive ring around the heart of the city. Each flak tower consisted of a pair; a Command Tower that received and relayed targeting information from the giant Wurzberg radar to the Gun Tower, a massive four-cornered tower with 128mm twin mounted flak guns at each corner with a range of up to 35,000 feet. On platforms lower down the towers were lighter calibre flak guns, 28 and 37mm. These formidable defences were linked to searchlight batteries. A master searchlight with its blue beam would pick out a target and then three satellite searchlights would lock on to it, 'coning' it in the glare. Radars tracked the aircraft's height and speed and fed their predictions to the guns. Their priority targets were planes at the front of the bomber stream, in other words, the Pathfinders.

Arriving over Berlin, Bill found that the predictors had correctly assessed their height. The guns maintained a constant barrage; wave after wave of flak streaked through the air and burst around them. He felt JB-361 shudder as flak slammed into her. They started the bombing run and Reg, now lying flat out in the nose, gave final directions to Bill before finally pressing the little button that would unleash thousands of pounds of high explosive onto the target. The aircraft leapt up, suddenly released from the tremendous weight of the bombs. There was the usual agonising pause waiting for the bomb photo, and then at last Bill turned for home, manoeuvring the Lancaster through the curtains of flak that the German gunners drew across the sky.

While JB-361 had sustained comparatively light flak damage, several members of the squadron were not so lucky. Two were severely damaged by the heavy flak, while another reported, 'Starboard wing tip cut off in collision with Lancaster at 20,000 19.46 hours. Collision occurred as bombing runs started'.[14]

As New Year's Eve approached, the crew wondered if they would be working. The betting was that they would be, but tentative plans were made just in case they got a chance to celebrate. The 31st was a Friday. On checking the board, Bill discovered he would be spending his New Year's Eve over Germany. At the briefing it turned out to be the 'Big City' again. There were light-hearted promises to make it a New Year that Hitler would not forget, but in their bellies the crews felt the old familiar tightening at the thought of yet another visit to Berlin. In preparation, Bill took JB-361 for a flying test. However, once again the weather intervened and the operation was cancelled. On this occasion, the news was met with shouts of absolute delight, and plans were swiftly made to celebrate New Year's Eve in true RAF style.

CHAPTER EIGHTEEN
THE BLEAK MIDWINTER

When he awoke the next day, Bill, like many others, wondered what the new year would bring. 1943 had seen the war slowly turning in the Allies' favour. In February, Hitler's armies had suffered their first major defeat at Stalingrad and throughout the year the Soviet armies continued to advance. The Germans had been defeated in North Africa in May and the autumn had seen the Allied invasion of Italy. In the middle of the year, the Battle of Hamburg had been a major success for Bomber Command. However, the Battle of Berlin would be a different story. This winter saw the men of Bomber Command facing their worst months. Aircrew casualties mounted rapidly as Arthur Harris focused on attempting to destroy Berlin.

Morale in the Command was already low. Men could not help but be aware of the increasing losses or the realisation that their chances of surviving a tour were decreasing all the time. In the long, freezing, dark winter nights they faced countless lengthy trips to the most well-defended targets. Not only this, but a decision had recently been taken to increase bomb loads. This meant a loss of performance and manoeuvrability, with the result that the crews were more vulnerable to flak and enemy fighters and had to spend more time over the target. The autumn had already seen an increased rate of 'early returns', with aircraft turning back due to real or imagined equipment failures. For some crews this additional risk was asking too much and, to lighten their load and improve performance, they would drop their 'Cookies' in the North Sea on their way to a target. Despite their fears, though, most crews continued to show a devotion to duty and truly exemplary fortitude.

Bomber Command and the Luftwaffe were engaged in an ongoing tactical contest. If one side developed a new technique, the other would devise a countermeasure. In the summer of 1943, the introduction of 'Window' had given the RAF the upper hand. The Germans responded with the expansion of a technique known as *Wilde Sau* or Wild Boar. Previously, the radar-controlled fighters were limited to attacking within the confines of their 'boxes'. Wilde Sau involved freelance night fighters sent up over a target city to seek out and attack the bombers visually when they were at their most vulnerable as they flew straight and level on their bombing runs. Of course, they then ran the risk of getting caught in their own flak, but to prevent that, Flak Commanders would restrict the height of their gunfire to below an agreed limit and the fighters would keep above that. These fighters proved very effective and the majority of Bomber Command's losses were due to attacks by these night fighters.

Another plan had also been devised in the summer of 1943; this was *Zahme Sau* or Tame Boar. However, this plan could not be put into operation immediately, as it called for the introduction of a new airborne radar, the Lichtenstein *SN-2* that operated on a frequency that could not be jammed by Window. Zahme Sau involved twin-engined night fighters attacking the bomber stream on the way to and from the target. To do this, German ground controllers had to be able to track the bomber stream on its way to the target. This they did by means of radar that could detect H2S transmissions. The knowledge that Bomber Command used H2S for major raids enabled the controllers to identify which was the main target and ignore diversionary tactics. Controllers would report the progress of the bomber stream by radio and the fighters would head for that area, sometimes holding at beacons until the stream arrived. From there, the fighters would rely on their own radar to pick up a bomber and then close in on it.

It came as no surprise to the crews when they heard that Arthur Harris had chosen to open the new year with a raid on his favourite target, Berlin. Bill and his crew were to act as Blind Backers-Up on this raid. Take-off was originally planned for mid-evening, but once again it was put back due to the weather. The hours of waiting passed slowly. Bill, like many others, found it difficult to relax, his mind filled with thoughts of the night ahead over Berlin.

The original plan had been for a long route north over Denmark before turning south towards Berlin, but with the change in take-off time, the route had to be shortened to one directly across Holland so that the bomber stream could return before dawn broke. It was not until after midnight that Bill took off into the icy night sky. It was dark and overcast as the Lancaster climbed slowly up through layers of cloud. Approaching the Dutch coast, huge flashes could be seen lighting up the thick, unbroken cloud as the anti-aircraft guns started firing. The crews had been warned that there would be cloud over Berlin and that they should descend to 18,000 feet when over the target to see the original markers. As Blind Backers-Up, they were to use H2S to locate and re-mark the target but on this occasion, as on so many others, the H2S set broke down and so they bombed on a cluster of Wanganui flares.

It was to be a long trip back. The routing was first to the southwest then south of the Ruhr and over Belgium. Battling against the strong headwinds, Bill wove his way along the tops of clouds, anxious to avoid the icing conditions within them. Tom Shaw, the flight engineer, kept an eagle eye on their fuel consumption. A whitish blur was all that could be seen below as they flew towards the coast of England. Once again, it was shrouded in fog. After descending through thick mist, they found snow flurries greeting them nearer the ground. When they were finally overhead Bourn, Jim McLeish broke radio silence to ask for permission to land. They touched down at 7.20 am. Numb with cold and exhaustion, they slowly emerged. In the dull morning light, a cold white world greeted them as wisps of snow drifted slowly down, blanketing sounds. Their breath made clouds in the icy air as they walked, feet softly crunching across the snow-covered tarmac, to the waiting transport.

Bill's logbook states, '1st Marker Trip (Blind B.U.) Y U/S. Easy but tiring trip. Little flak over target. No fighters seen. 10/10th'. In this at least he was lucky. Twenty-eight Lancasters went missing that night, almost all due to fighters; one was a 97 Squadron aircraft. P/O Mooney's crew did not return. 'Y' refers to the H2S set and '10/10' indicates the target was completely hidden by cloud.

The ORB for that night states, 'Slight fighter activity and many scarecrow flares'.[1] In the autumn of 1943, crews started reporting seeing explosions, often with no evidence of an attack. They were told that these were scarecrow flares, pyrotechnic devices that simulated a fully loaded bomber exploding with the aim of demoralising the RAF crews. However, post-war research has found no evidence of such a weapon. What crews were seeing was actual bombers being shot down, usually by night fighters using another new technique known as *Schrage Musik*, literally 'slanting music', the contemporary slang for jazz.

A fighter equipped with Schrage Musik had two cannon mounted obliquely upwards. So armed, it was able to creep up unseen in the blind spot under the belly of the target before firing at the unprotected underside of the aircraft. Instead of normal tracer, they used 'dim' tracer, which, almost invisible, did not serve to attract the attention of the bombers' gunners. Sometimes they dispensed with tracer altogether. Once underneath the bomber, the fighter pilot could see its silhouette clearly against either sky or cloud and the bomber was a sitting duck. The only thing the fighter had to beware of was an own goal if they were too close and the exploding bomber brought them down as well. This happened on several occasions. For this reason, the fighters preferred to fire into the fuel tanks in the wings rather than into the bomb bay, where the resulting explosion might blow them out of the sky too.

Unbelievably, despite clear and ample evidence visible on damaged aircraft, Bomber Command remained officially unaware of the deadly upward-firing cannons used in Schrage Musik for many months. In view of all the evidence, this was extraordinary. During the long winter nights in 1944, the Luftwaffe were able to employ this weapon with impunity, inflicting mounting casualties on Bomber Command.

By the time the crew had been debriefed and had had breakfast it was 9.30 am. Drawing the curtains to shut out the daylight, Bill fell wearily into bed and was asleep immediately. Other officers could be heard coming and going but he remained oblivious. Around lunchtime, an unwelcome voice drifted into his dreams. A hand was gently shaking him awake and informing him that he was on ops that night and there was a briefing to attend. Opening his eyes, he found his batman waiting to hand him a cup of strong RAF tea. Forcing his bleary eyes to focus, Bill picked up the cup and slowly drank the tea. It didn't help – every inch of his body cried out for more sleep. Wearily he forced himself out of bed and dressed quickly in the chilly air. Frost was etched on the window and it was still snowing, the light flakes drifting gently down, hiding the ugly cinder paths and softening the crude outlines of the Nissen huts. A wash of whitish mist hung in the air, broken only by the snow-clad branches of trees reaching up towards the lowering sky. Surely there would be no flying today.

After the demanding sortie last night with the late return, it was expected that operations would be cancelled. However, Harris had other ideas and to everyone's amazement another raid was ordered to go ahead.

In the afternoon Bill made his way to the briefing. Tired crews sat slumped in their chairs and the usual cigarette fug filled the air as the men waited. The mounting tension was broken as the Commanding Officer arrived and walked up to the map. As he pulled away the curtain, all eyes followed the ribbon to the target. They watched with disbelief as they took in where the ribbon ended. Berlin. A murmur swept around the room and a wave of shock and incredulity washed over the tired faces. After last night it seemed inconceivable that they should be sent back again barely twenty-four hours later. The reaction was the same elsewhere. In another Pathfinder Squadron that had also been to Berlin the night before, the crews' reactions were noted by Wing Commander Philip Patrick, a Flight Commander in 7 Squadron:

> That was the nearest thing I ever saw to mutiny in the R.A.F., when the guys walked in and saw the map showing Berlin again. There was a rumble of what I might call amazement, or horror, or disbelief. The Station Commander quietened the chaps down and there was no trouble, but you can imagine what it was like to be dead tired and then having to go again.[2]

At Bourn too there was no trouble. Harris was known as 'Butch' or 'Butcher' to his men, so, no surprise that he was living up to his nickname. The murmuring quickly died down and the men settled down with a weary acceptance of what was being asked of them. Navigators took down details of turning points, heights and timings. The forecast weather en route was not promising, with icing conditions and cloud extending up to 28,000 feet. At the briefing, a warning was issued telling crews to beware of '… fighters operating over our own and enemy coasts. It is suspected that some of our aircraft were shot down by them last night'.[3]

The target was not the only cause of concern. The route was to be almost straight in and straight out again, with a short 'dog leg' a little before Berlin to allow the bombers to take advantage of a strong northwesterly wind. There was to be no attempt to disguise the main target and keep the Germans guessing. The approach led over the Zuider Zee, and this would be the eighth time in ten raids this route had been used. The German night fighters knew it well and would no doubt be waiting.

Anyone who could be spared was now set to work clearing snow from the runways. At the dispersals the ground crews worked flat out under arc lights preparing the recently returned Lancasters for yet another sortie. All maintenance was done outside. The 'Erks', as they were known, worked in the bitter cold, hands sore and chapped, racing against time to sort out damage and problems reported the night before and to complete the comprehensive daily inspection of all the aircraft systems. Then the fuel bowsers started on their ponderous rounds, stopping to refuel each aircraft. Snow-dappled ammunition trains followed them shortly afterwards.

Take-off time was late. Around 22.00, Bill and the crew were driven to their dispersal. They were to act as a Blind Backers-Up once again. It was midnight before they took off. The forecast for the weather en route was bad, clouds up to 28,000 feet with embedded CBs (thunderstorms). This meant there would be ice and turbulence to deal with. They would have to pick their way through this to even get to the target. Once out over the North Sea, they found themselves already in heavy cloud. Purple strands of static electricity danced across the windscreen (St Elmo's fire) and Bill felt the controls become heavier as ice began to build up on the airframe. He struggled on but many aircraft found themselves unable to continue. The weather was every bit as bad as forecast and the heavy icing caused problems for several 97 Squadron Lancasters. One Lancaster reported, 'Aircraft late on target due to ASI icing up before reaching enemy coast', ASI being the airspeed indicator, a vital piece of equipment. Another Lancaster became so heavily iced-up over the North Sea that it was only able to reach 13,000 feet. Unable to continue, they bombed Texel airfield in the Netherlands as a last resort before turning back for home.[4]

That night saw '...the highest rate of early returns in the whole of the Battle of Berlin'.[5] Sixty bombers turned back. Even allowing for the fifteen that returned in error when they received a recall signal meant for some Wellingtons deployed on a mine-laying operation, it was an abnormally high rate of returns. It can only have been a reaction to the demands being made on crews in the winter of 1944. The combination of mounting losses, extremely bad weather, heavier bomb loads and longer trips meant the strain was telling. The repeated sorties to Berlin were resulting in sheer physical and mental exhaustion in those who did manage to return, and so many did not.

There were no diversionary raids planned that night and so, on the approach to Berlin, the fighters were waiting and wasted no time in attacking. In his logbook, Bill mentions the many fighters and fighter flares lighting up the sky, turning night into day and making the bombers hideously visible. Approaching the target, Bill had started weaving when suddenly, slightly below him, a fighter appeared, closing in on a Lancaster just ahead. A stream of tracer laced through the air, hitting the right wing which erupted in a sea of flame as the fuel tank ignited. Bill and Tom, the engineer, watched horrified as the Lancaster turned into a huge ball of fire lighting up the sky. A few seconds later, it exploded, sending a blaze of multi-coloured flares arching across the sky. The end of yet another Pathfinder. Bill struggled with the controls as the shock waves threw JB-361 up in the air. No time to think about that crew; just keep on going; get back on track and start the bombing run. Shards of flak sounded a constant patter on the fuselage. Through the intercom, the crew heard the rasp of Reg's voice calling for the bomb doors to be opened and held their breath as he gave Bill the last corrections before finally uttering the words they were waiting for: "Bombs gone." Then long, long seconds till the bomb photo was taken before Bernie gave Bill the new course to steer and they turned sharply for home.

The return was even worse. By now, the Germans had sent all available fighters to Berlin. As well as being lit by the fighter flares, crews now found themselves silhouetted against the thin cloud by searchlights. The bomber stream was less concentrated than usual because of the number of early returns, and the fighters exacted a heavy toll on the returning Lancasters. Bill landed at 6.30 am. Slowly, the crew made their way out. Their legs stiff with cold, they clambered down the ladder. In the bus, no one said a word. Bill, in his usual understated way, wrote that it had been a 'Tiring trip'. Pathfinder casualties were particularly heavy that night, with ten aircraft and crews lost.

The ORB for 3 January states, 'Most crews resting'.[6] The last two nights' raids had stretched crews to the limit and beyond; the men were suffering from profound mental and physical exhaustion.

Flying a Lancaster was a physically exhausting task as it bucketed, yawed and rolled, buffeted by the slipstreams of other aircraft en route and then tossed around by exploding flak over the target. Then there were the engines, the four roaring Merlins battering the senses for hours on end. Despite the mounting exhaustion, there was the need for constant alertness, the knowledge that a minute's loss of concentration might bring disaster on them all. Always somewhere at the back of the mind the thought: would it be their turn tonight to 'Fail to Return'? The stress endured by aircrew for months on end was exacerbated by the constant reminders of their ever-decreasing odds of surviving in the form of missing places in the mess each morning. Inevitably, this had an effect on morale in Bomber Command. Perhaps the greatest surprise of all is that so many managed to cope and continue.

Bill and the crew were not part of the next operation when the squadron sent twenty aircraft to Stettin on the 5th. Yet another two 97 Squadron crews 'Failed to Return' from this operation. For those that remained there was no let-up in training. When the weather permitted, there were air-to-air firing, fighter affiliation and bombing exercises, and also practice in using H2S and SBA.

During the full moon period from 6 January there were no major operations planned by Bomber Command. The squadron had a new commander. Wing Commander E.J. Carter took over from Squadron Leader Dunnicliffe on 7 January. Operations resumed on 15 January with a raid on Brunswick when twenty-one crews from 97 Squadron were dispatched. Bill and the crew were not on the Battle Order. Once again, two crews failed to return.

The weather over the next few days was so bad that, exceptionally for Bomber Command, no operations were launched for five days. When on 20 January the weather cleared, dawning bright and sunny, Harris immediately returned to his main target, Berlin.

It had become clear to the Command that the straight-in routes to Berlin were no longer an option. The Luftwaffe knew the route too well and would just lie in wait till the bombers appeared, and pick them off. Alternative routes would have to be found, but these would be yet-longer routes that would be even more tiring for the crews. More fuel would be needed so the bomb load would have to be further reduced. The route chosen for this night was to the north, the planners hoping that it would look as though the raid would be on Kiel. To this end, diversionary raids by Mosquitos on Kiel and Hanover were also planned.

The take-off time was earlier than usual, being in the late afternoon. A weak winter sun hung low in the sky and cast long shadows over the airfield as the crew were driven to their dispersal. The last rays played over them as they stood around in the fading light. The crew were acting as Primary Blind Markers, setting down the initial target markers for this operation, a role demanding the utmost accuracy. Settling into 'their' aircraft, Lancaster JB-361, Bill and the crew began their checks. In this role, they would be at the very front of the stream and they were the first of the squadron to take off, becoming airborne at 17.45 and setting course over Cromer. As darkness fell, the skies over the east of England slowly filled as 769 aircraft climbed, heading like flocks of giant birds to merge into one stream out over the North Sea. From his lonely seat in the rear turret, Robbie Roberts watched as wave after wave of aircraft slowly formed up in the skies behind them.

As they approached Germany, the weather worsened and the temperature plummeted. Once again, they found themselves flying in a thick layer of cloud. This had been forecast and the cloud had one benefit as it prevented some German fighters from taking off. Not all, though, and a substantial number were dispatched to beacons to await the arrival of the bomber stream. The diversionary raids were identified as such and ignored, and Berlin was again accurately identified as the target. The attacks started as the stream turned southeast towards Berlin.

At the head of the bomber stream, Bill approached Berlin to find it completely blanketed in cloud. Batteries of searchlights played underneath the cloud layer silhouetting the bombers above it and making them an easy target. Reg Pike lay stretched flat out in the Perspex nose, adjusting the bombsight. He took his time, far too much time for the rest of the crew, until he called, "Bomb doors open," gave final instructions to Bill and, at last, reported, "Bombs gone." After dropping the target indicators and bombs, they continued south before turning west towards Holland. The Luftwaffe fighters that had abandoned them over Berlin to dodge their own flak now reappeared.

The new Tame Boar tactics meant that attacks were no longer concentrated around the target, but fighters were positioned to attack all along the route. As they approached Munster, a fresh wave of fighters attacked. Immediately ahead, a vast brilliant orange explosion lit up the sky; yet another Lancaster would not be coming home. Suddenly they felt the thud of cannon fire run through the fuselage. At the same time, Robbie, the rear gunner, yelled, "Corkscrew, left. Go go." Adrenalin flooded through his body as Bill threw the aircraft into a steep dive, twisting and turning in a classic corkscrew manoeuvre. Robbie and Archie, the gunners, peered out into the darkness, waiting to get the fighter lined up in their sights if he followed them down. They hung onto their guns, anxiously quartering the sky. Finally, Robbie reported on the intercom that he had gone. Bill heaved with all his might on the controls, calling for Tom to help him. Together, they slowly wrenched the control column back and JB-361 finally levelled out and then slowly started climbing. Bernie called out the new heading and, with aching arms and somewhat breathless, Bill turned them back on course. The well-practised corkscrew had saved them. Timing was vital. If the gunner called for a corkscrew too early, the fighter could just follow the bomber down, but, when called at the right moment, the fighter, whose speed was greater than the bomber, would overshoot the bomber's turn. Back at Bourn, the ground crew found that cannon shells had passed through the radiator of the starboard engine but luckily not the engine itself. They immediately set to work to change it. JB-361 had had a lucky escape. Another had not; F/O Wakley and his crew failed to return to Bourn that night.

The ORB for 21 January states, 'Weather unfit for flying, no NFTs carried out for tonight's operations for which 21 aircraft are detailed'.[7] The fact that there had been no test flights of the aircraft may account for the problems some of the squadron experienced that night, especially with their notoriously unreliable H2S sets. The chosen target was Magdeburg, just 60 miles west of Berlin. Magdeburg was a rail and road hub with war-related industries that included engineering works, the manufacture of explosives and synthetic oil production. The RAF had not 'visited' it before. There was to be a diversionary raid on Berlin itself.

Once again, Bill and the crew were to act as Primary Blind Markers and also as Wind Finders. This was the system introduced in late December 1944, with selected crews in the first wave of bombers sending back data on the actual winds found so that this data could be broadcast to the bomber stream for navigators to amend their plots.

The briefing was at 13.00 but, as happened so often, the take-off time was delayed, leaving the crews with the usual hours of nervous waiting. It was almost 20.00 before the twenty-one Lancasters rumbled out of their dispersals and joined the line, weaving along the perimeter track. Running off the track was all too easy in the dark, and one aircraft did just that and became bogged down in the soft ground. The following Lancaster paused, then with infinite care the pilot just managed to edge it past the stranded aircraft. Slowly, the rest followed.

The bomber stream set course over Cromer. As it set out over the North Sea, German controllers were monitoring it and fighters were directed on to it even before the stream reached the German coast. Bernie had trouble identifying the target and they bombed Brandenburg in error. Clearly, they were uncertain as to their whereabouts even as they bombed for, as Bill recorded in his logbook, they had retained their target indicators. Standing orders were that, for obvious reasons, Primary Markers' target indicators should not be dropped unless the target was positively identified. Another 97 Squadron crew, that of S/L Peter de Wesselow, also misidentified the target and bombed Dessau in error. The winds were much stronger than forecast that night, which probably contributed to these errors. Both crews reported seeing fires burning in Magdeburg on their way back. Bill was not at all happy with this result, noting in his logbook, 'A poor trip'.

Bomber Command lost fifty-seven aircraft on this raid, a disastrous loss rate of 8.8%. The Halifax squadrons suffered worst: their loss rate was a devastating 15.6%. As was now the norm, yet another 97 Squadron crew, that of F/L Roberts, failed to return. The new Tame Boar tactics were proving alarmingly effective. However, this night also saw the deaths of two of Germany's leading fighter aces. One was Major Heinrich Prinz zu Sayn-Wittgenstein, who had shot down eighty-three aircraft and was a German hero and holder of the Knight's Cross with Oak Leaves. This was upgraded after his death to the very rare Oak Leaves with Swords. The other German ace killed that night was Hauptmann Manfred Meurer, the commander of 1/NJG/1 (Group I of Nachtjagdegeschwader), based at Venlo in Holland, who had downed sixty-five aircraft. The bomber he had attacked blew up above him, causing his Heinkel 219 to crash.

The next five days saw a break in operational flying. On the 25th, the crew saw their names once more on the Battle Order. At the briefing at 15.00, the crew were given the routing for the target and afterwards went straight to the mess for their pre-operation meal. At 16.25, the route was changed, the orders being relayed by teleprinter from Bomber Command. Immediately, the navigators started frantically reworking their figures. At 16.40 once again the teleprinter stuttered into life with the news that the operation had been cancelled. By this time, all the planning had been done, twice in the case of the navigators. After all this preparation and tension, this was not a wholly welcome respite. Every man found his own way of coping with the tension of an incipient operation, but the stress as they geared up mentally for the task ahead was cumulative and it would now all have to be gone through again on another occasion.

The respite was not for long. On the 27th, Bill and the crew were to operate as Blind Backer-Up. As they tramped into the briefing, some felt sure that the relentless focus on Berlin would have shifted. Once again, though, when the board was uncovered, the ribbon led straight to Berlin. A groan ran around the room. The forecast was, once again, for cloud cover over Berlin and icing conditions en route. After the terrible losses on the last operation, the route to and from Berlin had been carefully planned with a substantial diversionary raid, including aircraft with H2S being laid on ahead of the main force.

The routing was ingenious – after crossing the North Sea, the stream turned southeast on a course that appeared to miss Berlin and threaten towns such as Leipzig, Hanover or Brunswick. Then, while Mosquitos continued on this course dropping massive amounts of Window, the main force suddenly turned northeast and headed for Berlin. It had been hoped to bomb visually but the weather over the target was reported as worsening, and a couple of hours before take-off this was changed to targeting using the H2S radar.

This devious route did largely prevent the Luftwaffe attacks en route but once over the target the fighters were active once more. The return route was a long drag southwest over Germany, then across Belgium and France, entailing nerve-racking hours spent trying to stay alert for night fighters. Bill's voice came over the intercom at regular intervals, checking up to see all was well with his crew. He was particularly concerned about Robbie Roberts, completely isolated in the rear turret. It was 1 am before Bill landed back at Bourn. The strain of those long hours over enemy territory is evident from his logbook which states, 'Very long stooge back across France. Tiring trip'.

The pressure was on. The squadron were ordered to take part in a maximum-effort raid the following night. Bill and the crew were flying again, as were most of the crews that had flown the night before. Men shuffled into the briefing room, their careworn faces sallow and pinched. When the target was announced, there was a moment's stunned silence before murmurs of dismay ran around the room as men looked at the map: it couldn't be Berlin yet again. It was. Bad weather meant that the take-off time was put back twice, ratcheting up the tension and leaving the crews on tenterhooks. It was not until 01.15 that they finally took off. As so often, ice was a problem, with one Lancaster becoming so heavily iced up that it had to return.

Once again, Bomber Command was imaginative in its planning. In the afternoon and early evening, Mosquitos bombed Berlin and airfields in Holland while Halifaxes and Stirlings laid mines in Kiel Bay. The route planned, both outbound and inbound, was well to the north over Denmark and the Baltic. While this was out of the range of many Luftwaffe night fighter bases, the longer distance meant a reduced bomb load and extra exhausting hours flying.

As the main operation got underway, yet another diversionary raid was laid on, this time to Hanover. These diversions were successful and the bomber stream arrived overhead Berlin relatively unscathed. Acting as a Blind Backer-Up, Bill arrived to find Berlin covered in thick, icy cloud. However, the aiming point was successfully identified using H2S, and Reg, the air bomber, watched with satisfaction as the marker flares cascaded swiftly down, followed immediately by the target indicators and bombs before they turned northeast for the return trip. For once, flak was not a problem, as it was aimed rather low that night. The downside of that was that it allowed the fighters free rein to seek their prey. Suddenly Robbie's voice came over the intercom from his rear turret, warning Bill as he saw a dark shape sweep past. All held their breath and listened intently. However, the Messerschmitt 110 either did not see them or had another target in his sights and they flew on unhindered. Around them, others were not so lucky as the Wild Boar fighters attacked fiercely over the burning city. P/O Raalte in another 97 Squadron Lancaster was attacked and severely damaged, and his rear gunner, F/Sgt Laurie, was killed before he finally managed to evade the fighter and limp home on three engines.

Returning, they faced a long haul back following an almost identical route over the Baltic and Denmark. Not only was there thick cloud and icing conditions but they had to punch into a strong headwind. Crossing Denmark, Tom, the flight engineer, watched the fuel gauge intently; the long route and icy conditions meant that fuel consumption needed careful monitoring. Once over England, the grey morning light revealed a bleak, frost-coated countryside. It was 08.00 as they landed. Heavy with fatigue, they filed slowly out, fumbling with fingers numb with cold for much-needed cigarettes. There was still the debriefing to be got through before they could rest. As usual, in the Ops room, they were waiting for the aircraft to return, the WAAFs chalking up the landing times beside the pilots' names as they came in. The Ops room staff knew the latest time an aircraft could be expected to return safely but always waited a little longer. That morning, a WAAF had to write the bleak letters FTR (Failed to Return) against two more 97 Squadron crews' names.

Bill wrote that he found the 'Danish route excellent', as it had kept them out of the way of some of the heavy fighter activity they had experienced previously. However, this long route took its toll and an unknown number of aircraft came down in the sea. Some were close to the English coast and were rescued. Many were not. Often, men would not survive the initial ditching. When a Lancaster ditched in the sea, the tail section usually broke off and sank immediately, trapping the men inside.

The squadron was rested on 29 January and Bill and his crew were not among the twenty-one crews scheduled for an operation to Berlin on the 30th. This must have been some sort of record, as no fewer than six crews were led by Squadron Leaders and one crew by the newly promoted Wing Commander Dunnicliffe. While they all returned safely that night, another two crews from the squadron did not.

97 Squadron had now lost eleven crews in the nine operations carried out in January. A total of seventy-eight men had died in four weeks. These were terrible losses, and following so soon after the disastrous night of 16 December when eight aircraft were lost, it left squadron morale at rock bottom. The odds were all too easy for the crews to calculate. During the Battle of Berlin, the loss rate had risen to such a degree that there was almost no chance now

of completing a tour. The statistics make chilling reading. In 1943, one crew out of six would survive a first tour. Bad enough, but for a crew on a second tour, the odds dropped considerably to a mere one crew out of forty.[8] Newcomers were the most vulnerable. Pilot Officer Wakley and his crew were lost on their first sortie on 20 January, and Pilot Officer Hart and his crew were lost on their second sortie on 30 January. Four other crews had only a few trips under their belts. However, while skill and experience improved the odds, they were no guarantee of survival – five of the lost crews were very experienced, most of them on their second tours.

CHAPTER NINETEEN
THE RISING COST

February dawned grey and overcast. Dark clouds hung low in the sky, threatening rain. Visibility was poor, the airfield fading away in the distance in the dull wintry mist. There would be no flying. In the cold that afternoon, some of the officers and men of the squadron attended the funeral of F/Sgt Laurie, the Air Gunner killed over Berlin on 28 January. The 23-year-old Australian was buried in the Air Force Plot at Cambridge City Cemetery. It was a sombre start to the month.

The next two weeks provided a brief respite; there was a lull in Bomber Command operations due to the full moon and bad weather. The squadron were kept busy doing 'make and mend', training and attending lectures. Snow prevented flying training on some days but, whenever possible, day, night and Bullseye exercises were undertaken.

At Bourn there were frequent air raid warnings and on 3 February some of the squadron who had been on a training exercise had to be diverted to other bases due to the threat of 'hostiles' operating in the area. On 21 January, as Bill was on a sortie to Magdeburg, the Luftwaffe had begun a series of attacks on London. These became known as the 'Little Blitz'. Although not on the same scale as the Blitz proper, there were heavy raids on London and targets in southeast England. Winston Churchill wryly remarked, "It's quite like old times again!"[1]

Efforts at keeping aircrew occupied included a lecture on 'Photographic Interpretation of Bomb Damage', with Squadron Leader Morris explaining how much could be revealed by the bomb plot photos; perhaps this was an effort to try and convince the crews that the hated extra minute flying straight and level over the target to take the photo was worthwhile. Of more practical use to the aircrews was a lecture on 'Evasion and Escape' by F/L Durnford. The men listened attentively to this. Crews had all heard stories of men being machine-gunned as they dangled helplessly from parachutes, and shot out of hand or lynched by mobs as 'Terrorflieger' if brought down over Germany. In 1943, Heinrich Himmler had stated that it was not the business of the police to interfere when civilians clashed with 'Terrorflieger'.[22] This amounted to no less than open season on aircrew – civilians were to be allowed to do as they pleased with downed airmen. Bailing out was a terrifying prospect at any time, but over Germany it was understood that the chance of survival was minimal. Bill shifted uneasily in his seat – with his family background, it was a particular worry.

By the 11th, the CO was running out of ideas for how to occupy his men. As a result and to their dismay, the men found themselves condemned to a morning spent doing various sports. This was not a popular idea at any time, but especially not in midwinter. The following day, an icy wind whistled around the Nissen huts and overhead the skies were again white and lowering. The temperature plummeted. In the late afternoon, it started to snow, soft white flakes covering the bleak functionality of the airfield in a white blanket. Men glanced out of windows, watching and calculating the odds on operating that night. The flakes were larger now and falling faster. By 18.00, it was clear there would be no flying that night. Twenty-one crews who were due to take part in a night navigation exercise had a riotous evening in their messes instead.

First light on the 13th revealed a gentle coating of pristine snow. It lay across the airfield, merging the familiar shapes of buildings and aircraft with the ground in a seamless blur. Frost glazed the windows and wind whipped the snow into small drifts against buildings. The runways were invisible. This beautiful transformation did not last long, though, as all free aircrew were swiftly dispatched with shovels and brushes to clear the runways and dispersals.

Twenty-four crews, including Bill's, were on the board for a sortie that night. As they heard the night's target, many felt their stomachs knot. Berlin again. Bill and the crew were to act as Blind Markers. The squadron geared up, crews attended briefings, navigators worked on their plans and radio operators made notes. After the pre-op meal, they went through all the usual rigmarole that kitting-up involved and were bussed to their dispersals. The crews were actually boarding their aircraft when word came through that the operation had been cancelled. Once again, all the effort of mental and physical preparation was to be wasted. Crews, their adrenaline already flowing, now had to try to wind down and face the fact that they would probably have to go through the same ritual again tomorrow.

The next day saw the snow slowly turning to rain, but it was not until 15 February that the raid on Berlin was on again. The two-week respite had allowed Bomber Command to re-equip the depleted squadrons with aircraft and crews, and that night saw the largest force yet sent to Berlin with a total of 891 aircraft taking part: 561 Lancasters, 314 Halifaxes and sixteen Mosquitos. Bill and the crew in JB-361 were acting as Blind Backers-Up. It was an earlier take-off than usual and JB-361 was airborne at 17.15. Once again, they were taking the long route over Denmark that lay too far north for many of the German fighters. The operation had been carefully planned, with two diversionary measures. One was a mine-laying sortie over the Kiel Bay and the other a simulated raid on Frankfurt. The Germans ignored both and their controllers picked up the bomber stream as it crossed the North Sea. However, once the Germans had identified Berlin as the target, they ordered their fighters not to attack over the city in order to allow the flak gunners free rein. Many fighters ignored this and attacked relentlessly as the bombers arrived over the city. Unteroffizier Benno Gramlich, a Junkers 88 pilot, was one such young pilot: 'I decided to fly into the flak. The earlier night-fighter crews had gained their successes in the box fighting but we "young crews" had to find our bombers wherever we could'.[3]

En route over Denmark, Robbie Roberts, the rear gunner, got on the intercom and reported that his turret was partially inoperative. After some discussion, it was decided they would carry on. The rear turret was a vulnerable enough position when it was working; a malfunction could well be lethal for its occupant and probably the whole aircraft as fighters nearly always attacked from the rear. Bill asked Archie Barrowman in the mid-upper turret to keep an extra-sharp lookout.

Berlin was completely covered in cloud but the visibility was good above it. German fighters made the most of this and homed in on the heavily laden bombers. Unable to visually identify the target, they bombed using H2S, six seconds early according to Bill's log. As Bernie plotted their progress home, he was delighted to find they were making good time thanks to a following wind. They landed back at Bourn after more than seven and a half hours in the air. It had been another long, demanding night.

Bomber Command was satisfied. This raid caused enormous damage to the city, mainly in the centre and to the important industrial area of Siemensstadt to the southwest. In all, twenty-six Lancasters and their crews failed to return. One of them was P/O McLean and his crew from 97 Squadron.

On 16 February, twenty-one crews, including Bill's, were working. As men trudged through pouring rain on their way to the briefing, they glanced at the scudding low clouds, wondering about the weather and what awaited them. The curtain covering the operational map was pulled aside and the jaded crews looked on in horror: it was Berlin yet again. With weary resignation, the crews wrote down the details and made their preparations, only for the sortie to be cancelled. With frayed nerves, the crews dispersed to their messes to slowly wind down.

The next day, the 17th, Bomber Command detailed the raid on Berlin again. Once more, the crews were briefed and the aircraft prepared. Again, the weather intervened, turning colder with sleet showers and once more it was cancelled. On the 18th, there was a sense of incredulity as the crews found themselves attending a briefing yet again for Berlin, and yet again, late in the day, the operation was cancelled.

To have an operation cancelled night after night was devastating. It left crews wound up, demoralised and frustrated. To repeatedly have to go through all the mental and physical preparation and then not to be able to have it count as one of your sorties ratcheted the tension up a little more each time, tightening nerves already at full stretch. Commanders were well aware of this but had no choice but to leave such decisions to the last possible moment in the hope of taking advantage of a sudden improvement in the weather. Earlier in the war, in 1942, an RAF report on operational stress noted 'the disastrous effects upon morale of repeated cancellation of sorties, especially when late in the day'.[4] These cancellations came at a time when the heavy squadron losses were already playing on crews' minds.

On the 19th, twenty 97 Squadron aircraft were briefed. The crews were pleased to see that for a change the target was Leipzig. Bill and his crew were to act as one of seven Primary Blind Markers. This raid was the start of Operation Argument or 'Big Week' as it came to be known. The plan called for a concentrated attack on German aviation industries by Bomber Command by night and the USSTAF (United States Strategic Air Forces in Europe) by day, with the aim of annihilating the Luftwaffe before the invasion of Europe.

Leipzig, situated on the Weisse Elster river on the confluence of the Pleisse and Plarthe rivers, was one of the leading cultural, commercial and industrial centres of Germany. Both Johann Sebastian Bach and Felix Mendelssohn had spent time there, and Richard Wagner was born there. For centuries, the city had been, and still is, famous for its trade fairs. It was also a rail hub, with enormous marshalling and goods yards and the largest railway station in Europe, Leipzig Central Station, which had no less than twenty-six platforms. Among the important war industries based there were the Erla assembly plants building Messerschmitt Me 109s and Heiterblick, a supplier of major aircraft components. Other local industries included machine tools, arms, ammunition and ball bearings.

This was an important target. A perfect match for the criteria of the Pointblank Directive with its focus on the destruction of aircraft and associated industries. The city had been attacked a number of times before but this was to be the largest raid yet, with 823 aircraft taking part.

There was an air of restless, edgy anticipation at the briefing. Three days of operations being 'on/off' and the losses the squadron had suffered affected everybody. Take-off was to be late in the evening, leaving hours of time to kill.

This time, there was no cancellation, and Bill and the crew in JB-361 took off at 23.40, heading out once again over Cromer and the North Sea beyond. The meteorological flight had indicated that while low cloud could be expected over Leipzig, there would be good visibility above it. This meant that the Pathfinders would have to skymark the target using the Wanganui method. After identifying the target with H2S radar, red target indicators on parachutes would be dropped to provide Main Force with a visual aiming point.

Bomber Command had organised a diversionary mine-laying raid on Kiel Bay. However, German fighters were waiting for the bomber stream when it crossed over the Dutch coast near Groningen, and the fighters that had been sent north to Kiel were quickly recalled to attack as well. Charles Owen, another 97 Squadron pilot, reported, 'Intense fighter opposition on the whole route in, and we saw many more aircraft shot down than usual'.[5] On the long flight over enemy territory, the fighters had plenty of time. Another airman described how, 'We were flying a corridor of flares and, of course, the fighters were waiting on the outside and just coming in and bumping off the bombers'.[6]

Bent over his maps, Bernie soon realised that the forecast winds were wrong. The forecast headwinds were in fact strong tail winds. In their role accuracy was vital. That extra time would somehow have to be lost en route in order to arrive overhead Leipzig at zero hour. Getting on the radio, he told Bill that they would have to dogleg to avoid arriving early. He also warned Bill to keep a good lookout; other aircraft were doing the same, making collisions more likely as they crossed each other's tracks. According to Bill's log, they 'wasted 45 minutes en route'. It could not have been a worse night for such a thing to happen when the Zahme Sau (Tame Boar) night fighters were particularly active and decimating the bomber stream. For the crews, it was a long drawn-out nightmare.

Main Force bombers arriving overhead early also had to stooge around the sky. As they waited for the Pathfinders to drop their markers, they too faced being picked off by the flak and fighters. Crews became desperate to drop their bombs and head away. With the mass of bombers weaving and diving overhead, collisions were inevitable and four aircraft were probably lost in this way.[7]

As JB-361 approached Leipzig, they could see the searchlights. Shell bursts lit up the sky and huge red explosions rocked JB-361 as aircraft nearby were blown to bits. As Bill struggled to bring the aircraft into position to drop the marking flares, another Lancaster directly ahead of him was coned with searchlights. Seconds later, there was a huge, blinding flash as it exploded. Bill wrestled with the controls as the shock wave hit and debris filled the air. There was no time to avoid it; he flew straight through it. On the run-in, the flak seemed focused directly on them and the agonising minutes waiting for the photo flash seemed to last forever. Finally, they were free to weave their way through the mayhem around them and head northwest for home.

There was a choice of return routes. The shorter route was to the south of Leipzig, passing north of Frankfurt and then northwest past Antwerp. However, this route skirted the heavily defended Ruhr with its daunting batteries of anti-aircraft guns and searchlights. Bill chose the longer route north, passing between Osnabruck and Hanover. Constantly weaving and with every pair of eyes that could be spared looking out, they made their way back. At last, Bernard's voice came over the intercom to tell them they had passed over the Dutch coast and were out over the North Sea. Flasks were brought out and the ritual coffee drunk, warming and comforting despite its dubious taste.

As they approached the English coast, dawn was breaking and Bill could just make out the dunes of Haisborough Sands on the Norfolk coast in the dim first light. Nearing Bourn, the static in their headsets filled with voices asking permission to land as radio silence was finally broken. In the distance, the flares lining the runway were just visible. Finally, it was their turn. The controller said, "Hello, 'B' Beer, QFE one zero zero three, pancake, pancake." QFE being the barometric pressure setting for their altimeter, giving height over ground rather than sea level, and 'pancake' their permission to land. It was 6.30 am when they landed. As always, the ground crew were waiting; relief that 'their' crew had made it back softened their tired faces as they enquired how the trip had gone and what problems there were. After debriefing, the crew's eyes flicked to the Operations Board as usual to see who had returned, and who had not. To their amazement, they found that in the mayhem of this night, all of 97 Squadron's aircraft had returned safely to base.

This night was a disaster for Bomber Command; it suffered the greatest losses of the war so far. Seventy-nine aircraft failed to return that night, a total of 553 men killed in one night. The shock of these figures reverberated throughout the Command. It is highly significant that for the first time Bill recorded the losses in his logbook. In a terse little entry, he noted, '79 aircraft lost'. Bill, thoughtful, brave and determined, had always been realistic about the chances of survival, but the effects of the relentless pressure of these long night flights to heavily defended targets deep in Germany and the ensuing mounting losses were telling. Bill was stoically acknowledging the fact that even the slightest chance of survival seemed to be vanishing. The men of Bomber Command found themselves drawing deep on reserves of courage – such reserves could not be inexhaustible. 'Butch' Harris was well aware of the valour of his men, noting perceptively:

The courage of the small hours, of men virtually alone, for at his battle station the airman is virtually alone. It was the courage of men with long drawn apprehensions of daily "going over the top". Such devotion must never be forgotten.[8]

In the beginning, the odds had been stacked against survival. Now they were so slim as to be almost negligible. In 1943, during the Battle of the Ruhr, losses had averaged 4.3%. During the Battle of Berlin, the losses rose to 6.3%.[9] On this operation, the loss rate was a horrifying 9.5%. The losses on Halifaxes were the worst, totalling around 13%.[10]

The events of this night galvanised Bomber Command into making three immediate operational changes. The Halifax loss rates led to earlier types of Halifax being withdrawn from operations over Germany. Secondly, it was decided that 'Zero Hour' should be flexible, allowing for a change in timing to be broadcast with the usual wind broadcasts if unexpected winds led to the bomber stream arriving early over target. However, it was the third change that would make the most difference to the men of Bomber Command. Although they were not aware of it, Sir Arthur Harris decided to curtail the Battle of Berlin. There seemed to be no defence against the latest German night fighter tactics, and it was likely that the events of the Leipzig raid would be repeated on further raids on Berlin. The Command was suffering unsustainable losses, and to continue raids in Northern Germany with its heavy concentration of night fighter bases was no longer viable. Harris was not giving up his campaign, though; he now turned his attention to cities in Southern Germany where the bomber stream could route over France rather than Northern Germany.

It was almost 9 am before the crew got to bed. Not for long. All too soon, Bill's batman woke him with the news that he was to be on operations again that night. Wearily, he shaved and dressed before walking to the mess. Men trickled in and like automatons they went through the motions of eating and drinking. Little was said. Thoughts turned to tonight's operation; the fuel load indicated it would be another long night.

Briefing was at 17.00. Twenty-one of 97 Squadron's aircraft were among the 598 detailed to attack Stuttgart. Bill would be operating again as a Blind Backer-Up. After the previous night's disaster, much planning had gone into this raid. Prior to the main attack, Mosquitos made a diversionary raid on Munich while others attacked airfields in Holland. A training exercise out across the North Sea was also planned to mislead the night fighters. These tactics, together with the change to a target in Southern Germany, were much more successful. Only ten aircraft were lost. The target was marked and re-marked successfully and vast explosions were seen. Many crews remarked on the glow that was visible many miles away on their return trips.

As always, Bill's remarks in his logbook are brief but revealing. He noted that this was an 'Easy trip. No fighters but heavy flak over target. Only 10 lost'. Such typical understatement speaks volumes about the nightmare nature of every trip and the amazing tenacity and devotion to duty shown by aircrew. That morning, the front pages of the newspapers had been full of reports of the terrible losses suffered on the Leipzig raid on the 19/20 February. It was clear that night fighters, always a terrible threat to the vulnerable Lancasters, had now become an even greater menace. Only after the carnage of the previous night could this Stuttgart sortie have been seen as an easy trip. One of the ten crews lost was that of F/L Emerson of 97 Squadron. In the melee over Stuttgart, he had had a collision with another aircraft and had also suffered severe flak damage. F/L Emerson had nursed the badly damaged Lancaster all the way back to England. He had warned Bourn on the radio of his situation and, as was usual to prevent a damaged aircraft crashing and blocking the runway, was asked to wait until all the other aircraft had landed. He would have waited patiently, nursing his damaged aircraft and watching as all the others landed before it was his turn. In an extraordinarily cruel twist of fate, the aircraft crashed on the final approach, just 300 yards short of the runway. There were no survivors.

The next day, twenty-one aircraft were on the board for operations. The crews were out at their dispersals when the operation was cancelled. The following day, exactly the same thing happened when operations were cancelled yet again.

On 24 February, the funeral took place of the crew killed on the Stuttgart raid. Once again, officers and men from the squadron made their way to the cemetery in Cambridge to witness the ceremony. It was a familiar ritual now.

That night, on a sortie to Schweinfurt, yet another 97 Squadron crew failed to return.

CHAPTER TWENTY
MARCH 1944

The gaps in Bill and Reg's logbooks indicate that they took the six-day leave every six weeks to which aircrew were entitled at this time. The next entry in both logbooks is for 2 March when the crew were detailed for a low-flying exercise.

On 3 March, the squadron had an important visitor when Air Vice-Marshall D.C.T. Bennett spent a day with them. In the afternoon, he gave a lecture to the most vulnerable members of the crews, the air gunners. Bennett still sometimes flew on operations to see what was going on; he was the only one of the Group Commanders to do so. Aircrew knew that he understood exactly what he was asking of them. He considered '…that each one of these operations was equivalent to a major battle which in either of the other two services would be regarded as the experience of a life-time'.[1] This description puts into context the tremendous continuous pressure aircrew were under. In the other services, men went into battle sporadically, while bomber crews faced the equivalent of going into battle several times a week, for months on end, with ever-decreasing odds on surviving.

During the next ten days, six operations were planned by Bomber Command with 97 Squadron crews ordered to take part. On receipt of these orders, all the diverse sections of the squadron immediately set to work. In the Operations Room, Squadron and Base Commanders would meet and have a telephone conference with Group HQ and other squadrons operating that night to decide the type of Pathfinder operation, the route to and from the target, the bomb and flare loads and the fuel the aircraft would require. After the crews due to operate had done their brief flying tests, engineers would work flat out to repair any problems that had come to light. The Lancasters were checked again, refuelled and armed. Timings were worked out for briefings, meals and transport. Briefings took place, radio frequencies and routes noted. The operating crews themselves were psyched up for the night ahead. For five consecutive days from 4 March, the squadron went through all this planning and preparation only to have the operation cancelled. On one occasion, this happened only an hour before take-off, when crews were already with their aircraft. The repeated build-up of pre-operation tension was an enormous source of strain. Another operation was cancelled on 10 March. The ORB for that day reads: '10.3.44 21 aircraft detailed for night operations – cancelled in early afternoon. Games and PT arranged for remainder of day for aircrews'.[2] Occupations of very limited appeal to the stood-down crews.

The time was filled with yet more lectures or ground training. Various lectures on the old favourite 'Escape and Evasion' and on 'H2S' are mentioned in the ORB. However, whenever possible, flying exercises were undertaken. Between 4 and 15 March, Bill and the crew undertook various air tests, and an air-sea firing exercise. On one afternoon, several crews, including Bill's, were practising bombing at the range at Rushford in Norfolk when they were recalled to base, as German fighters were detected in the area. Bill also flew Standard Beam Approaches; aware of the need for constant practice, he also did a stint in that uncomfortable device, the Link Trainer.

At 09.47 on 15 March, RAF Bourn received orders from Group HQ stating that the target for tonight would be 'Barbel' – Stuttgart. The operation was to be a 'Newhaven', the method used to accurately mark a medium-sized target. This involved aircraft identifying the target with H2S and dropping flares over it to enable others to mark the aiming point. If the target was obscured by cloud then skymarking (Wanganui method) would be used, dropping target indicator flares suspended on parachutes.

Twenty-four crews were detailed for the operation, four Blind Marker Illuminators, one Visual Marker, four Blind Backers-Up, seven Visual Blind Markers and eight Supporters. Bill and his crew were listed on the board to act as Blind Marker Illuminators; that is, they were the initial markers who would open the raid, in this case by dropping white flares followed by green Target Indicators.

The bomb load was calculated and passed to the armourers at 11.23. However, it was found that the 'BMI [Blind Marker Illuminator] load too heavy at present. On each A/C carrying 5 x 4 hooded flares reduce the load by 1 x 1000 MC. 9042 [lbs] total load. Petrol 1870 gals'.[3] The 1 x 1000 MC was a 1000 lb Medium Capacity bomb. The flares were made of magnesium and the hoods had been developed to enable the Pathfinders to illuminate targets without dazzling their bomb aimers.

Unusually that morning, they did an air test on Lancaster ND 452-E before testing their own aircraft, JB 361-B. There were no problems on either aircraft. The briefing was at 15.30 and there was a feeling of relief when the target was revealed as Stuttgart rather than the 'Big City' again. On the squadron's previous operation on Stuttgart on 1 March, they had found the city lightly defended and had not been much bothered by searchlights, flak or night fighters. All aircraft and crew had returned safely.

Men confronted the possibility of their own mortality in their own ways. Letters were written to loved ones, some immersed themselves in books while others played games to distract themselves from the night ahead. On this day, with an early evening take-off, there was only an hour before it was time for the pre-flight meal at 17.00. Then the transformation from individual to crew began. Pockets were emptied, stripping away all personal items. Such items were carefully locked away in the locker; the shedding of an identity to be retrieved again later, for now they were all elements of a composite, the crew, whose existence was tied to their aircraft.

The crew buses started running at 17.45, slowly trundling round the peri-track before stopping at each dispersal to drop off a crew. The men sat, bulky in their flying gear. There was not much chatter as minds focused on the task ahead. At their dispersal Bill checked with the ground crew that there had been no last-minute snags. All through that freezing winter since Bill had joined 97 Squadron, the same 'erks' had looked after JB-361, and ground crew and aircrew now knew each other well. The Lancaster loomed above them as Bill and Tom walked around doing visual checks; little stabs of red flared briefly out of the dark as last cigarettes were finished.

Clumsily, they climbed the steps and groped their way through the dark fuselage before settling into their positions. Gear was sorted and stowed away and the many pre-flight checks begun. Up at the front, Bill and Tom ran through their checklist before firing up the Merlins. One by one, coughing and spluttering, they roared into life. Temperatures and pressures were checked and the hydraulic flaps tested. On the ground the 'erks' disconnected the starter battery and pulled away the chocks. Slowly, JB-361 moved out onto the peri-track and zigzagged her way to the holding point where the usual gaggle of WAAFS and RAF personnel were waiting to wave them off. As one of the Primary Markers, Bill ensured that JB-361 was ready and waiting and, on receiving the green light, they were the first to take off from Bourn, becoming airborne at 19.20, almost an hour ahead of the last aircraft to depart, which was airborne at 20.20.

After take-off, Bernie gave Bill their first headings. They routed south over Reading and out over the Channel at Selsey Bill. The route then continued across France almost as far as the Swiss border on Lake Constance before turning north for Stuttgart. Bomber Command intended that this routing would make the Germans think that Munich was the intended target, and to back this up, they dispatched ten Mosquitoes to drop target indicators and bombs on Munich. These tactics did delay the German fighters to some extent, but on the whole they ignored the Munich diversion.

Seeing the general southerly routing of the bomber stream that night, the German controllers called in night fighters from Northern Germany as well as more locally based groups. Among the German squadrons called into action were fighters from *Gruppe II* of the *Nachtjagdgeschwader*, NJG/II. The top German ace, Major Heinrich Prinz zu Sayn-Wittgenstein, had commanded this group before his death on 21 January 1944. The squadron flew the night fighter version of the Junkers Ju 88, the Ju 88C, considered to be Germany's most effective World War II night fighter. Improved and modified since its inception in 1936, the Ju 88C, carried on its nose the antler-like array of aerials that constituted the Lichtenstein FuG 220 SN-2 radar. This enabled it to identify and track Allied bombers. It was immune to Allied jamming at this time. Another aid that had been recently introduced was *Naxos*, a radar detector that could home in on H2S transmissions. The most lethal equipment the Ju 88C carried was its two upward firing MG 151 Schrage Musik 20 mm cannon, which were mounted obliquely on the fuselage. The night fighters were scrambled early and held at navigation beacons along the supposed track of the bombers. From there, they were directed onto the bomber stream and they then hunted individually using their own radar equipment to find their targets.

Stuttgart was not an easy target to find using H2S; it lay well protected within a long, narrow valley. The route took the bombers well to the south till the turning point at the northerly tip of Lake Constance. Until then, the German controllers and fighters could not be sure of the target; both Munich and Augsburg were other possibilities. Reaching the turning point, JB-361 turned to head north on its final run for Stuttgart some 50 miles away. Unbeknownst to them, there were several German fighters lurking in the vicinity. One of them was Hauptmann Horst Heinz Hissbach. At twenty-eight, Hissbach was an experienced and successful fighter ace from 5/NJG/II. As the trace of a bomber appeared on his Lichenstein radar, he turned to track it.

After Bill turned JB-361 north towards Stuttgart, it was time to identify the target using H2S. To do this, they had to fly continuously straight and level with no weaving or manoeuvring to allow the gunners to peer under the aircraft. Crouched over his navigation table, Bernie was calculating timings and the distance still to run. That night, the winds were stronger than predicted, making his task difficult. Blind Markers setting the initial target indicators played a vital role in the success or failure of a raid and it was crucial that their timing should be absolutely accurate.

In the rear turret, Robbie was keenly aware of their vulnerability now they were flying straight and level, and both he and Archie in the mid-upper turret quartered the skies for the slightest sign of fighter activity. Flying above a layer of broken cloud, the visibility was good, but they, like all RAF aircrew at the time, were unaware of the Schrage Musik technique now practised by German fighters.

Meanwhile, in the Junkers Ju 88C, the *Naxos* radar detector had picked up the emissions from JB 361-B. Following the H2S signature and aided by his Lichtenstein radar, Horst Heinz Hissbach now closed in. Flying at a lower level than the Lancaster, he manoeuvred his Ju 88C into position below it to positively identify the aircraft before dropping slightly back into the perfect firing position. Hissbach took careful aim through the sight in the roof of his cockpit and fired, probably hitting the tail turret first and then directly into the port wing between the engines where the vulnerable main spar and highly inflammable fuel tanks lay.

Cannon shells now ripped through the JB-361's fuselage, tearing through Perspex and metal, the whole aircraft juddering as shells slammed into her. A fire warning must have lit up on the instrument panel. The port inner engine was ablaze, the glow of orange flames visible beneath the engine. Bill would have ordered Roy Shaw, the engineer, to feather (shut down) it and press the extinguisher button before getting on the intercom to check on his crew. There would have been no response from the rear turret; Robbie Roberts, the rear gunner, was killed outright. It is likely that Roy was asked to go back to check on Robbie and look for damage where the flying controls ran down the port side. Grabbing a flashlight, he would have struggled back through to the narrow fuselage as smoke filled the air with the smell of burning oil and flames flickered hungrily through holes in the fuselage.

A shell had smashed through the Navigator's station, sending shards of sharp metal flying and wounding Bernard Starie on the side of the head. Someone, probably Reg, got permission and fought his way back to grab a dressing from the first aid kid and bandage Bernard's head. In the cockpit, lit by flames from the burning engine, Bill would see the whole port wing was now ablaze, fiery fingers of flame curling up the inner wing, licking their way towards the fuselage. There was no longer any hope. As smoke infiltrated the cockpit and the crackle and roar of the flames grew louder, Bill must have given the order for everyone to bail out as he fought to maintain control and give them time to jump. The aircraft was diving now, plunging down, engines screaming. An enormous explosion shook the aircraft as fuel tanks in the port wing exploded, taking the port wing and part of the tail plane off. The aircraft was now uncontrollable and dived blazing towards the snow-covered ground where, narrowly missing a tiny village, it crashed into a field. There were no survivors.

CHAPTER TWENTY-ONE
THE AFTERMATH

Nestling against the mountains 50 miles south of Stuttgart lay the little hamlet of Zillhausen. Hidden in a valley in the Swabian Alps, Zillhausen had remained isolated and almost untouched by the war. The rhythm of life in the farming village continued much as it always had, largely dictated by the seasons. The winter of 1944 had been particularly severe, bringing with it repeated heavy falls of snow. On 15 March, thick snow covered the village and the fields, glinting in the starlight of the winter's night and occasionally cascading gently from the branches of the trees in the forest onto the hillside.

In the late evening, the village was quiet and still, the little cluster of houses shrouded in darkness. No cracks of light from windows or doors – blackout precautions prevented that. In any case, the inhabitants were mostly already asleep. A solitary figure plodded through the snow, slowly making his way along the street. Kurt Schneider, a schoolboy aged fourteen, was going home from the weekly Hitler Youth meeting, which had finished promptly at 22.00. Hitler saw the youth movement as a vital means of indoctrinating the young in National Socialist ideology, and programmes were set up for both boys and girls. The movement put an emphasis on physical and outdoor activities, incorporating basic military skills. Membership of the movement was compulsory, and attendance at the weekly meetings was obligatory. Like most young boys, Kurt found the heady mix of propaganda, exhortation and 'Boy Scout' activities exciting. Kurt's parents understood the rationale behind the movement and were not happy about it but were powerless to prevent their son's attendance. Mr Schneider was one of the few men left in the village, exempt from military service due to his occupation as the local blacksmith, a vital role in a small farming community.

Yet though the village was silent, there were sounds in the night air. Sounds Kurt had heard many times before, the distant angry drone of aircraft engines in the sky above. Zillhausen lay close to routes frequently used by the bomber streams from England.

Kurt stopped and turned. Scanning the night sky, his attention focused on an area over the mountains southeast of the village. There, dim flashes arched across the night sky – it was tracer fire and barely visible. He saw the target, an aircraft; it was easy to spot now, a yellow glow illuminating the underside. It had been hit but continued steadily on. As he watched, the glow got brighter but the aircraft continued. Now the glow was spreading; he could see the flames creeping relentlessly along the wing towards the fuselage, and the aircraft started to dive. Soon it was plunging down, the pitch becoming steeper and steeper until the aircraft seemed to be diving in an arc straight for the village.

Night turned into day as the burning aircraft now lit up the sky. Kurt could see flames curling across the fuselage, the engines screaming as the speed built up, straining the airframe to the limits and beyond. The noise was overwhelming; Kurt stood transfixed, horrified, and quite unable to move. While he watched, a tremendous explosion tore through the aircraft sending fiery pieces spinning through the air as it disintegrated. Quickly, Kurt ducked as the flaming main body of the fuselage passed right overhead. It plunged into a nearby field, the ground shuddering under the impact. Immediately after, there came another shattering explosion as the 4,000lb 'Cookie', that had been thrown clear, impacted and exploded further up the hillside. Shock waves from the blast hit Kurt as he took to his heels and ran towards the crash site. As he ran, explosions shook the night air as the smaller bombs flung from JB-361 B detonated on impact.

When he reached the field, it was lit up as if a spectacular firework display was in progress. Awestruck, he watched as the many marker flares JB-361 B carried erupted from the wreckage, their reds, greens and yellows like multicoloured rockets streaking across the sky while on the ground chains of bullets crackled and exploded in the flames. Flames had engulfed the fuselage and now soared high in the night sky, blazing through the darkness. It was impossible to approach the wreckage and quite obvious that no one could have survived. Soon other villagers were stumbling through the snow, coats and boots hastily donned, and Kurt was pulled back to a safe distance. All watched silently, stunned by the inferno as munitions continued to detonate in all directions, whistling through the air. Now the snow was no longer white but transformed, lit with red and gold as the flickering fires and explosions were reflected in it, the blazing wreckage illuminating the whole field.

Burning fuel now ran from the aircraft, carving a fiery path through the snow and flowing down to the little brook, the Roschbach, at the bottom of the field. Later that night, as Kurt finally walked home, he saw to his astonishment that the little brook appeared to run with fire rather than water as the flames, flickering and reflecting on its snow-covered banks, created a river of fire that flowed down through the heart of the village.

The next morning, Kurt returned to the field. Bomb shrapnel and debris were scattered everywhere. The wreckage was still smoking but now the police and soldiers guarding it chased him away. All that day he could not get what he had seen out of his mind, and he determined that he would return and search the surrounding fields, taking a roundabout route to avoid the soldiers. After school, he and a couple of friends cut across the fields and through the trees, slipping as they staggered up the snow-clad hill above the crash site. Here, the snow was despoiled with tangled pieces of metal, twisted and re-forged into strange shapes by the furnace of the fire.

Stumbling along, they spotted a large piece of cockpit wreckage and rushed over to inspect it; they froze, panting, their breath clouding in the icy air. Half out of the wreckage of the cockpit, covered by the twisted metal and shards of Perspex, lay the body of a man; he was lying on his left side with his head downhill. He wore his oxygen mask, though no oxygen could help him now. The airman was wearing a leather flying jacket, and in his pocket he carried a large bar of chocolate which had fallen half out. His left arm was stretched out in the snow and on his wrist was a beautiful gold watch. Hearts beating wildly, the boys stood there silently, stunned and too fearful to approach, despite the temptation the chocolate bar presented. Finally, they crept around the body at a distance. Shocked, they stumbled on and came across another body some way away. Shards of Perspex surrounded the airman and even in death, he was still holding a wound dressing to his head. Some 10 metres away, a long dark shape lay in the snow. Gathering their courage, they went to investigate and found a half-opened parachute; someone had tried to escape from the aircraft, without success. The young airman lay, partially covered by his parachute, as though resting in the snow. The light was fading now and it was growing colder. The boys huddled together, their shivers not entirely due to the chill air. Slowly, they retraced their steps down the snowy hill and quietly went home.

Motor transport was difficult in wartime and in this small hamlet there was no mechanised transport, only farm carts. Both lorries and the fuel to run them were in short supply, and so it was not until the following day, 17 March, that the bodies were recovered. A lorry had to be requisitioned from the Seeger soap factory in the nearest town, Balingen. Two local farmers, Jakob Jentner and Christian Pfeiffer, were ordered to bring down the bodies. They hitched up the horses to the sleigh and plodded slowly through the snow up the hillside to fetch the three bodies. The airmen's bodies were loaded onto the sleigh and brought down to where the burnt-out fuselage lay. Cannon shells had completely destroyed the rear turret. Kurt watched, horrified, as the remains of the rest of the crew were added to the sleigh and then brought down to the village. There, he and other villagers stood silently as the bodies were transferred onto the lorry. The terrible sights Kurt had seen had shaken him to the core and left him deeply shocked. Until now, the war had been an impersonal thing. Now he had seen what war could do. He would never forget it.

The bodies were carefully draped with their parachutes before being taken away. Bill, Archie Barrowman and Bernie Starie were identified by their identity tags and Reg Pike by something he carried. The remains of Robbie Roberts were found in what was left of the rear turret, but the others were not identified at this time. The bodies were taken to Balingen for burial. There was a service at the ancient Friedhofskirche Church, attended by a British Officer from a nearby POW camp. Then the crew of Lancaster JB-361 OF-B were interred in the cemetery there on 17 March 1944.

By this time, Nazi officials and Luftwaffe personnel had arrived to examine the crash site. The fire had been so severe that at first they thought it was a Wellington bomber. However, it was soon identified as a Lancaster Pathfinder Aircraft. As such, the Germans knew it would be fitted with the latest navigation aids and the next day a specialist military unit came to examine the wreckage for any trace of the equipment on board.

In the aftermath, a team from the Todt Organisation arrived. The Todt Organisation had been founded by Fritz Todt, an engineer high up in the Nazi hierarchy. It was a semi-military organisation responsible for civil and military engineering and the labour necessary for such projects. While the organisation had first conscripted German workers, it now used both concentration camp inmates and prisoners of war, effectively treating them as slave labour. One of their tasks was clearing away the wreckage of aircraft.

The violence of the explosion had scattered wreckage in all directions, the once pristine snow now pockmarked with tortured, jagged metal pieces. The remains of one wing and two fuel tanks had been flung almost a kilometre away; amazingly, the tanks still had fuel in them. One engine was found further up the hillside towards the enormous crater left by the exploding 'Cookie'. The tail plane was found months later in the nearby woods. Most of the bombs had exploded on impact, but one was found unexploded on the hillside. A cart, drawn by oxen, was used to tow it down through the nearby village of Streichen, presumably having been defused first. Surprisingly, there is a photo of the devastation taken immediately after the war ended. It clearly shows the various craters scarring the landscape that were caused by the exploding munitions. It is a mystery as to why the Allies should have taken such a photo and raises questions that remain unanswered to this day.

Shock waves from the 'Cookie', as it detonated, were felt throughout the village. The force of the blast badly damaged twelve houses in Zillhausen; some villagers still remember their doors being blown in by the explosion. An orchard on the hillside was completely destroyed. Many had fled their houses that night. One lady, with great presence of mind, carefully carried with her the stew that had been cooking at the time.[1]

There was a feeling of stunned disbelief throughout the village. Until that time, the realities of war had passed them by; now the war had come to their doorstep. As news of the crash spread, people came from miles around to see the crash site for themselves. The whole village realised that they had had a very lucky escape that night.

CHAPTER TWENTY-TWO

FINAL ACTS

At Bourn, the ground crews waited patiently. The first aircraft to return landed at 02.05 and during the next hour the other Lancasters returned, the last that night being that of S/L Mansbridge, who landed at 03.05. Still JB-361 B's ground crew lingered in the icy cold at their dispersal. Rubbing their hands, they waited, peering up at the sky, until finally the flare path was switched off and it was clear there could be no hope. In the Ops Room they waited too, filling in the landing times against the pilots' names until only one blank space remained. Finally, a WAAF marked the fateful letters 'FTR' (Failed to Return) against Bill's name and a well-practised ritual began. A phone call was made to the Air Ministry to report the crew as overdue. Personnel were dispatched to the crew's quarters to collect their personal belongings. The RAF was keen to remove evidence of losses as quickly as possible to avoid reminding aircrew of their probable fate. In the morning, though, the empty beds and spaces at the breakfast table could not be hidden.

It was not a very successful raid. Bomber Command's final report states that 'Adverse winds delayed the opening of the attack and the same winds may have been the cause of the Pathfinder marking falling back well short of the target'.[1] W/C Dunnicliffe, who flew that night, noted with some surprise in his report that he was the first aircraft to drop any markers, and several other 97 Squadron pilots reported that the first target indicators and Wanganui flares were only seen at 23.10. It is sad and ironic that on a night that many of the Pathfinders and main force were late over the target, JB-361 and her crew would have been on time. With commendable accuracy, the crew had managed to keep to their schedule despite the strong winds. On a night with a comparatively low loss rate of 3.7%, they had the misfortune to be leading the bomber stream and to come up against one of the Luftwaffe's ace fighter pilots using Schrage Musik – equipment that crews were unaware of.[2]

The following day, the Air Ministry sent a telegram to the crew's families informing them that their son/husband was missing in action. The Commanding Officer of 97 Squadron, Wing Commander E.J. Carter, also wrote to the crew's families. Given below is part of the letter the Commanding Officer of 97 Squadron wrote to Mr and Mrs Pike. In it he makes clear that they were one of 97 Squadron's most valued crews:

> Your son had completed forty-two operational sorties with the Squadron, a record to be proud of. He was a most conscientious and efficient Air Bomber and had done much good work at instructing. Being a member of one of our most reliable crews he was therefore undertaking a most important duty.[3]

A mixture of anguish and hope must have been felt when these letters arrived, as families clung to the thought that the crew might have been able to bail out. They were aware it was unlikely. After a couple of months, the personal effects were returned to the families, accompanied by a businesslike letter asking for a receipt and advising on the disposal of uniforms should the airman's death be confirmed. The actual inventory of Reg Pike's possessions survives. It makes heartbreaking reading, as listed are deeply personal items, precious possessions that obviously had a special meaning for their owner. Items such as a 'St Christopher Medallion on chain', '1 Odd Cufflink', '2 Bundles of Letters and Photos' and a 'Boy Scout Bracelet', the latter invoking happy childhood memories.

Months passed and it was not until July that the RAF wrote again to the families informing them that, having received information from the International Red Cross, the crew should now be considered to be 'missing believed killed' on the night of 15/16 March. It was not until December 1944 that death was officially confirmed.

There was one final act. In June 1946, after the war had ended, each of the crew's families received a registered parcel. Unwrapping the brown paper, they found inside a book with a blue cover with the owner's name written on the front. These were the crew's personal logbooks. They contained a complete record of their time in the RAF. In it were listed their qualifications, types of aircraft flown, where stationed and all their flying experience from early training until March 1944, all carefully written up in their own known hands. That is, until the entry for 15 March 1944; the entry was there but it had been written up in a different hand to complete the record.

They had been a quite outstanding crew. Their skill, dedication and courage had led to every one of them having previously received an award for bravery. This was quite exceptional; it was very rare indeed for every member of a crew to have been so honoured.

Bill had known better than most what he was fighting against. Prior to the war, he had seen first-hand the changes that came over his parents' much-loved country. He had watched in dismay as the ruthless fanaticism of National Socialism gripped Germany when Hitler came to power. When Bill volunteered, Britain stood alone in the world, a last bastion of liberty in a Europe overrun by Nazi aggression. He knew full well the odds against survival in Bomber Command. Like thousands of others, he was determined to serve his country, to defend its freedom and to do his part to ensure it remained as a symbol of hope in the midst of the subjugated nations of Europe. At that time, the bombers of RAF Bomber Command provided the only means of attacking Germany directly. In September 1940, Churchill summed up the importance of Bomber Command when he stated, "The fighters are our salvation but the bombers alone provide the means of victory." The courage and devotion to duty of the men of Bomber Command was truly exceptional.

After the end of the war, the Canadian Government instigated an original and charming scheme to remember and honour all Canadian servicemen who had lost their lives. Geographical features such as lakes, islands and bays were to be named after the soldiers, sailors and airmen who never returned home. There are currently some 3,900 such features in Saskatchewan, and one of them is named for Archie Barrowman. Lake Barrowman lies to the northwest of Lake La Ronge Provincial Park. It is an area of great natural beauty and there Archie's name lives on amidst the forests and lakes of northern Saskatchewan.

On 28 December 1944, a small and poignant notice appeared in the In Memoriam section of *The Times*. It is representative of the feelings of so many grieving families. It read:

> In deep gratitude and loving memory of William, dearly loved only son of Mrs. E. Meyer, of 52 Pont Street, London SW1, on his 35th birthday, who on the night of 15th March, 1944, together with his gallant crew, gave his life for his country on operations over Stuttgart.

Despite the terrible losses the men of Bomber Command suffered, they never received a campaign medal after the war. It was only in 2013 that their bravery and service were formally recognised with the award of the Bomber Command Clasp. It took some sixty-seven years for the magnificent Bomber Command Memorial to be built in Hyde Park to honour the 55,573 airmen who lost their lives. The memorial depicts a crew who have just returned from operations. They stand, exhaustion writ large on their faces and bearing, looking skyward, watching for other crews to land safely. It is a poignant reminder for generations to come of the courage and sacrifice of these young men. The words 'Lest we forget' echo down the years, reminding us of the heartbreaking 'what might have been' of so many lives curtailed and the enduring loss suffered by those who remained.

Isle de Chausey Combat by Michael Turner. Bill Meyer's Lancaster WS-U 'Uncle' beating off the second attack from a Me. 109 night fighter.

A Steeplechase Across Denmark by Michael Turner. Bill Meyer's Lancaster crossing the coast of Denmark low level en-route to Stettin.

Sinc's wedding to Eileen, December 1944 with Darkie as his best man

Lancaster JB 361 OF-B 'Beer' 97 Squadron RAF Bourn 1943.
Left to right: Archie Barrowman, Bernie Starie, Tom Shaw, Jim McLeish, Robbie Roberts, Reg Pike (IBCC Digital Archive)

Lancaster JB 361 OF-B 'Beer' the aircraft Bill flew in 97 Squadron
(IBCC Digital Archive)

Reg Pike when he was a flight sergeant in early 1943 (left), *James McLeish at RAF Bourn 1943* (middle), *Reg Pike after his promotion to Pilot Officer late 1943* (right)

 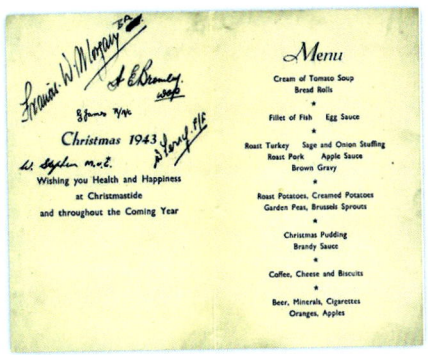

Bill's medals and log book (left) *and Christmas menu 1943* (right)

Bill's logbook February/March 1943, page 51 with Bill's brief but telling comments

Zillhausen. Brett and Luella with Kurt Schneider at the crash site which is marked by the brown area of grass that is still visible just behind them

The Mayor of Balingen, Oberbürgermeister Herr Reitemann, speaking at the unveiling of the memorial, with Brigitte Lorch beside him translating. Some of the men from IX (B) Squadron are on the left 4 April 2009

The crash site is just to the right of the red roofed building, the brown area of grass is just visible April 2009

After the ceremony at the memorial. Left to right Dr. Schimpf-Reinhardt, Kurt Schneider, Dorle Steingraeber, Mayor Reitemann, Luella, Brett, Brigitte Lorch 4 April 2009

Memorial after wreaths had been laid

IX Squadron officers' mess RAF Waddington March 1943. Bill second from right

Herr and Frau Jenter. Herr Jenter helped retrieve the crew's bodies from the crash site and found the pieces of OF-B in the forest

The memorial. The crew's names are on the front with descriptions on each side, one side in German and one in English (left) and The blackened piece of the bomb bay door from Lancaster JB 361 OF-B, the bristle edging is down the right hand side (right)

Wing Commander Nick Hay (4th from left) and the men of IX (B) Squadron visit the memorial and lay wreaths in 26 June 2010

The beautiful Lake Barrowman in Saskatchewan, Canada, named after Archie Barrowman

Durnbach cemetery in Bavaria. The graves of William Meyer, Reginald Pike, Bernard Starie and Archibald Barrowman are in the front row with James McLeish, Albert Roberts and Thomas Shaw in the row behind

Durnbach cemetery in summer from the air

Durnbach cemetery in winter from the air

William Meyer's grave

THE AFTERWORD
TRACING THE PAST

In the last twelve years, many more records have been computerised and my task would have been much easier. When this research started, this was not the case.

The Search Begins
The wallet and plaque revealed where Bill had trained in the USA; the next step was to find any records of the Polaris Flight Academy. The National Archives in London hold among their vast archives the records of the RAF during the war. Among the treasure trove of documents there is a file on No. 2 BFTS, Lancaster, California. This turned out to be a large, overstuffed folder filled with papers. Rustling through the folder, I found a page that listed the names of the cadets under their course numbers. Also noted were the dates when some of them had been subsequently killed in action. Looking through the survivors of Bill's course, I searched for an unusual surname that might be possible to track down. One name stood out: a Mr K. H. Gilderdale. Brett then ran through the electoral roll and sent out letters of enquiry to various 'Mr K. Gilderdales'.

A week later, we received a reply from Mr Ken Gilderdale saying that he had not only trained at Polaris with Bill but that he remembered him well. This was our first piece of luck, and on a bright, sunny summer's day we drove down to Sussex to meet

Ken. Ken filled us in on life at the Polaris Academy, and the epic journey they had getting there. He remembered it clearly and it was fascinating to hear first-hand of what their training had been like. We were shown photos as well as the Polaris magazine and other papers, and these helped fill in the period of Bill's life after the Initial Training Wing in Devon and during the voyage on the *Pasteur* and training in America.

Bardney IX (B) Squadron
To find out what squadrons Bill had served with, we turned to Bill Baxter and his excellent Bomber Command website. Bob informed us that Bill had served with RAF IX (B) and 97 Squadrons. Further research revealed that while, sadly, 97 Squadron no longer exists, not only does IX (B) Squadron still exist but it also had a very active Association and its own historian, Roger Audis. Roger actually lived in Bardney, the 'spiritual home' of IX Squadron, and so we drove up to meet him. We are greatly indebted to him for the tremendous amount of help he gave us. He not only provided information but he also took us to see where the airfield had been. The airfield was disposed of in 1963 and is now private land, but Roger kindly arranged with the farmer to show us around.

As we drove through what had been the main gate, we could see the box-like two-storey concrete building that was the Control Tower. It still stands looking out across the field and is now used by the Bardney Flyers Model Club. Climbing the stairs to the upper floor, we walked out on the balcony that runs around the outside. This was where men once stood eagerly peering out and willing the laden aircraft safely into the air and then watching anxiously again for their safe return, counting them home during innumerable long nights. Looking out over the stubbly grass that covers the field, the long line of the main runway can be traced by the buildings that edge part of it; it is now used as a poultry farm.

Slowly, we drove onto the peri-track where so many Lancasters once made their way weaving and snaking till they reached the end of the runway. It is now rutted and pitted and water-filled holes pockmark the surface. On the edges of the field, the grey utilitarian shapes of some wartime aircraft hangars can still be seen. Bumping along the peri-track, we followed it round, turning the corner where it skirts the Austacre woods. We could see some traces of the turn-offs that led to the dispersals; they were just visible, running into the trees and bushes to the hard standings where once mighty Lancasters stood. Roger told us that this was where Bill's flight, 'B' flight, had their dispersals. Getting out, we walked across the uneven ground. Brushing aside twigs and leaves and looking down, we caught glimpses of concrete though the undergrowth. We followed to where the concrete widened into what had been the circular hard standing. A tree lay fallen across the dispersal pan. The wood is slowly reclaiming its own, brambles, nettles and bushes inching out, covering ground that once echoed with the sound of Merlin engines crackling and thundering into life. All that could be heard now was birdsong and the buzz of insects but somehow, perhaps in my imagination, something in the atmosphere still seemed to remain, the faintest echo of what once had been.

On leaving the airfield, Roger pointed out where the living quarters used to be; they had been a little further on down the road on the opposite side. It is woodland now and almost nothing remains of the many huts that once formed the offices and messes, just the odd ivy-draped piece of masonry signifies that something once was there. It was hard to imagine the immense bustle and activity that once pervaded these woods in the quiet countryside now.

Birth Certificate
The Commonwealth War Graves Commission records showed that William Meyer was buried at Durnbach War Cemetery in Southern Germany. His gravestone revealed that he was thirty-four when he died. A birth certificate would tell us the names, addresses and occupations of his parents. At the time, the National Archives held copies of the Births, Marriages and Deaths records on well-handled and sometimes misfiled microfiches. However, after repeatedly going through the records, I could not find an

entry. A letter to the General Register Office asking for a formal search came back with the reply that there was no entry for that name. Puzzled and frustrated, we tried another line of research and applied for a copy of Bill's will and the grant of probate.

The arrival of these documents provided further clues. For the first time we learnt that there had been a family business, William A. Meyer Ltd. The will also revealed that Bill left his entire estate, including the family business, to my father with the proviso that it should go to his mother should he predecease her.

We now also had an address. On a quiet Sunday morning, we drove up to Hampstead to see if we could find the house. Would it still be there? Eton Avenue turned out to be a peaceful, tree-lined road with thirties-style large red brick houses. It looked as though most houses still stood, although many had been converted into flats. As we drove down the road, the houses became more substantial. Then on a corner plot we found it. Nearly hidden from the avenue by tall trees there stood an enormous three-storied house, also in red brick, with three massive chimneystacks towering above an ornate gabled roof. There were several driveways, one up to the porch and front door and the other round to the back of the house, while yet another led to what must have been garages at the back. Clearly, Bill's family had lived in great comfort and style. We got out and walked up the drive to the front door; there were several names by different bells indicating that this house too had been turned into flats. Thankfully, no one seemed to be around so we walked on through the garden looking around at flowering shrubs and bushes that now ran wild. A mass of pink roses rambled over the brickwork of the house, giving it a homely look despite its size. There had obviously been a garden at the back of the house, but the land had been sold off and built on. We walked slowly, looking around and wondering which of the many windows would have been that of Bill's room and trying to imagine what his life had been like when he lived here.

An application was sent off to Companies House for the records of William A. Meyer Ltd. and shortly afterwards we received an enormous file of documents; it was this that contained the bombshell. The papers dated back to the formation of the company in 1930. The firm bore the name of Bill's father, William A. Meyer, and showed that it had been a substantial company with offices in Southwark. The company had been importers and agents for a variety of industrial hardware, mostly from Germany. Their most important agency had been for Primus, well known to generations of campers for their Primus stoves and associated equipment.

Trawling through this file, we came to the page that gave the personal details of the directors. Glancing through it, we stopped in disbelief. Bill's parents, William A. Meyer and Emmy Meyer, were duly listed together with their nationalities; they were not British, but German. There had been no hint or indication of this beforehand. What is more, his parents had never given up their German nationality. When we told Alan Hart, a member of Bill's first crew, he was so astounded that he refused to believe it at first. Bill had appeared a typical well-spoken Englishman. Unsurprisingly, he had never given any hint of a connection with Germany. It took some time to take in the implications of this discovery. It opened a Pandora's box of possibilities and gave a totally new dimension to our research.

Reading through the file, we learnt that after the death of Bill's mother, Emmy Meyer, the firm had continued in existence till the 1990s. It was finally wound up with the Primus agency being bought back by the parent company in Sweden. The names and addresses of the directors were listed, so we hoped to find one of them who might have known the family and give us further information.

Once again, we were lucky. Dialling a number, Brett found himself talking to Richard Lovelace, a man who had spent his working life with the firm. Starting out as an office junior, he had ended up as a director of the company. He had not known Bill or his father but remembered briefly meeting his mother, Emmy Meyer, when she came to the company offices for meetings in the 1950s and '60s. Even then, she still spoke with a heavy German accent. She revealed little about her son to them and seems to have led a comfortable but rather sad and lonely life after the war, living in an apartment on Piccadilly overlooking Green Park. She died in 1964. In her will, she left the shares of the company to its two directors, with the touching request that the company should always bear the name 'William A. Meyer Ltd'. Brett was told that the company had originally got the Primus agency through a chance meeting in the 1920s. William Meyer senior had been having a relaxing drink in a London pub and had started chatting to someone there. This man turned out to represent Primus and a deal was done there and then. We discovered that, immediately after Bill's death, my father took over running the family business for Mrs Meyer. Post-war, business quickly resumed with links with Frankfurt swiftly re-established. Metal milk churns for the Milk Marketing Board were the first items imported to the UK from Germany.

When the company was wound up in the 1990s, Primus bought back the agency and the directors came over to London to sign the papers. They knew the history of the company and were full of admiration for Bill's wartime record, so much so that they made a point of visiting the Air Forces Memorial at Runnymede to pay their respects. They were puzzled not to find Bill's name among the 20,000 airmen commemorated there who have no known grave.

We learnt that William Meyer senior had died just before the war and so Brett applied for his death certificate and will. His death certificate contained another shock. William Meyer had died of Nembutal poisoning at the end of August 1938. The certificate stated it had been taken orally in unknown circumstances and that the coroner had recorded an open verdict. An open verdict is usually recorded when suicide is suspected but there is no evidence of intent. Nembutal is a barbiturate that was often prescribed at that time for insomnia, although it is now considered too dangerous and has been superseded. It is possible that an overdose was taken in error but doctors we have talked to consider this unlikely due to the amount that would have had to be taken to cause death. It is not hard to imagine the dismay with which the Meyers watched the rise of Nazism and the coming to power of Hitler in their beloved country. In 1938, the writing was well and truly on the wall. In January that year, Mr Meyer senior had made Bill a director of William. A. Meyer Ltd. Another factor that must have played on Mr Meyer's mind was the prospect of internment. Not having adopted British nationality, he would have been classed as an enemy alien and interned for the duration. He had already endured this once during World War I.

This will contained a reference to his son as 'Alex Wilhelm Meyer, commonly known as William Alexander Meyer'. Bill's name had been anglicised. Despite living in England for all this time, the Meyers had retained their German citizenship, an indication of an enduring feeling for their home country.

National Archives

The next step was back to the National Archives to look at their copies of the Squadron Operational Record Books. Fortunately, officers' movements are listed in squadron records and so I set out to fill in the details of Bill's RAF career starting from the known points of his training in California and his postings to IX and 97 Squadrons. It was a slow job; the ORBs are on microfilm and hours were spent winding and rewinding, not only looking for operational details but for the vital hints as to where Bill was posted from and then where he was sent to next. The trail led backwards and forwards, with the occasional maddening gap that left me flailing about looking in all sorts of files with varying degrees of relevance and with varying degrees of success. IX Squadron records revealed Bill had been posted there from No. 82 OTU at RAF Ossington. Using the same process, it was possible to work backwards and discover the various places Bill had trained at: 1660 Heavy Conversion Unit at RAF Swinderby, 19 Operational Training Unit at RAF Kinloss, No. 3 Advanced Flying Unit at South Cerney, Initial Training Wing 1 at Babbacombe and back to where he enlisted at the Aircrew Recruiting Centre at Euston.

A look at the 97 Squadron ORBs revealed that Bill had been posted there from the Pathfinder Navigational Training Unit at RAF Upwood. Having roughly mapped out Bill's progress through the RAF mill, it was time to find out as much as possible about the various places. The list of all the files/documents that might be relevant soon assumed alarming proportions. Some information was straightforward and easy to find, but often little gems of information would emerge from the lucky ordering up of some document on the fringes of relevance. Weeks were spent happily reading through absorbing archives and trying to stay focused on the relevant ones.

The range of information preserved is extensive and the flavour of wartime life leaps off the page. Attitudes are revealed in reports such as that by an RAF officer who had a crash crew on standby to receive damaged aircraft at Bourn. Deciding to test their alertness, he toured the runways in his car without provoking any reaction before finally finding the whole crash crew sound asleep at their posts. 'Bad show', he reported. The language may be dated with sorties rated as a 'Wizard prang' or a 'Bad show' but the feeling and atmosphere comes through clearly.

Finds could be unexpected. Browsing through books on Lancasters in the National Archives library one day, I came across a photograph that stopped me in my tracks. It was of Lancaster WS-U, the aircraft that by now I knew that Bill flew for most of his first tour, and the photo showed her nose art, a pawnbrokers' sign featuring three golden balls. The photo was credited to an N.R. McCorkindale. Neil McCorkindale had been the navigator in Bill's IX Squadron crew; it had to be his photo. Fortunately, McCorkindale is an uncommon name and, after a trawl through the electoral roll, Brett wrote off to some twenty possible candidates. Although not spot-on, our luck held and a relative contacted us. He told us that although Neil McCorkindale had survived the war, he had since died. However, he said that his widow was happy for us to contact her. This we did and received a charming letter back from her son, Ken McCorkindale, offering to show us their memorabilia. This turned out to be a treasure trove of documents, navigation charts, Neil's logbook and some wonderful photos.

A Living Link

Ken also provided us with the next and very exciting link to the past in the form of a list, compiled many years before, of roughly where the crew members had lived and what had happened to them. Although we knew their names, those with common names would be impossible to trace without some indication of where they came from, and this list provided clues. Instantly, one name grabbed our attention. One of the crew was listed as surviving and living in Leicestershire; his name was Alan Hart. Was he still alive? It was back to the electoral roll again until we found him. We wrote to Alan and soon received a gracious reply and arranged to drive up to meet him.

Alan was a wonderful source of detailed information. He was able to fill in bare facts with some great anecdotal stories and generally give us a feeling of Bill's personality and that of the rest of the IX Squadron crew. He also had some photographs and, of course, his logbook, which we were allowed to copy. His memory was phenomenal and he kindly took the trouble to make tapes of his memories for me to work from.

After tracing Bill's service career as far as possible, there were still a few gaps and, knowing that the RAF only release service records to immediate family, I realised it was going to be difficult to fill them. However, archivists at the National Archives informed me that the RAF had discretion to release service records to non-family members in the interests of serious research and suggested I write off to RAF Personnel Management explaining what we were doing. Personnel Management were most helpful and in view of the exceptional circumstances released Bill's service record to me. This was a treasure trove of information. It gave Bill's exact date of birth and that in turn made it finally possible to find his birth certificate. On our reapplying to the Registrar of Births, Deaths and Marriages, they managed to track down the correct certificate. Bill had been registered as Alex-Wilhelm Meyer-Braselmann. In the Registry, the family name is indexed under the last name; hence, it was filed under 'B' not 'M'. It was common in Germany to add the wife's maiden name to the family name.

The certificate revealed that Bill was born on 28 December 1910 at a house in Chinbrook Road in Lewisham. The name of the house was 'Rhenania', a name indicative of a nostalgic link with Germany with its reference to the great river Rhine and German university clubs of that name. We hoped to find this house too but this time we were out of luck. Chinbrook Road has since been largely redeveloped and although a few older houses remain, the majority are post-Second World War.

The birth certificate proved that the Meyers must have arrived in the UK some time before Bill was born in 1910. It has proved impossible to find a record of the exact date. The family would have been in the UK during the First World War when all enemy aliens were rounded up and interned. Mr Meyer had spent the whole of the First World War in an internment camp on the Isle of Man. It must have been a difficult experience for a younger man, for a man of sixty-six it would have been even harder to contemplate, suggesting a possible explanation for Mr Meyer's death in 1938.

Filling in the Gaps
As well as filling in some gaps and giving various family addresses, the Service Record also mentioned an accident Bill had when acting as 'screen' at RAF Ossington. The accident card in the archives at RAF Hendon then revealed details of the cause of the crash, the hospital where he was treated and the length of time he was off flying.

In due course, another piece of the puzzle fell into place, again totally unexpectedly. We knew that Bill's mother had left his logbook and medals to the RAF in her will. We contacted them to see if we could access them. A deeply embarrassed officer told us that in the 1960s the RAF had decided it could no longer store all the logbooks and artefacts that had been left to them. Where possible, families were contacted and warned that the logbooks would be destroyed if they did not want them. Unbelievably, this happened, and thousands of wonderful irreplaceable records went up in flames. We were informed Bill's would have been one of them. There was nothing more to be done.

However, a couple of years after we first met Roger Audis, the IX Squadron Association Historian, he got in touch with us to say that he had had a rather mysterious phone call asking for information about a Pathfinder pilot; the pilot was William Meyer. To cut a long story short, it turned out that Bill's logbook had not gone up in flames but it, and his medals, had actually been sold to a collector in the USA in the 1960s under somewhat mysterious circumstances. Being a Pathfinder pilot, Bill's logbook and medals were now extremely sought-after and valuable. The collector had recently died and the artefacts had been bought by a collector in England who was now searching for information about Bill to enhance their sale value. We immediately offered to buy the medals and logbook. Negotiations started but the collector seemed reluctant to sell and so we gave up. Or so I thought.

While I was away for a week, Brett decided to go and see the collector in person, with pockets filled with large denomination notes to help things along. He was both determined and persuasive. When he left some hours later, his pockets were absolutely empty but in his hands were the logbook and medals!

On my return, I was handed two parcels. Somewhat surprised, I started unwrapping the first, slowly unravelling layer after layer of tissue paper until there, lying in the last sheet of paper, lay a row of medals. One of them was a silver cross with a distinctive white and purple striped ribbon, the Distinguished Flying Cross. Beside the medals there was a small gold badge in the form of an eagle, the prestigious Pathfinder Badge. I knew instantly that I was holding Bill's medals and badge. I could hardly believe it.

I opened the next parcel and my eyes blurred with tears. The parcel contained a logbook; pale blue, a little faded and slightly dog-eared. On the cover was printed 'Royal Canadian Air Force'; obviously, it had been issued in America. Underneath it stated 'Pilot's Flying Log Book' and beneath that, in the space beside 'Name', was written 'Meyer, W.A.' This was Bill's very own logbook that I had in my hands, written up by him all those many years ago. As I slowly turned the pages, the entries were revealed, carefully filled out in Bill's neat and precise hand.

Later, on reading through it, I thought about him writing it, sometimes exhilarated in the early days, often worn and exhausted and always understating what he had gone through. What emerges is a sense of his courage, tenacity and a sheer dogged determination to do the job well. Bill underlined the names of the target cities and made brief notes beside them, giving details of each sortie. Despite their brevity, a sense of what his feelings were at the time comes through very clearly. There is a marked difference in tone between the entries from the winter/summer of 1943 and the dreadful winter of 1944. The dates, times, aircraft type, the nature of the flight (training, operations, etc.) and whom he flew with are all recorded, but it is the little notes that give this record the tremendous sense of intimacy that official records lacked. What thoughts, what searing memories had gone through his head as he made the small but significant comments in it? The satisfaction when an operation had gone well and the disappointment when it hadn't are obvious. Operations in daylight are written in blue, while night flying is in red ink. The red ink stands out on the pages, its clarity highlighting each entry and what it represented, yet another exhausting night on ops. facing flak, night fighters, freezing cold and equipment failures, not to mention seeing other planes and their crews blown out of the sky all around you. It must have taken extraordinary courage to face this, night after night, knowing that your chances of survival were diminishing all the time. Of all the sources I have been able to draw upon, this has been the most personal and the most moving.

Tracing Relatives
We had managed to trace the relatives of a couple of the 97 Squadron crew, Bernard Starie and James McLeish, but, despite our efforts, had been unable to trace the others. However, one year on the anniversary of the crash, 15th March, we drove to Durnbach to visit the cemetery and had another lucky break. As we walked in, we could see a splash of red on one of the crew's graves. Drawing near, it became clear that there was a poppy

wreath resting on Reginald Pike's grave. Someone must have visited the grave fairly recently. Quickly we knelt down and tried to make out the faded writing on the card. It read, 'To my brother Reg on your 83rd birthday. You are still sadly missed. Tich, Nancy, Percy, Edna and Beryl'. Obviously, Reg had come from a large family and his brothers and sisters were still alive. But how to find them? 'Tich' was obviously an abbreviation or pet name, but for what? Reg had been twenty-one when he had died, so he must have been born in 1923. The wreath was fairly recent so his birthday would probably have been in February or March. We hoped the visitors' books might contain further details, but although we found signatures, that was all.

Back in London, the first thing to look for was the record of Reg's birth. That would give his mother's maiden name and I could then look for the births of Nancy, Percy, Edna and Beryl with the same mother's maiden name. 'Tich' would be impossible to trace. The quarterly Births Records revealed two Reginald C. Pikes born in the right period. Now it was time to look for the siblings. It would involve working around dates ten years before and after Reg's birth. This took some time. It was not until the records for the summer of 1930 that there was a record for the birth of a Percy Pike with a mother with the same maiden name, Killinger, as one of the Reginald C. Pike births. Continuing the search, I came across a record of the birth of an Edna, in 1932, again to a mother with the maiden name of Killinger. Feeling increasingly sure that this was the right family, I ploughed on and found the record of the birth of Beryl in 1935. These last two births had been recorded in Deptford, which gave a starting point for the next step in the search.

The girls might well have married and have different surnames, so the best hope was to look for the only certain male name: Percy Pike. The records revealed numerous Percy Pikes but, in the hope that he had not moved away, we wrote to all the Percy Pikes in East London. We were only just in time as, sadly, it turned out that Percy had died recently. However, his widow forwarded our letter to Tich, who was now revealed to be Dennis Pike.

After several letters and phone calls, we arranged to meet up with the family. It turned out that Beryl now lived in Australia, but we spent a wonderful day with the rest of the family and some of their children, while they told us all about Reg. The family had proudly kept many of Reg's papers, including school reports, RAF official letters, his logbook and several photos. These they had kindly brought with them and allowed us to make copies of. We spent the afternoon going through the many pieces of fascinating memorabilia and, in a sense, getting to know Reg.

Germany
RAF records had revealed the name of the village, Zillhausen, in Southern Germany where Bill's aircraft came down. The nearest large town was Balingen in Baden-Württemberg, capital of the district of Zollernalbkreis. Brett sent an email to the local councillor for Zillhausen asking if they had any information or documents about the crash. With truly impressive efficiency, they replied within a couple of hours with some astounding news. They told us that a local man, who had been an eyewitness of the crash, had written an article about it in the local paper just two weeks before. It seemed like an incredible coincidence and we asked the councillor to contact him on our behalf to see if he would be prepared to meet us. They also sent us a copy of the article.

So it was that a few weeks later we were on our way to Zillhausen to meet Mr Kurt Schneider, the eyewitness who had written the article. We were invited to his home, and there we met his partner, Dorle Steingraeber, and the archivist, Dr Schimpf-Reinhardt, from the nearest large town, Balingen. He had kindly retrieved some documents, maps and photos relating to the crash from the archives and brought them for us to see. One document detailed the members of the crew who had been identified. William Meyer, Bernard Starie and Archie Barrowman were identified by their military identity discs and Reginald Pike through something on his person. The rest of the crew were unidentified at that time. The documents showed where the wreckage had been found, and there were also details of the damage caused to villagers' properties. Dr Schimpf-Reinhardt also told us that the crew had originally been interred in a local church, the Freidhofkirche, in Balingen. Kurt related all that he had seen that night, telling us how the event was seared in his memory, never to be forgotten. He told how it had shaken him to the core and what a terrible shock it had been to the whole area.

In our excitement at the totally unexpected opportunity of finding someone with first-hand information, we must have overwhelmed Kurt with questions, but he not only suffered our grilling with good grace but took us to see the crash site.

We drove through the village of Zillhausen and turned onto a small road that slowly petered out in the fields above the village. The road became a path that wound on between peaceful meadows before vanishing into the woods that covered the hills in one direction. To the north, the meadows rose up a hillside, dotted with the occasional apple tree and some firs. To the south, close by stood a line of tall trees edging the Roschbach, the small brook that ran at the bottom of the fields. It was a sunny day, the air filled with birdsong and the buzz of insects. On the hillside, complacent Black Angus cattle tore contentedly at the rich grass. Yet this beautiful and peaceful place had once been the site of such a disaster.

We noticed one small corner of the meadow nearest to the path was fenced off. The grass there was discoloured, yellow and coarse, quite unlike the lush green growth everywhere else. This, Kurt told us, was where the main part of the fuselage tore into the ground. We walked around, taking in the scar that remains to this day. Then slowly we climbed up the steep hill, pushing our way through the long grass while the cattle raised their heads to watch. Halfway up the hill, Kurt stopped. This was where the cockpit had come down. We stood in silence.

Further up the hill, we were shown an enormous deep hole, carefully wired off to prevent the cattle falling into it. This was where the 4,000lb 'Cookie' had exploded, gouging a massive crater deep into the earth. Brambles and bushes now cling to the sides and at the bottom a tree has grown up. It is so deep that now, some seventy-five years later the upper branches have only just reached the top of the hole.

We had been somewhat nervous at that first meeting, unsure how people there would feel about our research into a British bomber and its crew. Later, we discovered that our German friends had been equally apprehensive as to what our attitude would be to the events of the war. We made clear our view that these events were history; the Germany of today is not the Germany of 1944, and our interest was purely to find out exactly what happened that night.

In Memory

Having discovered so much, we felt we would like to arrange for something tangible in memory of Bill and his crews. We came up with two ideas. The first was to commission a painting. With this in mind, we went to talk over our ideas with Michael Turner, the well-known aviation artist.

After much debate, it was decided that the extremely low-level sortie to Stettin would be the subject. This was when the Danish people flashed 'V' signs with their torches as the bombers swept over the Danish coast. Lots of elements were combined in the picture: the Halifax of Eric Brown, the Lancaster of Sergeant Evans, who had such an eventful sortie, and one of the windmills that line the Danish coast. As Michael said, "It would look good." It did, and it also had a connection, as Brett's family were mill owners in Denmark in the eighteenth century. The picture captured the feel of that night so well that we commissioned another picture. This would be of the faithful WS-U in which Bill and his first crew completed most of their first tour. This time, their combat with an ME 109 after the sortie on St Nazaire was depicted, the Lancaster twisting and diving and the ME 109 plunging seawards in the moonlight with smoke pouring from her. The pictures are at present on loan to the IX Squadron Warrant Officers' and Sergeants' Mess.

A second idea also slowly took shape. Perhaps a more public form of commemoration might be possible in the form of a small memorial at the site of the crash. Concerned that the idea might cause offence, we somewhat hesitantly asked our German friends what they thought. Much to our relief, they liked the idea. We then asked them to see what people in the village thought about it and again the response was very positive. Now we had to see if the landowner would allow the memorial to be placed there. It turned out that the town of Balingen owned the land. Our friend and translator, Brigitte Lorch, kindly asked her sister Karin, who worked for Balingen Council, for help in approaching the Council.

Thanks to our friends' efforts, a few months later we received the necessary permission and went over to Germany once again to make some plans. We went to see a local stonemason to discuss the design of the memorial. We wanted a simple design that blended in with the countryside where it would stand. After much discussion, we decided on a plain four-sided piece of dark grey polished granite with a slanting top. On the top in a dull gold would be the insignia of the RAF and RCAF, for one of the crew had been Canadian, while on the front panel would be the names of the crew in pale grey. On each side panel would be a brief history of the night's events, one side in German and the other in English.

We settled on Saturday, 4 April 2009 for the unveiling ceremony. We were able to leave the supervision of the memorial and the final arrangements to our German friends. Without their help and hard work, it would have been impossible to get everything sorted out.

We wrote off to invite the relatives of the crew members we had traced to attend. We were delighted when no less than fifteen family members said they would be coming. As 97 Squadron was disbanded in 1967, we wrote to IX (B) Squadron, the squadron where Bill had completed his first tour, to tell them what we were doing and invite them to send a representative, although we felt it unlikely that this would be possible. Nothing was heard for several weeks and then a letter with the IX (B) Squadron logo on the envelope arrived. Opening it in expectation of a polite refusal, we found that not only were the Squadron interested but they wanted to know if they could send two Tornados, their crews and their ground crews as well. This was totally unexpected, and an immediate reply was sent to say they would be very welcome indeed. The RAF had hoped to do a flypast with the Tornados, but this was not allowed due to local noise regulations.

Emails flew back and forth, sorting out travel arrangements and hotel bookings. The whole contingent, RAF crews, families and ourselves, were duly booked into the Thum Hotel in Balingen. The families all arrived during the afternoon and evening of 3 April. There was so much to talk over that it turned into a very late night for all.

To everyone's relief, Saturday dawned sunny and bright. A quick trip out to the site revealed how busy our friends had been. A lectern and microphone had been set up, benches laid out and Kurt had prevailed upon the local fire brigade to lend their marquee. Tables decorated with flowers were laid out to serve tea, coffee and cake from after the ceremony. Meanwhile, Brigitte had spent days struggling to translate everyone's speeches, some into German and some into English. Now she faced the exhausting task of reading both sets of translations at the ceremony.

By lunchtime, the eight members of IX (B) Squadron had arrived, looking splendid in their uniforms and medals with toecaps you could see your face in. There had been articles in the regional papers and on the news about the ceremony, but even so, we were surprised and delighted when around a hundred local people turned up. There were speeches by the Mayor of Balingen, Oberbürgermeister Herr Reitemann, Kurt, ourselves and representatives of each family present. The Mayor unveiled the memorial and spoke of it as a symbol of reconciliation and of the importance of remembrance. We all considered the memorial as a means of honouring the sacrifices made by these young men and ensuring they are not forgotten. The presence of the RAF with the attendance of the men from IX (B) Squadron formed a direct and moving link to the past.

Towards the end of the ceremony, we were startled to see Kurt dart off and disappear behind some bushes while Brigitte announced that he had a surprise present for us. He reappeared clutching a very large, rectangular piece of slightly blackened metal; it seemed to consist of three panels riveted together. For a few seconds, we just stared, wondering what on earth it could be. Then it dawned on us. This was a piece of Lancaster JB 361-B. We came forward to collect it with tears in our eyes, utterly amazed. So many years later, a part of Bill's Lancaster had survived and was now in our hands. Afterwards over tea, we heard the story of how it had been found.

During the war, it was strictly forbidden to collect and keep any part of an enemy bomber. The penalty was death. After the crash, the site and surroundings had been scoured for wreckage and it had all been taken away. So the Luftwaffe thought. However, one day a couple of weeks after the crash, Jakob Jenter, the man who had brought the bodies down from the crash site, was collecting firewood in the woods close by. He had his sledge with him to pile the wood onto. As he pulled out a branch and shook the snow off it, he saw something shiny below it in the undergrowth and, brushing aside more snow, found a large piece of metal. Delving further into the snow, he dug out two more large pieces of blackened metal. One piece was clearly stamped with a Lancaster part number. Mr Jenter was in no doubt as to what the pieces were, but the impossibility of getting hold of any metal sheeting during the war made him decide to risk taking it home and keeping it. Unloading the wood off his sledge, he carefully placed one piece of metal at the bottom and then covered it with logs, brushwood and a few dollops of snow and set off for home. He repeated the trip a couple more times until he had safely retrieved all three pieces. Living in the country, the Jenters had always kept chickens. They lived at the end of the garden in a makeshift run with a tumbledown wooden hencoop at one end. With the wartime food shortages, their eggs were a precious form of food and the hens were in need of decent protection. Mr Jenter decided to use the metal panels to provide them with a new roof.

And so it was that for more than sixty years, the three pieces of the Lancaster provided waterproof roofing for generations of the Jenter family's chickens.

The week before, having heard about the ceremony, Herbert Jenter had approached his old friend Kurt and casually remarked that he had three pieces of the Lancaster in his possession and did Kurt think that we would like them? Kurt could hardly believe his ears, for all this time, pieces of the Lancaster had been there in the village and no one had known. He assured Herbert that we would like them very much indeed.

After the unveiling, refreshments were served and Mayor Reitemann kindly presented each family with beautifully illustrated books about Balingen. Then, all our German friends and the many local people who had helped us joined us for dinner at a local restaurant. Together with the families and the members of the RAF, some fifty of us sat down to dinner at tables decorated with flowers and festive menus made especially for the occasion.

Language problems vanished, wine and beer flowed and new friendships formed. The evening ended back in our hotel room with the RAF displaying their usual excellent planning skills; cases of beer suddenly appeared while we provided whisky. It was a long and memorable night.

Happily, the connection with IX (B) Squadron continues to this day. We were invited to join the Squadron Association and, on Association days, we were able to meet and talk to veterans who had actually flown Lancasters. IX Squadron's archives hold a wealth of information and photos that the Squadron Association Historian, Squadron Leader Dicky James, kindly showed us. On one occasion, the RAF Memorial Flight's Lancaster PA-474 flew in and, to my amazement, we were allowed to climb on board. It was a wonderful and memorable experience. From the outside, the Lancaster looks enormous, but inside it is a different matter. The narrow dark structure with its bare ribs and stringers climbs steeply upwards. The difficulty of moving around became only too apparent as I clambered over the huge main spar. The cockpit was filled with sunlight and something else... a rich aroma, an evocative blend of oils and leather, the distinctive smell of a wartime Lancaster. Slowly I climbed onto the pilot's seat and, looking around, took in the view that Bill would have seen so many times. The instrument panel ahead, and looking out, the great Merlins and the wingtips beyond. A shiver ran through me.

In the summer of 2010, the squadron were on detachment, based at Lechfeld in Germany. Wing Commander Nick Hay (now Air Commodore), then their Commanding Officer, told us he would like to visit the memorial and bring along some of his men while they were in Germany. We planned a lunch so the RAF contingent could meet our German friends before we visited the memorial. Once again, we all stayed at the Thum Hotel where the owners, Herr and Frau Meyer (no relation of Bill), arranged a wonderful lunch on their terrace. Over the table, a little tin plane (a toy from Herr Meyer's childhood) was tied to honour the RAF; a lovely touch.

After lunch, we visited the memorial and wreaths were laid. Kurt explained exactly what had taken place that night so long ago. One of the aircrew told me how important they all felt it was to remember; he said that visiting such memorials gave them a sense of comfort, knowing that if something happened to them on active service, their sacrifice would not be forgotten.

After the ceremony, we drove back to Balingen to meet Dr Schimpf-Reinhardt, the town archivist. He had kindly arranged to show us the place where the crew were originally buried in the Freidhofkirche cemetery and also some of the historical parts of Balingen. The Freidhofkirche Church is situated in grounds surrounded by a stone wall that separate it on one side from the River Eyach. The church itself is very old, with parts of it dating back to the eleventh century. The cemetery is beautifully kept with large stone monuments, headstones and flowers everywhere. Walking slowly around, we passed a row of German war graves headed by simple black crosses and stopped to read the names. At last we reached the place where the crew were originally interred and looked around. The place was to the rear where the western wall separates the churchyard from the river. Trees on the riverbank spread their branches over the wall, shading the spot, and neatly trimmed bushes covered the ground. In the background could be heard the constant murmur of the river. It was a quiet and peaceful place.

After a brief tour of the town, we adjourned to the old Zoller Castle. The Mayor, Herr Reitemann, had kindly invited us to a reception he held for us there. It was very hot. The RAF contingent in their smart but heavy uniforms were slowly roasting, so that when we entered the cool of the old Zoller Castle it was quite a relief.

Afterwards, we had another lengthy dinner and, as before, we ended up back at the hotel, cases of beer and wine appeared and it turned into a long night. It was very quiet at breakfast the next day. It would hardly be fair to say who was the last down… but seniority does have its privileges.

The RAF contingent wanted to see the two largest pieces of the Lancaster. We had just managed to take the smallest piece home in the car the previous year but Kurt had kept the other pieces for us. One piece is instantly recognisable as part of the bomb bay door. After all this time, the bristles are still in place on the closing edge. Its size was a problem, as it was far too big to fit in a car. The RAF came to the rescue. They offered to take it back with them to RAF Marham in the VC 10 they used for logistics. We all felt that it was singularly appropriate that parts from an RAF Lancaster, so long in Germany, should now be returning home in an RAF VC 10.

Two years later, it became apparent that Mr Jenter was not the only one to find pieces of wreckage in the forest. We received an email from Mr Franz Scheck who lives near Zillhausen. He wrote to tell us that a friend had found a piece of Lancaster JB-361 in the forest and, knowing his interest in flying, had given him a little piece of it. Franz is a pilot himself and he and a friend were building their own light aircraft at the time. He had always known about the Lancaster crash in Zillhausen and so he decided to incorporate the little piece of JB-361 into the fuselage of his light aircraft in memory of the crew. He then took the trouble to put in a formal application for a modification of the original design to the German Civil Aviation Authorities. The modification was duly approved and the piece riveted into place. He wrote saying, 'We see this sheet metal part as the soul of our plane… So I think the soul of the Lancaster is still alive and airborne and also the poor crewmen will be with us and hold their hands over us all the time we are airborne'. A lovely thought and a very touching gesture.

Finally, after all this research, I feel that I have come to know Bill. Talking to men that knew him, looking at photos, reading his comments in his logbook, his own letter to Mr McCorkindale and myriad small things have all come together to form a picture of a man whose quiet exterior hid an iron determination and great courage. A natural leader, his care and concern for both his crew and his mother speak volumes of a kind and thoughtful nature, while pre-war photos show a great sense of fun. He overcame differences in age and background to become a well-liked, trusted and much-admired 'Skip'. Throughout the war, Bill quietly carried the added burden of his German parentage and connections, never telling a soul. My mother described him as 'a wonderful man'. He was.

A Final Resting Place
At the end of the war, the Commonwealth War Graves Commission realised that sites for new War Cemeteries would be needed. A search was conducted for a location that would become the final resting place for casualties previously interred in Southern Germany and Austria. Durnbach, situated to the south of Munich, was chosen by British Army and Air Force officers together with officers of the American Occupation Forces in whose zone it lay.

The cemetery faces south, looking out towards Lake Tegernsee, the Alps that rise up beyond it providing a majestic backdrop to the lake. Trees planted along the sides and to the rear of the cemetery form a dark green background for the long white lines of headstones that stretch away in perfect serried ranks into the distance. Flowers and shrubs – roses, lavender, delphiniums, violets and thrift – mingle and frame the headstones. They are homely flowers, especially chosen to evoke the peace and tranquillity of an English country garden. There are 2,934 graves in this serene and beautiful place. Among them are the graves of William Meyer and his crew.

Simple wrought iron gates form the entrance of the cemetery and the crew's graves lie past the stone Cross of Sacrifice, at the far end on the right-hand side close to the pergola at the back. If possible, the Commonwealth War Graves Commission made a point of burying crew members together, but the crew's graves are slightly separated. William Meyer, Reginald Pike, Bernard Starie and Archibald Barrowman lie side by side in the right-hand front row, and James McLeish, Albert Roberts and Thomas Shaw lie in neighbouring graves one row behind.

As you walk through the cemetery past the rows and rows of headstones, the names stand out clearly from the austere Portland stone, each a remembrance of someone's son, husband or father and of the sacrifice they made. So many of those buried there are aircrew that the cemetery is known as 'The Wings Cemetery'. Near the centre of the cemetery, drawing the eye as you enter and when you leave, stands the great altar-like Stone of Remembrance. Carved on both sides of the Stone are the words chosen by Rudyard Kipling to ensure that the sacrifice made by so many is never forgotten by us or by future generations. The words read, 'Their Name Liveth For Evermore'.

NOTES AND REFERENCES

Chapter 1 Standing Alone
1. *Hansard's Parliamentary Debates* 4 June 1940, vol 361, cols 787-98
2. *Hansard's Parliamentary Debates* 18 June 1940, vol 362, cols 51-64
3. http://www.aviationancestry.com/Recruitment/RafRecruit/RafRecruit-Aircrew-1941-2.html

Chapter 2 Joining Up
1. Richard Hough, *One Boy's War* (London: Heinemann, 1975), p.8
2. Ibid, p. 11

Chapter 3 A Journey to the USA
1. T. Killebrew, *The Royal Airforce in Texas* (University of North Texas Press, 2009), p.152
2. National Archives, AIR 29/501Wilmslow No. 2. PDC
3. Ken Gilderdale, 1941 Diary
4. Richard Hough, *One Boy's War* (London: Heinemann, 1975), p.15
5. Ken Gilderdale, 1941 Diary
6. http://www.moncton.ca/Visitors/City_Attractions.htm
7. Hough, p.16
8. Ken Gilderdale, 1941 Diary
9. *The Challenger* http://www.northeast.railfan.net/classic/CARdwgs19.html
10. Hough, p.18

Chapter 4 Polaris Flight Academy
1. National Archives, AIR 29/626 No. 1-6 B.F.T.S. p.89
2. *Salute*, No. 1
3. Hough, p. 22
4. *Salute*, No. 1
5. Hough, p.26
6. National Archives, AIR 29/626 No. 1-6 B.F.T.S.
7. *Salute*, No. 1
8. National Archives, AIR 29 /625-7 No. 1-6 B.F.T.S.
9. *Salute*, No. 1
10. National Archives, AIR 29/626 No. 1-6 B.F.T.S.
10. *Salute*, No. 1
11. *Salute*, No. 2
12. *Salute*, No. 1
13. *Salute*, No. 2
14. Hough, p 30
15. Ibid, p.30
16. Ibid, p.30
17. Ibid.

Chapter 5 Advanced Training
1. National Archives, AIR 29/553 No. 3 Flying Training School and No. 3 (P) Advanced Flying Unit
2. Ibid.
3. General Directive No.5 (S46368/111 D.C.A.S)
4. National Archives, CAB 66/28/4 Memorandum. Bomber Command, p. 33
5. Robin Havers, *The Second World War: Europe, 1939-1943, Volume 4*. (Abingdon, Oxford: Routledge, 2003) p.69
6. Charles Webster, Noble Frankland, *Strategic Air Offensive Against Germany 1939-1945* (Naval and Military Press, 2006), Annex 3 4.27
7. Station History Website RAF Kinloss http://on-target-aviation.com/kinloss_history.html
8. RAF Kinloss Squadron History http://www.raf.mod.uk/rafkinloss/aboutus/history.cfm

9. National Archives, AIR 29/662 Squadron Operational Record, No. 19 OTU September 1942
10. Tape of Alan Hart's reminiscences of his time in IX (B) Squadron
11. National Archives, AIR 29/662 08/09/42

Chapter 6 An Introduction to the Lancaster
1. Taped reminiscences of Alan Hart
2. Letter from Alan Hart
3. Taped reminiscences of Alan Hart
4. Ibid.
5. Letter from Bob Lasham DFC
6. National Archives, AIR 2/7964 RAF Squadrons and Units (Code B, 67/34) Conversion Training Units. Letter 23.03.43 Air Commodore P.E. Maitland MVO, A/FC to Air Vice Marshal A.J. Capel DSO, DFC

Chapter 7 IX Squadron
1. National Archives, AIR 20/857 Notes on Situation regarding SBA. Letter 30/08/42

Chapter 8 First Ops
1. National Archives, AIR 27/127 9 Squadron Operational Reports January – December 1943
2. London, Imperial War Museum, Miss M.J. Barclay Private Papers 99/86/1. p. 26
3. Neil McCorkindale private papers. This account was written just after their first sortie and sent to his family
4. Taped reminiscences of Alan Hart
5. National Archives, AIR 27/127
6. London, Imperial War Museum, Sound Archive 2164. Richard Dimbleby's recording when flying with Wing Commander Guy Gibson on a sortie to Berlin in January 1943

Chapter 9 Uncle
1. Martin Middlebrook & Chris Everitt, *Bomber Command War Diaries. An operational record book 1939 – 1945* (Ian Allan, Revised edition 1995), 2 February 1943

2. Taped reminiscences of Alan Hart
3. Ibid.
4. National Archives, AIR 27/127 9 Squadron Operational Reports January – December 1943
5. Interview with Alan Hart
6. Ibid.
7. National Archives, AIR 27/127
8. Memorandum C.C.S. 166/1/D by the Combined Chiefs of Staff, 21 January 1943: United States Department of States p.781

Chapter 10 The Battle of the Ruhr
1. Harry Yates DFC, *Luck and a Lancaster Chance and Survival in World War II* (The Crowood Press, Airlife Publishing 2001), p.148
2. Middlebrook & Everitt, *Bomber Command War Diaries*, 1 March 1943
3. Letter from Bob Lasham DFC, describing one of his many visits to 'Happy Valley'
4. Interview with Alan Hart
5. National Archives, AIR 14/3410 Final Raid Reports, March 1943
6. National Archives, AIR 27/127 12/03/43
7. Neil McCorkindale, Logbook 12/03/43
8. National Archives, AIR 14/3410, p.62
9. National Archives, AIR 14/3410, p. 61
10. National Archives, AIR 50/179/53 Combat Report. Lancaster V ME 109, 24/03/1943
11. Taped reminiscences of Alan Hart

Chapter 11 Rest and Recreation
1. Alan Hart, Notes
2. Patrick Bishop, *Bomber Boys Fighting Back 1940 – 1945* (London: Harper Perennial 2008), p. 266

Chapter 12 The Squadron Moves
1. London, Imperial War Museum Sound Archive 2170
2. Don Charlwood, *No Moon Tonight* (Manchester: Crecy Publishing Ltd, 2007), p. 181

3. Eric Brown, Logbook 03/04/43
4. National Archives, AIR 27/127 9 Squadron Operations Record Book
5. Ibid.
6. London, Imperial War Museum, 5828 67/90/1 Miss M.J. Barclay Private Papers, p. 18
7. Taped reminiscences of Alan Hart
8. National Archives, AIR 14/3410 Final Raid Reports, April 1943, p. 143
9. National Archives, AIR 14/752 Group Orders and instructions
10. Eric Brown, Logbook 20/04/43
11. National Archives, AIR 14/3410, p.168
12. Eric Brown, Logbook 20/04/43
13. National Archives, AIR 27/127 20/04/43
14. Middlebrook & Everitt, *Bomber Command War Diaries,* 20 April 1943
15. National Archives, AIR 14/3410, p. 167 Night Raid Report No.315
16. Ibid.

Chapter 13 Experience
1. Charlwood, *No Moon Tonight,* p. 117
2. National Archives, AIR 2/8591 Aircrew who refuse or are unfit to fly: disposal policy
3. National Archives, AIR 27/128, 129-9 9 Squadron Operational Reports January – December 1943
4. O.K.L. Fighter Claims Chef für Ausz. und Dizsiplin Luftwaffen-Personalamt L.P. (A) V Films & Supplementary Claims from Lists. http://www.airmen.dk/pdfs/p114v3reichwest.pdf
5. Middlebrook and Everitt, *Bomber Command War Diaries,* 12 May 1943
6. National Archives, AIR 27/127, January – December 1943, p. 79
7. Alan Hart, Interview
8. National Archives, AIR 27/128
9. Middlebrook and Everitt, *Bomber Command War Diaries,* 29 May 1943
10. Eric Brown, Logbook 29/05/43

11. National Archives, AIR 2/8934 Decorations, Medals, Honours and Awards (Code B, 30) Non-immediate awards Coastal and Bomber Command
12. Letter from William Meyer to Mr McCorkindale senior, 24 August 1943

Chapter 14 Training Others
1. Alan Hart letter
2. Royal Airforce Museum, Hendon. Accident Card for Wellington X-HE265

Chapter 15 The Pathfinders
1. Sir Arthur Harris, *Bomber Offensive* (Pen and Sword Books, 2005), p.130
2. National Archives, PREM 3 20/9 Sir Arthur Harris to Winston Churchill
3. National Archives, AIR 14/2058 Pathfinder Force Instructions, Instruction No. 5, p.21

Chapter 16 97 Squadron
1. Letter from Reginald Pike to his father, 15 June 1942, sent when he was training in Ontario, Canada
2. Letter from Gordon and Catherine Taylor, relatives of James McLeish
3. National Archives, AIR 2/9148 Decorations, Medals, Honours and Awards (Code B, 30) Non-immediate awards Coastal and Bomber Command
4. National Archives, AIR 8/435 Air Ministry and Ministry of Defence: Department of the Chief of the Air Staff: Registered files. Bombing of Berlin
5. Martin Middlebrook, *The Berlin Raids* (London: Cassell, 2002), p. 8

Chapter 17 Life and Death
1. Middlebrook, *The Berlin Raids*, p.177
2. London, Imperial War Museum, Group Captain Charles Owen, DSO DFC. *Operations Diary*

3. National Archives, AIR 14/2555 RAF Bourn: flying control log. Watchkeeper's Log 16/12/43
4. Air Vice Marshall Sir Donald Bennett, CB CBE DSO. *Pathfinder* (Manchester: Crecy Publishing Ltd, 1998), p. 214
5. Alan Hart, Taped Reminiscences
6. National Archives, AIR 27/767-770 97 Squadron Operational Record Book 16/12/43
7. National Archives, AIR 14/2058 Pathfinder Force Instructions, p.11
8. Charlwood, *No Moon Tonight*, p. 170
9. Ibid.
10. National Archives, AIR 27/ 767-770 20 December 1943
11. London, Imperial War Museum, Group Captain Charles Owen, DSO DFC. *Operations Diary* 23/12/43
12. National Archives, Air 14/3002 Attacks by Pathfinder Force and Main Force on Enemy Targets.
13. Middlebrook, *The Berlin Raids,* p. 197
14. National Archives, AIR 27/767 97 Squadron Operational Record Book December 1943

Chapter 18 The Bleak Midwinter
1. National Archives, AIR 27/ 767-770 97 Squadron Operational Record Books 1 January 1944
2. Cited in Martin Middlebrook, *The Berlin Raids* (London: Cassell), 2002 p. 210
3. National Archives, AIR/2545 RAF Bourn: Watchkeeper's Log 02/01/44
4. National Archives, AIR 27/767-770 97 Squadron Operational Record Books 1943/44
5. Middlebrook, *The Berlin Raids* p. 211
6. National Archives, AIR 27/ 767-770 3 January 1944
7. National Archives, AIR 27/ 767-770 21 January 1944
8. Jonathan Falconer, *Bomber Command Handbook* (Sutton Publishing, 2003), p. 51 quoted in Patrick Bishop, *Bomber Boys* (Harper Perennial, 2008), p 230

Chapter 19 The Rising Cost
1. Winston Churchill quoted in *Time* 28 February 1944

2. Patrick Bishop, *Bomber Boys. Fighting Back 1940 – 1945* (London: Harper Press, 2007), p. 178
3. Middlebrook, *The Berlin Raids*, p. 267
4. Bishop, *Bomber Boys*, p. 157
5. London, Imperial War Museum, Group Captain Charles Owen DSO DFC. Private Papers 3574 85/16/
6. Kevin Wilson, *Men of Air* (London: Weidenfeld and Nicholson, 2007), p. 83
7. Middlebrook, *The Berlin Raids*, p. 271
8. Sir Arthur Harris, *Bomber Offensive* (Pen and Sword, 2005)
9. Bishop, *Bomber Boys*, p. 230
10. Middlebrook and Everitt, *Bomber Command War Diaries*, 19 February 1943

Chapter 20 March 1944
1. Air Vice-Marshall Donald Bennett CB CBE DSO, *Pathfinder* (Manchester: Crecy Publishing Ltd, 1998), p. 133
2. National Archives, AIR 27/767 – 770 97 Squadron Operational Record Books 10 March 1944
3. National Archives, AIR 14/2545 RAF Bourn: Watchkeeper's Log 15 March 1944

Chapter 21 The Aftermath
1. Stadtarchiv Balingen. Papers relating to crash March 1944 and compensation claims August 1944

Chapter 22 Final Acts
1. Middlebrook and Everitt, *Bomber Command War Diaries* 15/16 March 1944
2. Ibid.
3. Letter by kind permission of the Pike family

BIBLIOGRAPHY

Beech, Joan, *One WAAF's War* (D.J. Costello publishers, 1989)
Bennett, Air Vice Marshall Sir Donald, CB CBE DSO *Pathfinder* (Manchester, Crecy Publishing Ltd, 1998)
Bishop, Patrick, *Bomber Boys Fighting Back 1940 – 1945* (London: Harper Perennial, 2008)
Charlwood, Don, *No Moon Tonight* (Manchester: Crecy Publishing Ltd, 2007)
Currie, Jack, *Lancaster Target* (Goodall Publications Ltd, 2004)
Currie, Jack, *Battle Under the Moon* (Air Data Publications, 1995)
Falconer, Jonathan, *Bomber Command Handbook* (Sutton Publishing, 2003)
Garbett, Mike & Goulding, Brian, *Lancaster at War* (Ian Allen, 1985)
Gray, Jennie, *Fire by Night: The Dramatic Story of One Pathfinder Crew and Black Thursday, 16 December 1943* (London: Grub Street, 2000)
Harris, Sir Arthur, *Bomber Offensive* (Pen and Sword Books, 2005)
Hastings, Max, *Bomber Command* (Pan Military Classics, 1999)
Havers, Robin, *The Second World War: Europe, 1939 – 1943, Volume 4* (Abingdon, Oxford, UK: Routledge, 2003)
Holmes, Harry, *AVRO Lancaster The Definitive Record* (Airlife Publishing Ltd, 1997)
Hough, Richard, *One Boy's War* (London: Heinemann, 1975)
Killebrew, T., *The Royal Airforce In Texas* (University of North Texas Press, 2009)

Lewis, Bruce, *Aircrew: The Story of the Men Who Flew the Bombers* (Pen & Sword Books, 1991)

Middlebrook, Martin, *The Berlin Raids* (London: Cassell, 2002)

Middlebrook, Martin, & Everitt, Chris, *Bomber Command War Diaries. An Operational Record Book 1939 – 1945* (Midland, 2000)

Musgrave, Gordon, *Pathfinder Force A History of 8 Group* (Crecy Books Ltd, 1992)

Nichol, John & Rennell, Tony, *Tail End Charlies* (London: Penguin, 2005)

Overy, Richard, *Bomber Command 1939 – 1945 Reaping the Whirlwind* (Harper Collins, 1997)

Philips, J. Alwyn, *The Valley of the Shadow of Death* (New Malden: Air Research Publications, 1991)

Searby, John, *The Bomber Battle For Berlin* (Airlife Publishing Ltd, 1991)

Stooke, Gordon, *Flak and Barbed Wire* (Australian Military History Publications, 1997)

Thorburn, Gordon, *Bombers First and Last* (Pavilion Books, 2006)

Thorburn, Gordon, *Luck of a Lancaster* (Pen and Sword Books, 2013)

Webster, Charles & Frankland, Noble, *Strategic Air Offensive Against Germany 1939 –1945* (Naval and Military Press, 2006)

Wilson, Kevin, *Men of Air* (London: Weidenfeld and Nicholson, 2007)

Yates, Harry, DFC, *Luck and a Lancaster Chance and Survival in World War II* (The Crowood Press, Airlife Publishing, 2001)

Ziegler, Philip, *London at War 1939 – 1945* (Mandarin paperbacks, 1995)

INDEX

IX Squadron RAF, background 63–9
97 (Straits Settlement) Squadron RAF, background 162

Accident Card, 154
Airborne Cigar (Radio Counter Measure system), 150
Aircraft:
Airspeed Oxford, 40–2
Armstrong Whitworth Whitley, 47–8
Avro Lancaster, 53–62, 84–5 (*see also* 'Uncle' (WM's Lancaster Mk III))
Avro Manchester, 55–6
De Havilland Mosquito, 84, 150
Junkers Ju 88, 220
Messerschmitt ME 109, 57, 108–9
North American/Harvard AT-6, 31
Stearman PT 13, 27–8
Vickers Wellington, 147–54
Vultee BT 13-B, 30
Air Crew Reception Centre (ACRC), No. 1, 8–10
Air Gunner's role, 59–60
Air raid precautions, 6–7

All Through Training Scheme (ATTS), 14
Anderson shelters, 6
Area Bombing Directive, 44
Arnold Scheme (RAF training in USA), 14–15
Arrowsmith, Sergeant (No. 82 OTU student), 148
Art, aircraft nose, 85–6
Astrodome, 59
Atlantic, Battle of the, 39
Augment, Operation, 209

Babbacombe, Devon, 10–13
Balingen, Germany (WM's initial burial site), 227
Balnageith airfield, 47
Barclay, Miss (WAAF Intelligence Officer), 121
Bardney, RAF, 119–21
Barrowman, Pilot Officer Archibald, 165, 167–8, 227, 232
Battle of Britain Memorial Flight, 57
Bennett, Air Vice-Marshal Donald,

156–7, 160–1, 174–6, 216
Benzedrine drug, 74
Berlin, attacks on, 71–81, 99–100, 170–2, 182–6, 190–8, 201–3, 207–9
Beverley Hills Golf Club, party at, 36–7
'Big Week,' 209
Bishop, Patrick (author), 112
'Black Thursday' (16th December 1943), 176–7
The Blitz, 5–7
Blitzkrieg, 4
Bomb:
4,000lb 'Cookie', 88, 90, 127, 224, 228
incendiary, 68
Tallboy, 98
Bomb Aimer's role, 59
Bomb loads, 188–9
Bourn, RAF, 162–3
Bremen, attack on, 91–3
Britain, Battle of, 5
British Commonwealth Air Training Plan, 14, 167
British Expeditionary Force, 4
British Flying Training School (BFTS), No. 2, 25–38
Brown, Warrant Officer Eric, 117, 125
Brunswick, attack on, 196
'Bullseye' exercise, 65

Cambridge City Cemetery, 182, 205, 215
Camouflage, 57
Canadian geographical memorials, 232
Carter, Wing Commander E. J., 196, 230
Casablanca Directive, 64, 97, 170
Chadwick, Roy (aircraft designer), 56

Challenger (US train), 23–4
Charlwood, Don (IX Squadron pilot), 116–17, 129, 180
Charms, lucky, 179–80
Chicago, 23
Church Broughton, RAF, 147–8
Churchill, Winston, 4–5, 170, 205, 231–2
Clasp, Bomber Command, 232
Clothing, flying, 73–4
Codewords, 107
Colman, Ronald (film star), 36
Cologne, attack on, 97
'Colours of the Day' (Very pistol flare codes), 149
Combined Re-Selection Centre, 130
'Coning' by searchlights, 92, 105, 186
'Cookie' bomb *see* Bomb, 4,000lb 'Cookie'
'Corkscrew' evasion flying tactic, 100–1, 108–9, 198
Coventry, 5–6
'Creep-back' bombing pattern, 122, 181
Crew selection, 49–52, 54–5

Dambusters raid, 90
Dawson, Flight Lieutenant Stephen (97 Squadron pilot), 164, 166, 168–9
Decoy fires, 181
Deverill, Squadron Leader (97 Squadron pilot), 175
Dimbleby, Richard (broadcaster), 81
Disbury, Sergeant G. F., 42
Distinguished Flying Cross and Medal, 143–5
Dortmund, attack on, 134
'Double spoof' diversionary tactic, 185–6

INDEX

Duchess of York, SS, 38
Duisburg, attacks on, 66, 117–18, 131–3
Dunkirk, evacuation from, 4
Dunnicliffe, Wing Commander Charles, 164, 177, 203, 229
Düsseldorf, attacks on, 83–4, 135, 141–2
Dynamo, Operation, 4

Eastchurch, RAF, 130
Elliott, Sergeant J. (IX Squadron gunner), 140
Emergency equipment, 60
Emerson, Flight Lieutenant (97 Squadron pilot), 214–15
Empire Air Training Scheme, 14
Entertainments National Service Association (ENSA), 12
Essen, attacks on, 102–6, 116–17, 137–8
Evans, Sergeant (pilot with IX Squadron), 121, 125–7
Exhaustion, combat, 130–1

FIDO *see* Fog Investigation and Dispersal Operation (FIDO)
Fire by Night (Jennie Grey), 175
Firestorms, 139
First aid training, 42
First solo, 29
Flak (anti-aircraft fire), 91–3, 186
Flares, parachute, 90
Flares, scarecrow, 191
Flight Engineer's role, 58
Fog Investigation and Dispersal Operation (FIDO), 174–6
Forres airfield, 47
Foston Hall, Derbyshire, 147
Frankfurt, attack on, 178–82

GEE navigation aid, 72–3, 87
Gibson, Wing Commander Guy, 81, 90
Gilderdale, Ken, 19, 22–3, 32, 36, 40
Gilpin, Flight Lieutenant (WM's Lancaster instructor), 60
Glasgow, 17
Gomorrah, Operation (Battle of Hamburg), 169
Gosport tube intercom, 28
Gramlich, Unteroffizier Benno (Ju 88 pilot), 208
Gransden Lodge, RAF, 168–9
Graveley, RAF, 174–5
Greaves, Squadron Leader, 37
Grenville Hotel, Bude, 15
Ground loop, 28
'Guinea Pig Club', 155

H2S mapping radar, 81, 86, 101, 158, 189
Halifax, Nova Scotia, 20–1
Hamburg, attacks on, 86, 88, 169
'Happy Valley' (Ruhr), 66–7, 102, 104–5
Harris, Air Marshal Arthur T. 'Bomber', 43–5, 156–7, 170, 212–13
Hart, Alan (WM's first crew), 54–5, 112, 150
Hart, Pilot Officer (97 Squadron pilot), 204
Hathaway, G. D. (WM's Basic Course instructor), 30
Henlow, RAF, 164–5
Higginson, Flight Lieutenant, 103
Himmelstaub, L.A.C. Maier Ben, 34
Hissbach, Hauptmann Horst Heinz, 220–1
Hitler, Adolf, 5, 223

Hollywood, 36–7
Hough, Richard, 22–3, 29, 40
Hunter, Wilson 'Geordie' (WM's first crew), 51, 150

Icing, aircraft, 82–3, 86, 194
Immelmann turn manoeuvre, 30
Initial Training Wing, No. 1, 10–13
Instrument Flight Rules (IFR), 69

Jarrett, Squadron Leader G. W. J., 117
Jentner, Jakob (German farmer), 226
Johnson, Thomas 'Darkie' (WM's first crew), 51–2, 83, 149–51

Kammhuber line (German night fighter chain), 84
Kiel, attack on, 117
Kinloss, RAF, 45–53
Krupps armaments works, Essen, 102–3, 106

Lancaster, California *see* Polaris Flight Academy, California
Lasham, Bob, 102
Laurie, Flight Sergeant Lionel (97 Squadron rear gunner), 202, 205
Leave (holiday), 112–15
Leipzig, attack on, 209–12
Lend-Lease Act 1941, 14
Lichtenstein *SN-2* radar, 189, 220
Link Trainer, 31, 69
'Little Blitz', 205
Liverpool, 39–40
Lord's Cricket Ground, 8
Low flying, 124–6

McCorkindale, Neil 'Mac' (WM's first crew), 49–50, 76–9, 144–5, 150

MacIndoe, Sir Archibald, 155
McLean, Pilot Officer (97 Squadron pilot), 208
McLeish, Pilot Officer James, 165–7
'Mae West' lifejacket, 74
Magdeburg, attack on, 199–200
Mahaddie, Group Captain Hamish, 160
Mascots, 179–80
Memorial, Bomber Command, 232
Meteorological Flight, 159
Meurer, Hauptmann Manfred, 200
Meyer-Braselmann, Wilhelm-Alex *see* Meyer, William 'Bill'
Meyer, Wilhelm (WM's father), 2–3
Meyer, William 'Bill':
early years, 2
described, 55–6
joins RAF, 3–4
at No. 1 Air Crew Reception Centre (Lord's Cricket Ground), 8–10
at No. 1 Initial Training Wing (Babbacombe), 10–13
travels to USA for flying training, 14–24
at Polaris Flight Academy, California, 23–38
goes solo, 29
takes over as 'A' Course Commander, 34
passes 'Wings', 37–8
at No. 3 Pilots Advanced Flying Unit (RAF South Cerney), 40–2
promoted Pilot Officer, 41
at No. 19 Operational Training Unit (RAF Kinloss), 45–53
selects first crew, 49–52, 54–5
at No. 1660 Heavy Conversion Unit (RAF Swinderby), 54–62
flies Lancaster for first time, 60

INDEX

operational training in IX Squadron (RAF Waddington), 63–9
first operations, 66–86
with 1506 Beam Approach Training Flight (RAF Waddington), 69
with IX Squadron (RAF Waddington), 70–145
promoted Flight Lieutenant, 113
approach to crew welfare, 123
completes thirtieth operation, 140–3
awarded Distinguished Flying Cross, 143–4
writes to Mac's father, 144–5
at No. 82 Operational Training Unit (RAF Ossington), 147–50
injured in Wellington training crash, 152–5
at Pathfinder Navigation Training Unit (RAF Upwood), 161
with 97 Squadron (RAF Bourn), 162–228
anguish about attack on Frankfurt, 178–9
death, 221–8
In Memoriam notice, 232
Middlebrook, Martin (author), 170, 185
Middleton St George, RAF, 94
Mojave Desert, 32
Moncton, RCAF, 21–2
Moral fibre, lack of (LMF), 129–30
Munich, attack on, 103–4
Murrow, Ed (American broadcaster), 171

Nachtjagdgeschwader (German night fighter wing), 83–4, 220
Navigator's role, 58
Naxos radar detector, 88, 220
'Newhaven' target marking method, 217–18
'Nickels' (propaganda leaflets), 67, 104
Night fighter threat, 83–4
Northcliffe Hotel, Babbacombe, 11
Nuremberg, attack on, 95–7

Oboe blind bombing targeting system, 72–3, 84, 128, 158
Ossington, RAF, 147–9
Owen, Charles (97 Squadron pilot), 173

Pan American School of Navigation, 50
Parachutes, 74
Pasteur, SS, 18–20
Pathfinder Force, 72–3, 84, 86, 156–61, 179
see also 97 (Straits Settlement) Squadron RAF
Patrick, Wing Commander Philip (7 Squadron Flight Commander), 193
Peirse, Air Marshal Sir Richard, 43
Pelly, Sergeant, 117
Pfeiffer, Christian (German farmer), 226
'Phoney War', 4
Photoflash, 79–80
Pigeons, homing, 60
Pike, Pilot Officer Reginald, 164–6, 169–70, 222, 227, 230
Pilsen, attacks on, 124, 133
Pointblank Directive, 170, 210
Polaris Flight Academy, California, 23–38
Portal, Marshal of the RAF Sir Charles, 43
Powell, Sergeant R. (IX Squadron navigator), 138–9

Raalte, Pilot Officer (97 Squadron pilot), 202
Rationing, food, 7, 22, 114
Rauceby, RAF hospital, 154–5
Riley, H. T. (WM's first flight instructor), 28
Roberts, Flight Lieutenant (97 Squadron pilot), 200
Roberts, Flight Sergeant Albert 'Robbie', 165, 208, 221, 227
Robinson, Sergeant (IX Squadron bomb aimer), 138
Ruhr, Battle of the, 64, 101–10

St Elmo's fire, 194
St Nazaire, attacks on, 98, 107–8
Salute (Polaris Flight Academy magazine), 27
Sargent, Sergeant, 117
Sayn-Wittgenstein, Major Heinrich Prinz zu, 200, 220
SBA *see* Standard Beam Approach (SBA)
Schneider, Kurt (German schoolboy), 223–6
Schrage Musik (Slanting Music – German fighter technique), 191–2, 220–1, 230
'Screen' instructors, 147–9
Searchlights, 92
Sebastopol Inn, Minting, 123
Shaw, Flight Sergeant Thomas, 165, 168
Sinclair, Stafford 'Sinc' (WM's first crew), 51, 91, 115, 150–1
Skellingthorpe, RAF, 103, 152–3
Škoda works, Pilsen, 124, 133
'Skymarking', 90
Small Bomb Containers (SBC), 68
SN-2 radar, Lichtenstein, 189, 220

South Cerney, RAF, 40–2
Southwell, Wing Commander J.M., 66–8
Spam, 114
Specialisms, aircrew, 45
Standard Beam Approach (SBA), 69, 94–5, 173–4, 177
Starie, Flight Lieutenant Bernard, 164–5, 168, 222, 227
Stettin, attack on, 124–8
Stout, Sergeant, 118–19
Stuttgart, attacks on, 121, 214–15, 218–22
Survival and evasion training, 62
Swinderby, RAF, 54–62
Swire, Sergeant W. H., 117

Tain Bombing Range, 53
Target marking names, 160
'Terrorflieger', 206
The Times newspaper, 232
Tirpitz (German battleship), 64, 98, 157
Todt Organisation, 227
Toilets aboard aircraft, 134–5
Towers Scheme (RAF training in USA), 14–15
Training:
crew, 61–2
low flying, 89–90
night flying, 41, 89
survival and evasion, 62, 206
Tyrell, John, 34

'Uncle' (WM's Lancaster Mk III), 85–98, 122
United States Strategic Air Forces in Europe (USSTAF), 209
Upwood, RAF, 161

Van Note, Flying Officer, 116
Very pistol, 76, 91, 149

Waddington, RAF, 64–9
Wakley, Flying Officer (97 Squadron pilot), 198, 204
Wallis, Dr Barnes, 148
War Eagle Field *see* Polaris Flight Academy, California
Watkins, Flight Sergeant (No. 82 OTU student), 151
Wesselow, Squadron Leader Peter de (97 Squadron pilot), 199
Whitlock, Squadron Leader T. G., 26, 33
Wilde Sau (Wild Boar – German fighter tactic), 189
Wilhelmshaven, attack on, 90
Willbee, Donald 'Wilkie' (WM's first crew), 51, 58, 61, 114–15, 150
Wilmslow, RAF, 15–17
Wind Finders (Pathfinder role), 183, 199
'Window' radar countermeasure, 169, 189
Wireless Operator's role, 59
W. M. Meyer Ltd (WM's firm), 3, 6–7
Women's Auxiliary Air Force (WAAF), 74
Woodhall Spa, RAF, 136–7
Wright, Dr (IX Squadron's Medical Officer), 74, 131
Wuppertal, attack on, 138–40

Yates, Harry, 99

Zahme Sau (Tame Boar – German fighter tactic), 189, 198, 200, 211
Zillhausen, 223–6, 228

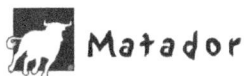

For exclusive discounts on Matador titles,
sign up to our occasional newsletter at
troubador.co.uk/bookshop